The Death of Zarathustra

NOTES ON TRUTH FOR THE RISK-TAKER

Graeme Donald Snooks

Institute of Global Dynamic Systems Books
Canberra

First published 2011
by **IGDS Books**
Canberra

© Graeme Donald Snooks, 2011

Printed in the United States of America by Createspace

National Library of Australia cataloguing-in-publication data
Snooks, G.D. (Graeme Donald)
The Death of Zarathustra
Bibliography.
    1. Philosophy
    2. Truth
    3. War on terrorism
    4. Strategic logos

ISBN: 978-0-9808394-2-5

For my grandchildren

Zachary William Snooks (b. 2004),

and

Maia Ann Snooks (b. 2008)

Contents

PROLOGUE: ZARATHUSTRA IS DEAD	**1**
Editor's Introduction	15
PART I TRUTH IN METROPOLIS	**25**
Editor's Preamble I	27
The State	29
The People	44
The Intellectuals	59
The Businesspeople	85
The Clergy	92
PART II TRUTH AND THE STRATEGIC *LOGOS*	**97**
Editor's Preamble II	99
The Strategic *Logos*	101
Strategic Desire	118
Strategic Cerebrum	123
PART III TRUTH THE DOUBLE-EDGED SWORD	**137**
Editor's Preamble III	139
Truth the Vivisector	141
The Subtle Art of Swordsmanship	152
PART IV DOES TRUTH HAVE A FUTURE?	**153**
Editor's Preamble IV	155
Notes From the Past About the Future	156
Editor's Notes	**161**
Glossary Of New Terms And Concepts	**172**
References	**188**
Acknowledgements	**193**
About The Author	**194**

List of Figures and Plates

Figure 1	The Strategic *Logos*	106
Figure 2	The Schizo-spectrum	145
Plate 1	"Zarathustra": model & image, © G.D. Snooks	1

PROLOGUE:

ZARATHUSTRA IS DEAD

Prologue: Zarathustra is Dead

1.

"Zarathustra is dead!" said an aging man, whose intense blue eyes belied his white thinning hair and beard. A man they called Old Realist.[1] He was at the head of a rectangular table around which a dozen or so people crowded. They were attending to their favorite real ales in the front, sun-lit, room of the "BG&E Tavern". It was mid-morning on the anniversary of their famous teacher's retreat from the world to his fishing lodge high in the mountains above Metropolis. They had been meeting like this each year for the past decade. This year they were shocked into silence by the news. "I tell you he is dead," insisted Old Realist as if they hadn't heard him earlier.

"When … where … how did it happen?," they demanded cacophonously. Their cries resounding around the tavern, penetrating even the gloomy back room, where some philosophers from the nearby National University of Metropolis (NUM) were drinking.

"In his fishing lodge in the mountains … just yesterday. Apparently he went mad a decade ago, soon after his retreat from the city. Long periods of sullen silence would be punctuated by loud singing and proclamations that he was the God who had died. They say Zarathustra's madness was his body's revenge against an intellect that had punished it for so long."

"Who on earth told you such terrible things Old Realist? Who kept him alive during his madness?," demanded those around the old tavern table.

"His two faithful fishing companions, Baldy and Adder, of course. They were the ones who told me when I went fly-fishing in the mountains."

"No doubt they were devastated," someone said resignedly, staring into his glass.

"I had expected the same, but they were strangely elated. They talked about a 'great noontide', and reminded me of what Zarathustra had told us all about the inevitability of his return," said Old Realist.

"Remind us, Old Realist! How are we expected to remember these things. It's a decade since Zarathustra left us and returned to his mountain retreat. You're not much of a storyteller," another of this company said, visibly upset.

"You're right, I'm not much of storyteller, that's why I've been a university teacher all these years. I don't have Zarathustra's gift or passion for stories. I won't be able to entertain you as he did."

"And your memory is deserting you too, Old Realist," said another with an indulgent smile. "Just give your account in your own way."

"Of course, I'll do my best. But you'll need to make allowances. Now where was I?"

"What Zarathustra told his companions," prompted the indulgent one.

"Right – what Zarathustra told his old friends Baldy and Adder. In anticipating his future death, Zarathustra told us a few decades ago" – and here

Old Realist attempted, rather comically, to mimic the way their teacher had spoken to them – "that:

> Now I die and decay ... and in an instant I shall be nothingness. Souls are as mortal bodies. But the complex of causes in which I am entangled will recur – it will create me again! I myself am part of these causes of the eternal recurrence. I shall return, with this sun, with this earth, with this eagle, with this serpent – *not* to a new life or a better life or a similar life: I shall return eternally to this identical and self-same life, in the greatest things and in the smallest, to each once more the eternal recurrence of all things, to speak once more the teachings of the great noon-tide of earth and man, to tell man of the Overman once more. I spoke my teaching, I broke upon my teaching: thus my eternal fate will have it – as a prophet do I perish!

It went something like that."

"It went exactly like that, my old friend," said the indulgent one, amazed at Old Realist's feat of long-term memory at a time when his short-term memory was less than perfect. "But your mimicry of Zarathustra's manner of speaking was truly terrible." At which Old Realist bowed his head in embarrassed agreement.

"If you know so much, tell us all when Zarathustra intends to return," burst out a more skeptical disciple. "And while you're at it, provide a few hints about how we're to follow the gospel of Overman. When Zarathustra was with us last, he taught that we would need to 'overcome' our fondest desires, our most powerful instincts."

"That's right," interjected one of the younger onlookers that morning at the "BG&E", "while your precious Zarathustra was a reasonable storyteller, he was off this planet when he insisted that his followers would have to give up the easy life to become 'higher men'. Get real! That sort of stuff could only appeal to wankers. Which is why I stopped coming to your meetings."

"And his ideas never cut any ice with university philosophers. We ... er ... *they* sneered at his naive storytelling, his rejection of their methodological 'dogmatism', and his emphasis on the body and its instincts rather than on the mind and reason. They say he was just a dilettante when it came to philosophizing – typical of a failed academic. They particularly disliked the passionate nature of his discourse and his mischievous way with words. He was too witty by half to be taken seriously by our famous university professors," said a well-known metaphysical philosopher – a pompous fellow who prided himself on his less-than-first-rate violin playing – who was drinking with other university philosophers in the gloomy back room.

"Only now that he is unable to defend himself are the academic philosophers breaking their cover and attacking Zarathustra," said Old Realist, with disgust, to his fellows, but loud enough to be heard throughout the tavern. "They were more cautious when he was still alive."

2.

"Zarathustra is not the only one to have died," said the pompous philosopher, swaggering closer to Old Realist's table.

"What do you mean?," the disciples demanded.

"It's ironical really," the philosopher intoned with a supercilious smile, "Zarathustra was the one who announced that 'God is dead', and that leadership in a godless world would pass to Overman".

"That's correct," said the indulgent disciple, "Zarathustra taught that man was merely a bridge between animal and Overman".

"Not a bridge, a rope," interjected the philosopher with a knowing sneer. "Zarathustra claimed, if I'm not mistaken" – and he said this as if he never was – "that

> Man is a rope, fastened between animal and Overman – a rope over an abyss. A dangerous going-across, a dangerous wayfaring, a dangerous looking-back, a dangerous shuddering and staying-still. What is great in man is that he is a bridge …

"There, I told you so – a *bridge*," exploded the indulgent disciple with uncharacteristic force.

> "… a bridge and not a goal; what can be loved in man is that he is a *going-across* and a *down-going*,"

continued the philosopher, pretending not to notice the tiresome interruption. The philosopher was well-known for ignoring inconvenient evidence about the real world.

"Yes, we know all that," said the indulgent disciple returning to the fray. "Zarathustra was always going-on about the going-across of man. What always puzzles me is the story about the rope walker who was half way between the two towers, when a buffoon suddenly appeared from nowhere, ran nimbly along the rope, and jumped completely over the terrified rope walker, causing him to lose his balance and plunge into the abyss."[2]

"There is no puzzle; the meaning is quite clear," said the philosopher, pleased to have the upper hand once more. "What it means is that anyone following Zarathustra's pseudo-philosophy will fail catastrophically! One is on firmer ground following the philosophy of successful university men, rather than failed academics like Zarathustra. As is well known, he obtained a chair in a provincial university even before he had finished his PhD. His resignation some ten years later, following the publication of a number of outrageously polemical works, merely demonstrated the lack of wisdom in appointing him in the first place. School teaching was about all he was fit for. But pity the poor children!"

"That sounds like sour grapes to me. University philosophers always feel inadequate in the presence of a truly imaginative thinker," the indulgent disciple interrupted.

"Nonsense! And would you refrain from interrupting," the philosopher said with considerable annoyance. "What I've been attempting to say is that there is a delicious irony here. Zarathustra came to teach us all about the death of God and the triumph of Overman whereas I have it on good authority that it is Overman rather than God who is dead."

"What authority ... when ... how?" came an uproar from the disciples' table.

"The Commissioner of Police, who attends my church – you know the Metropolitan Cathedral Church – told me last Sunday that his officers investigated the death of Overman.[3] His body was found at the base of the far tower of the harbor bridge. Foul play has been discounted. It would appear that he lost his nerve and fell, or jumped. The effort of 'going-across' was just too much for him, leading to a 'down-going' of a type not envisaged by Zarathustra." And here the philosopher paused, in anticipation of expressions of appreciation, at least from the other philosophers in the background gloom. But, as everyone in the "BG&E" just stared at him dumbly, the pompous philosopher continued: 'Well, you know what I mean, Overman just couldn't cope with all that truthfulness about himself. It was all too much for him. He became a manic-depressive – bipolar you understand – and ended lifeless at the base of the second tower." As this misguided attempt at wit failed as resoundingly as the earlier one, he quickly resumed his sorry tale: "What happened I leave to your imagination. The simple fact is that Overman is dead. And Zarathustra's preposterous promise to return some time in the future to 'teach once more the eternal recurrence of all things' and to 'tell man of Overman once more', has died with him. With the death of Overman, there is nothing more to tell!" With this final flourish, the philosopher folded his arms over an ample belly covered by an ill-fitting woolen cardigan, and assumed a self-satisfied demeanor that perfectly matched the pattern of deeply etched lines in his face.

3.

The disciples remained shocked and silent: first the death of Zarathustra; now the death of Overman! They appeared totally overwhelmed. The first to speak was an ethereal-looking man, wearing white, loose-fitting trousers and overshirt, with long, graying hair cascading over surprisingly delicate shoulders. "We shouldn't lose faith in the teachings of Zarathustra, despite the tragedy of Overman's death. We now need to embrace the eternal recurrence more firmly than ever."

"What good will that do?," whispered a dispirited disciple.

"It was precisely the eternal recurrence that gave us Zarathustra and Overman, just as it was the eternal recurrence that gave earlier eras Zoroaster and Ahura Mazda," said ethereal man firmly.

"What on earth is he rabbiting on about?," groaned one of the pompous philosopher's companions.

"I've no idea," said another at his table in the gloom. "He's been making such utterances ever since Zarathustra returned to his mountain retreat for the last time. What I want to know is how it is possible for everyone and every event to recur eternally. Absolute cant – or is that Kant?" Sounds of approval from the table of gloom.

"It appears puzzling, I know," conceded ethereal man, ignoring this new attempt at learned humor, "but the concept can be interpreted quite simply. Despite his extreme rhetoric, Zarathustra didn't *literally* mean that every person and every event would recur for all eternity, just that similar existential crises in history – the death of God and the death of Overman – will give rise to men who think in similar ways, and who can find satisfactory solutions to these crises. It is in this sense that 'Zarathustra' will return again and again. That is the meaning of the song he taught us. Remember – and he burst into a strangely ethereal voice:

> Now sing yourself the song whose name is 'Once more', whose meaning is 'To all eternity!' – sing, you Higher Men, Zarathustra's roundelay!
> O Man! Attend!
> What does deep midnight's voice contend?
>
> > 'I slept my sleep,
> > And now awake at dreamings' end:
> > The world is deep,
> > Deeper than day can comprehend.
> > Deep is its woe,
> > Joy – deeper than heart's agony:
> > Woe says: Fade! Go!
> > But all joy wants eternity,
> > Wants deep, deep, deep, eternity!"

"Sure, it's a good song, but what use is it now?", grumbled a dispirited disciple.

"What use? It reminds us of how we found the truth in the past and will do so again! Zarathustra was aware he fulfilled a role similar to that of Zoroaster in the distant past, and that someone else in turn would replace him. There is absolutely nothing mystical about this idea. Similar existential crises throw up similar great men. It is a matter of 'sleep' rather than death," said ethereal man passionately.

"Who is Zoroaster?," demanded the dispirited disciple, to a chorus of groans from the table of gloom.

"Zoroaster lived among the ancient Persians almost 3,000 years ago," replied ethereal man, ignoring the philosophers, "in an era before God died. Zoroaster was prophet to the God called Ahura Mazda – the Wise Lord – who created two primal spirits, one good and the other evil. The good spirit resided with Ahura Mazda, while the evil spirit, later called Ahriman, was filled with envy and attempted to destroy the good spirit. God created the world as a battleground for the great conflict between good and evil, light and darkness, Truth and Lie. Zoroaster taught the people that Ahura Mazda was the only God, that Truth was the supreme virtue, that good cannot come of evil, and that the Lie has only an allotted time to do its evil work, after which Truth will triumph and the world will end. Zoroaster, therefore, challenged mankind to reject the Lie of Ahriman and to follow the Truth of Ahura Mazda."

"Fascinating, I'm sure. But what has your Zarathustra got to do with the Persian prophet Zoroaster?," challenged the pompous philosopher. "Their teachings are very different. Zarathustra contra Zoroaster taught that good could in fact be created from the darker instincts in man through the will to power."

"The differences," said an animated ethereal man, "are more apparent than real. What I mean is that in the era before God died, virtue and truth were to be found in Him, and could not come of evil, which was the province of Ahriman, or the Devil. But with the death of God, all values were to be found in man, arising from his physiological characteristics. Again, before God died, the pursuit of truth brought about the destruction of the Lie, the end of time, and union with God. But after God died, this pursuit led to man's self-overcoming, the eternal recurrence, and the emergence of Overman. Remember what Zarathustra said about the pursuit of truth:

> And you too truth-seeker, are only a path and footstep of my will: truly, my will to power walks with the feet of your will to truth."

"You mean to say that a Zarathustra look-alike emerges whenever there is a major shift in the metaphysical circumstances of the world, in order to teach us the way to truth?," the philosopher spat out sarcastically.

"Absolutely," said ethereal man, smiling beatifically.

"Then you are an even greater fool than I hitherto thought. The best minds in my profession have been struggling with the truth ever since the great Plato told us about the Socratic revolution in philosophical thought. How can a born-again prophet compete against that great tradition? And what temerity to talk about the death of God in this Christian nation of Metropolis," the philosopher said with a self-righteous air.

"Of course," responded ethereal man, "you surely know what Zarathustra said about university philosophers."

"For the present it escapes me, but I'm sure it's totally irrelevant to this discussion. Or any other."

"Zarathustra made it quite clear what he thought about the dogmatism – the deductive logic – of all university philosophers from Plato to the present day. If I remember correctly, he said:

> The worst, most wearisomely protracted and most dangerous of all errors has been a dogmatist's error, namely Plato's invention of pure spirit and the good in itself ... to speak of spirit and the good as Plato did meant standing truth on her head ...

On another occasion he told us:

> You ask me about the idiosyncrasies of philosophers? ... There is their lack of historical sense, their hatred of even the idea of becoming, their Egyptianism. They think they are doing a thing *honor* when they dehistoricise it ... – when they make a mummy of it.

And on the matter of their dealings with the truth, Zarathustra said truly:

> In the case of philosophers ... their entire trade demands that they concede only certain truths: namely those through which their trade receives *public* sanction ... They know what they have to prove, they are practical in that – they recognize one another by their agreements over 'truths' – 'Thou shalt not lie' – in plain words: *take care*, philosopher, not to tell the truth ...

Zarathustra was, as you very well know, making the point that philosophy based on reason will not only fail to tell us anything useful about reality, it will also lead us into grievous error – into supporting the lie. It was Plato, that great model which all subsequent philosophers have followed, who threw his remarkable talents behind this lost cause. As Zarathustra told us, only those philosophical systems based firmly on a close and systematic attention to sensual experience can lead us out of this intellectual swampland. He looked past Plato, past Socrates, to the even greater Heraclitus. When looking forward again, he became so pessimistic about the profession of philosophy that he called for the abolition of all academic chairs of philosophy in Metropolis."

"What absolute nonsense," the philosopher burst out indignantly. "The senses are totally unreliable and will always lead us astray. And, as history is based on the senses, we do well – very well – to ignore it. We need to discover the *ultimate* reality underlying the world of appearances, and this can only be achieved by abandoning sensual illusion and focusing on deductive logic – on the product of the mind, God's great instrument in man (and woman of course). You empiricists are just mediocre fact grubbers rather than great rational thinkers in the Platonic tradition!"

4.

In the ensuing silence, most of those gathered in the "BG&E" stared gloomily into their glasses of ale. Only Old Realist noticed the perfect spring day outside, as the sun climbed steadily into the brilliant blue sky, like a mandala rising. Only Old Realist understood what needed to be said – and done.

"What we need," he said suddenly, breaking into the mesmeric atmosphere, "is an entirely new approach to life. While Zarathustra talked about replacing the metaphysical systems of philosophers with the historical systems of realist thinkers, he failed to live up to his own standards. Rather than employing a systematic historical approach, Zarathustra took the easy path by developing what he called 'a genealogy'. This genealogy, based upon etymology and logic rather than real history, led him astray. Zarathustra developed a vision of the world based not on realities but on his own prejudices. While I'm loath to admit it, his early training as a university philologist – the study of languages, in his case classical languages – was not up to the great task he set for himself."

"And you, Old Realist ('Old Imposter more like,' he said looking over his shoulder towards the other philosophers), have done what even Zarathustra failed to do, I suppose," scoffed the pompous philosopher, returning to the fray.

"Possibly," replied Old Realist.

"Well, go ahead then. Astound us!"

"Overman is dead. We have to face that fact squarely," Old Realist began, haltingly.

"Of course he's dead. I told you so. Just get on with it, as we all have better things to do with our time," the philosopher spat out impatiently, looking at his large gold wristwatch.

"More importantly," Old Realist continued in his own time, showing no recognition of this interruption, "Zarathustra's teachings about Overman are no longer relevant. What do I mean? Well, in the first place, Zarathustra was wrong about the will to power, and its associated will to truth, being the 'intelligible character' – the prime principle – in life. And, second, even if it were, man would be unable to generate appropriate social values from within himself. Not only would any attempt to do so be ill-conceived, it would also have a terrible impact on those who tried. The will to truth would strip an individual of his psychological defenses and expose him to the most destructive forces in life. While some can withstand greater exposure to the truth than others – and Zarathustra was definitely one of these – eventually we all succumb. Despite recognizing the dangers, both Zarathustra and Overman perished in the attempt to face the truth squarely and brutally. In his autobiography, Zarathustra tells us: 'One must never have spared oneself, *harshness* must be among one's habits, if one is to be happy and cheerful among nothing but truths'; and again, 'affirmation of reality is for the strong man'. They were spiritually strong, but they overestimated that strength and paid the price in terms of madness and death. Clearly, this is not the way most of us can, or wish, to live. As a society, therefore, we need to derive our values and ethics – our concepts of truth and untruth, of justice and injustice, and of good and evil – in other, more effective ways."

"The only way," interrupted the philosopher, "is through the exercise of rational thought."

"Definitely not!," exclaimed Old Realist, "Zarathustra spoke truly when he taught us to rely more on the sense and less on reason – to listen to the body as well as the mind. But he misled us about the will to power, which is not a realist force shaping our system of morality, but a dangerous ideal that can mutilate and destroy the body, which is the driving force, or dynamic strategist, in us all. It is a dangerous *ideal* – more dangerous even than the 'ascetic ideal'

Prologue: Zarathustra is Dead

of Christianity that Zarathustra attacked so uncompromisingly – which arose in the mind of a great thinker, who, despite his claims to the contrary, failed to construct a realist theory about the way the world works and how values are generated. A realist theory would have shown Zarathustra that the will to power is not the prime principle that he sought in order to explain 'the world seen from within', but rather a vivisector's instrument. The will to power is the road not to 'self-overcoming', but to self-vivisection. Zarathustra's madness arose not from physiological causes (such as syphilis) as he would have wanted but from the self-vivisector's blade. The pursuit of will to power led Zarathustra to abandon all the usual defenses of the psyche – convenient illusions as well as support mechanisms like family and professional organizations. This left him vulnerable – hypersensitive – to adverse changes in his physical and social environment. A vulnerability that increased over time until madness was his only refuge. The 'intelligible character' that he sought so persistently, therefore, needs to be found elsewhere. While Zarathustra is the prophet of 'historical philosophizing', he is not its great practitioner.

It is time, therefore, to tell you about strategic man and the strategic *logos*. We were wrong to believe Zarathustra that man is but a bridge – or a rope – between the animals and some transcendent being. We were wrong to believe that Overman could be created from within ordinary man. Even under the vivisector's knife, higher values cannot be liberated from mankind. If the effort was beyond Zarathustra, the most truth-hardy of men, then what chance of success would we ordinary men have? There are no 'higher men' of Zarathustra's imagining. The will to power is a dangerous and destructive *ideal* – not an instinct – which is capable of alienating an individual from both himself and his society."

"Just how is your 'strategic man' different?", demanded the philosopher impatiently, but curiously.

"How is he different?," Old Realist mused. "Well, strategic man doesn't indulge in self-vivisection – he doesn't wield that dangerous instrument of will to truth. Instead he is driven by a fundamental need – what I call strategic desire – to survive and prosper, rather than by a metaphysical *ideal* to achieve 'higher' values. Values such as truth, justice, and goodness – where they exist at all – are the unsought outcome of the strategic *logos*, of which man is just a component."

"The strategic WHAT?," exploded the pompous philosopher, with an accomplished look of scorn.

"The strategic LOGOS; the dynamic engine of life. It can be thought of as a circular process of interaction between man and his society, which is responsible for creating not only what we are, but also what our society is. The strategic *logos* is the creator of all values, all institutions, all culture, all material progress, even the creator of man himself. Man does not create these things out of himself through a mysterious act of will as Zarathustra claimed, rather they arise from man's interaction with his social environment in an effort to survive and prosper. In attempting to survive and prosper, man develops effective dynamic strategies which, as they are exploited and exhausted, generate a changing demand – a strategic demand – for a range of inputs required to fuel this life-giving process. In addition to material resources, the supply response to strategic demand includes values, institutions, religion, and culture, without which the strategic *logos* would break down. Strategic man is the active component in this *logos*.

Owing to the different dynamic strategies employed by different societies and at different times, societal values are relative rather than absolute. It all depends on the nature of strategic demand – and, in turn, on the strategic *logos* – to which individuals and societies respond. Am I making myself clear? Values are neither God-given as Zoroaster claimed, nor are they carved out of ourselves through an act of willpower as Zarathustra taught. Rather they are generated in the strategic *logos* as a necessary, but unsought and indirect, response to the strongest force in life – the desire of strategic man to survive and prosper. They are a response to logosian demand. This is the secret of the *logos*, a secret that could only emerge following the death of both God and Overman."

"And what will happen if the strategic *logos* breaks down as you suggest it might Old Realist?," asked a concerned disciple.

"If the strategic *logos* breaks down – if the cycle of life is interrupted – the society of man will collapse. This happens whenever a society exhausts, and is unable to replace, its life-giving dynamic strategy; or whenever a society is rocked by massive external shocks, such as war or invasion. The former, for example, occurred in Rome in the fifth century, and the latter in the New World in the early sixteenth century."

"You appear to be telling us that man, rather than seeking truth and virtue, seeks material gain through a variety of dynamic strategies," interrupted the philosopher.

"Exactly," replied Old Realist. "As far as mankind is concerned, truth and virtue, where they exist at all, are merely the means to a more important end – survival and prosperity. Just as there is no will to power, there is no will to truth or virtue."

"Nonsense!," sneered the philosopher, "everyone with any intelligence at all knows that we philosophers spend our lives seeking truth and virtue. Even Zarathustra, I'm sure you will agree, was a truth-seeker, albeit somewhat misguided. His problem was that he was a loner, an outsider, who spent too much time in the mountains, whereas we university philosophers are great team-workers, discussing our ideas with each other and writing joint work".[4]

"Men like Zarathustra are atypical," replied Old Realist thoughtfully, "they take a solitary and independent path through life. Their values never become society's values, unless there is a fortuitous logosian demand for them, as there was for the carefully reworked ideas of Jesus the Nazarene after, and only after,

Prologue: Zarathustra is Dead

the exhaustion of Rome's dynamic strategy of conquest. Typically, the prophet, whose values conflict with those of his society, is rejected, banished, even put to death: and typically he dies before this values have any impact on society. He is the antithesis of the prosperity-seeker.

While there is no general will to truth, these eccentric thinkers are driven by an aberrant curiosity to seek the truth no matter what the cost to themselves. Unlike the vast majority of mankind, they pursue truth at the expense of their own prosperity and, ultimately, survival. In their hands, truth becomes an instrument of self-vivisection. They run the risk not only of suffering mental disorders, such as severe depression and various forms of psychosis, but also of retaliation from those whose equanimity they threaten. These isolated and eccentric thinkers are the truth-seekers. And Zarathustra was one of them."

"And how do university philosophers fit into your schema? Are we also eccentric truth-seekers?," interjected the pompous philosopher.

"Not at all," said Old Realist emphatically. "University philosophers are, in the main, prosperity-seekers in both the senses that Zarathustra was a truth-seeker. As academics respond to what society expects of them – as they attempt always to meet logosian demand – they run the risk of neither self-vivisection nor retaliation. Their work, which largely amounts to exploring man in the way we like to see ourselves, usually contributes to the smooth working of our psychological defenses rather than undermining them. They, unknowingly, are apostles of the desire for survival and prosperity.

Accordingly they aim for, and achieve, comfortable university careers. While there are exceptions, most academic philosophers are more interested in material resources than in fundamental truth. Of course, as Zarathustra said, they are interested in 'certain truths: namely those through which their trade receives *public* sanction', but the larger truth is not their concern. I have, for example, witnessed a number of instances in the past in which philosophers at the National University of Metropolis turned their backs upon the truth when the disciplines and careers of their colleagues were being destroyed. Their only concern was to 'garner' more resources. At such times, when we might expect 'truth-seekers' to speak out about unjust and corrupt practices, university professors remain silent, and grow fat by *living* the lie. Academic philosophers, who substitute prosperity-seeking for truth-seeking, are strategists like the rest of the people of Metropolis from whom they like to distance themselves. What say you philosopher? Why are you leaving? Are you on the scent of a new truth?"

"But what does strategic man regard as truth and virtue?" said an onlooker, stepping aside to allow the pompous philosopher to push his way into the darkened depths of the "BG&E" to rejoin his friends, already bored with all this talk about truth in reality rather than in their virtual world of philosophy.

"The values of strategic man and his society are, as I suggested earlier, those that reflect their material interests. Those actions facilitating society's dynamic strategy are considered 'good', those hampering it are 'bad', and those threatening to overthrow and replace it with an antistrategic society – in which the strategists are oppressed and their surpluses confiscated – are 'evil'. Virtue is, and has always been, grounded in the dynamic strategies of human society. As the strategies unfold, or are replaced, once exhausted, by new strategies, society's "moral" values change. Moral values are strategic values. Their role is to facilitate the dynamic strategy of society by providing moral incentives for its citizens to do the 'right' thing – the strategic thing.

Moral values are an effective way of economizing on society's system of rules – its institutions. Imagine how difficult it would be to teach children a precise set of rules, together with rewards and punishments, governing how they should act in every conceivable situation in life. The list of rules would be impossibly long and completely unlearnable. Consider how much more economic and effective it would be to replace these endless rules with a handful of moral values that provide general strategic guidance in every possible situation. Such moral values could easily be imparted to our children, who, as they mature, would learn by experience and peer example that they need only be applied when not endangering the survival and prosperity of the individual. Only fanatics, we are told, take moral values to extremes."

"And truth?" queried the same onlooker.

"Truth," Old Realist replied, "is pursued by strategic man and his society only if it proves to be a useful strategic instrument. The lie is always preferred when it appears more beneficial than the truth. We respond more eagerly to stories than to reality. Like all values, truth is the outcome of the strategic *logos*, not the character of man or some sort of divine being. As I mentioned earlier, there is no *general* will to truth, precisely because it is only occasionally useful in man's strategic pursuit. For the same reason there is no *general* will to deceive, but deception is often a useful strategic instrument, and for some abnormal individuals deceit is an obsession. Truth and untruth, therefore, are strategic instruments, not moral attributes. But of course, it is always useful to take the high moral ground to accuse one's enemies of being followers of the lie! It economizes on the need to justify one's own position on any issue.

Truth, as is well known, can even be disastrous for our material and psychic well-being. Our very sanity depends on our ability to delude ourselves about the truth of our daily actions. It is vitally necessary to separate what we do and why we do it from the moralistic image we have of ourselves. While each day we act in a selfish, callous, cruel, even brutal way, we like – need – to think of ourselves as altruistic, sensitive to others, kindly, and merciful. Our rational minds find it difficult to acknowledge the strategic desire that drives us all. It is what I call existential schizophrenia – a mechanism for living with ourselves by looking the other way. While Zarathustra, for example, recognized the damage that that truth could do, he subjected himself to its full onslaught and, as we have seen, destroyed himself. Truth is a sharp weapon that must be handled carefully."

****

Prologue: Zarathustra is Dead

As Old Realist finished his speech, the group of old Zarathustrian disciples, and a few onlookers who had remained until the end, quietly finished their ales and dispersed. It now remained for Old Realist to take his message about strategic man and the strategic *logos* to the people of Metropolis, where the news of Zarathustra's death was spreading rapidly. He looked forward to the prospect, singing to himself: "Metropolis is my university, its bookshops are my library, its cafes and taverns are my refectory, and its thronging crowds are my colleagues". As he passed through the doors of the "BG&E" into the clear blue light of day, he noticed the midday sun high overhead.

EDITOR'S INTRODUCTION

Twenty forty-four. Year One of the dictatorship of Metropolis. Even as I write, the tentacles of the New Order are tightening around the city. In the name of peace and security, all critics of the regime are being rounded up and dispatched to "correctional institutions" in the desert far to the north of the city of Metropolis. These are nothing less than concentration camps.

The government media, which have taken over all forms of electronic communication, tell us that these men and women will be free to return to the city "once they have seen the error of their ways". Critical times, we are told, require decisive action. In our hearts we know they will never return. All their resources have been confiscated and have been invested in the armies of Metropolis, which even now are on their way to destroy our "enemies", who had objected to our conquest of oil-rich countries.

How did it come to this? How after 500 years of democratic evolution did Metropolis end in a radical-right dictatorship? Most of our intellectuals were shocked, particularly by the ready acceptance of the New Order by the people of Metropolis. In the beginning they claimed not to understand how the long-term "evolutionary" process by which democracy and liberalism emerged in Metropolis could suddenly be thrown into reverse. None of them had foreseen it. Yet most of them were indecently quick to embrace the New Order – to survive and prosper.

Only one of our thinkers – not to be confused with intellectuals – saw what was to come. An obscure figure. An outsider. He is known to me only because of the doctoral work I did a decade ago on unorthodox thinkers in political economy. His name was F.S.S. **Herac**. Although Frederick Herac had wide philosophical interests, my work focused on his unique dynamic theory of human society and the predictions he made about the political future of Metropolis. Most things he predicted have eventuated. It all seems so obvious now that it has happened, but forty years ago no one took any notice. His was a voice from the underground.

During the course of the second half of the twentieth century, the democratic governments of Metropolis lost their way. For the first time in the history of civilization, governments throughout the First World lost all sense of strategic leadership – leadership that facilitates the successful participation of individuals and corporations in their common strategic pursuit. This is the pursuit of survival and prosperity that has characterized human civilization for the past 10,000 years. Governments in the past had never failed on a widespread basis to recognize that their role was to support their fellow strategists by investing in strategic infrastructure, whether for conquest, commerce, or technological change. Unfortunately, with the emergence of ultra-liberalism, promoted by the unfolding technological strategy, the quality of Metropolis's political leadership declined in proportion to the reduction in its ability to generate personal wealth and power for government ministers. Former patricians in government became, of "necessity", robber barons in the corporate sector, and the political vacuum was filled by men and women of lesser strategic stature.

During the final decade of the twentieth century, Metropolis was governed by the Conservative Party (the "Old Fogies Party" as Herac called it), which accepted the philosophy and policies of neoclassical economics. This involved running down the long-term prospects of Metropolis by adopting a small government stance, refusing to invest in the infrastructure of knowledge on a large scale, and pursuing the anti-growth policy of zero inflation that was popular at the time. In turn this generated what Herac called **strategic frustration** in the people of Metropolis. This widespread frustration with the lack of long-run economic progress eventually led to the demise of the Conservative Party and to the triumphal return of the Social Democrats who had long been in opposition.

The Social Democratic leadership was dominated by a number of determined ideological interventionists, who were more interested in what the world "should" be like and in attempting to shape it according to their preconceptions, than in what it actually was like. They were easy targets for the growing climate-change lobby, which was obsessed with the *belief* that human activity was responsible for the beginning of a wave of climate change that ultimately would overwhelm the planet. These lobbyists had managed to convince themselves that only they, at the head of a massive program of government intervention, could save the human race. And they set about convincing the Social Democratic leadership that this was the "truth". It does not seem to have occurred to them that other attempts to launch and sustain programs of intervention on this scale – Akhenaten in ancient Egypt and the USSR in twentieth-century Europe – had completely failed. No one heeded the warnings of Frederick Herac (*The Coming Eclipse* [2010]) that the introduction of a massive climate mitigation program would require the establishment of a command economy of the type adopted so tragically in the USSR. No one believed that the establishment of a command climate-mitigation regime would derail the global dynamic process and that this would eclipse the forthcoming technological paradigm shift that Herac called the Solar Revolution. A revolution that Herac predicted would begin in the middle decades of the twenty-first century.

At the end of the first decade of the twenty-first century, the oddly automaton-like female leader of the Social Democrat government (who had learned nothing from the interventionist failures of the control-freak male leader she had recently ruthlessly replaced) took the first fatal step of establishing a climate-mitigation economy – the imposition of a carbon tax and the establishment of a Climate Commission to sell this idea to the people of Metropolis. This was the beginning of an interventionist process by which the market mechanism – the life-blood of the strategic *logos* – was displaced by a set of arbitrary decrees.

Predictably, even this was not sufficient to achieve the objectives of the Social Democrats, who soon changed their name to the Climate Pacification Party (CPP) to reflect their paranoid preoccupation.

In order to prevent the strategists of Metropolis ignoring their decrees, the mitigation government needed to enforce compliance. At first this involved direct government control of alternative energy programs, an attempt to "reeducate" and "motivate" strategists, an information program aimed at persuading the people of Metropolis that the future benefits of climate mitigation would be worth the higher cost of living, and the development of a massive network of regulations concerning both production and consumption. The mitigationists attempted to justify this massive degree of intervention on the grounds of "market failure". Apparently, the earlier long-term progress of Metropolis had been the outcome of a dysfunctional economy.

The Climate Pacification Party's (CPP) main advisor on climate change was Professor Nic Serious from the National University of Metropolis. Despite not understanding the dynamics of human society – he was an orthodox economist who had made a comfortable living from consulting to Third-World leaders on development issues – Serious had no hesitation in making dogmatic statements regarding climate change. His concern was not with the truth, but with the fame and fortune that accompanied this populist stance on climate change. By the time the truth was know for certain, his generation would have passed on, and its consequences would not be able to harm him. Clearly he highly discounted his long-term reputation. While Herac had been closely associated with Serious at NUM, our hero had been totally ignored both within and without the university. Herac was concerned not with fame and fortune but with the truth as he saw it.

Initially, the people of Metropolis, who had been brain-washed by the apostles of climate crisis through the Climate Commission and its subsequent incarnations, did not seem to be unhappy about this new direction for their society. But they knew no better, as the Climate Mitigation Party had assumed control of the national media and suppressed all dissent, "in the interests of the people of Metropolis". Predictably, the new alternative energy technologies (massive wind farms and solar farms that spread like a cancer over the land) were unable to successfully replace the suppressed fossil fuel technologies. As a result, the economy of Metropolis began to grind to a halt. Eventually even tight government controls were unable to completely suppress the growing waves of dissent. To make matters worse, China and India continued to use the old polluting technology in order to catch up with Metropolis as quickly as they could. This led to the rapid depletion of oil and coal reserves, so that by the 2040s a global energy crisis had emerged. Ironically, owing to its climate-mitigation fixation, Metropolis had lost its dominant role in the world, without being able to "save the planet".

As Herac had foretold, the mitigation policies of Metropolis had derailed the global dynamic process, resulting in the eclipse of the forthcoming Solar

Revolution. A technological paradigm shift that would have enabled radically new forms of solar power – such as satellites revolving around the Sun in order to beam back solar energy to the Earth – to replace the exhausting supplies of fossil fuel. The alternative energy sources – wind farms and solar farms – forced on Metropolis by the CPP, were part of the old exhausting industrial technological paradigm, and were totally inadequate for the strategic demands of Metropolis and the rest of the world. The problem was that the command mitigation economy of Metropolis had locked in this obsolete technology and locked out the new technology of the Solar Revolution. As Herac said (well before this outcome), "just imagine what would have happened from the end of the eighteenth century if our government had set up a command system that locked in water-mill and wind-mill power and locked out the steam engine! The Industrial Revolution would never have happened." How right he was.

Although the dissidents had initially been kept in check by Metropolis' newly formed secret police, their numbers in the early 2040s had become overwhelming. The level of violence on the streets of Metropolis escalated as the left and right battled for power. And the economy continued to deteriorate. Even total collapse seemed possible. In these chaotic circumstances, the old Conservative Party changed its name to the Restoring the World Party (RWP) and transformed itself to take charge of the winds of change. Owing to their contacts within the Armed Forces of Metropolis (AFM), the RWP organized and successfully prosecuted a military coup. Green dreamers, even of the fascist kind, are no match for the dogs of war.

Once in power, the leaders of the RWP reorganized the armed forces as an instrument both of internal control and overseas conquest. Within months of assuming control of Metropolis, our military forces were on their way to the oil regions of the Middle East. These battles were short but brutal. Once the oilfields, together with the means of storage, processing, and transport had been secured, the armies of Metropolis completely destroyed all social infrastructure and subjected the local populations to the status of slavery. Some of these slaves were put to work on extracting, refining, and transporting the essential oil supplies, while the rest were shipped off to Metropolis to work in our factories and on our construction projects. Flushed with the total success of this new conquest strategy, the leaders of RWP set their sights on capturing all remaining global oil supplies and overwhelming their global competitors, something the weak democratic government of Metropolis in the early years of the twenty-first century was unable to do.

Just as I put pen to paper, the armies of Metropolis are heading towards the Orient, following the use of tactical nuclear weapons. But not before China had launched a few of their own, with what we have been told is "minimal damage" – the loss of two of our "less significant" cities. Where this will all end only Herac could have told us.

****

Editor's Introduction

What is this book about? It is an edited collection of some of the later writings of F.S.S. Herac. But just who was he? There is considerable confusion about Herac's identity, in part because he employed a number of *nom de plumes*. As we have seen in the prologue, Herac sometimes referred to himself as the Old Realist. Also, all his published work appeared under the pen name Graeme Donald Snooks. Why Snooks? Because it is the well-known corruption of Sevenoaks – often spelt Sennocks in medieval times – the name of a town in Engle Land from which Herac's family originated. Herac's main publications, therefore, are listed under Snooks in the list of references, and are referred to as such in the editor's notes. It is all an elaborate deception for a self-proclaimed truth-seeker.

From my researches I've discovered that Herac had a highly successful early career at the National University of Metropolis (NUM). For thirty years he astutely played the academic game in the field of political economy, publishing clever papers, performing brilliantly at international conferences, and, by his early forties, becoming professor and head of his department. In this position he led a sustained intellectual attack on what he called metaphysical philosophy for its support of the deductive method. He wanted to gain general acceptance for a realist philosophy based on an empirical or inductive method. Never one to resort to dirty political methods, Herac was eventually ambushed by a coalition of metaphysical philosophers and rationalist neoclassical economists, who were intent upon expanding their resource bases. Disgusted by these base motives and ruthless tactics, Herac resigned his chair and devoted himself to private research and public teaching. But he retained his sense of humor, and could often be found humming a cheeky refrain: "NUM in name, NUM in brain".

In his subsequent work, none of which was published, Herac attempted to explain the significance of strategic man and the strategic *logos*. In doing so he held up a mirror to his fellow Metropolitans. Many did not like what they saw and contemptuously rejected his teachings. University philosophers in particular felt so uncomfortable in the face of his ideas that they boycotted them when they could and attacked them savagely when they could not. These university men felt uncomfortable because Herac's teaching about the strategic *logos* made it clear that they had been wasting their time all these years. Why? Because their arguments about ethics, religion, good and evil, and truth were based on faulty conceptions of the real world. They had become mired in theory about concepts and language rather than theory about reality. If Herac was correct, and they found themselves unable to refute him, much of their own work lacked meaning. It was essential, therefore, that the truth of his teaching be made to appear a lie.

After twenty-five years of rejection and abuse, Frederick Herac died. Long since had he resigned himself to the fact that his teaching would make little headway in his own lifetime. Instead Herac contented himself with the realization that he had sown the seeds of knowledge concerning the strategic *logos*, which he hoped would grow steadily in the minds of young truth-seekers in the difficult times ahead. Herac discussed these issues with his younger friends and committed his ideas to letters and notebooks. He preferred the concrete reality of ink and paper to the virtual reality of electronic systems, which he was convinced would lock up his ideas in their own technological obsolescence.

As it turned out, Herac had judged the intellectual climate, if not the electronic capability, of his era correctly. Metropolitans had no time for his teachings about strategic man and the strategic *logos*. They remained convinced about their own understanding of the "truth" – of the superiority of Metropolis's democratic political and social system. They saw their societal system as constituting the end of history. They were, of course, not correct in this matter. As we have since discovered, history has not ended; it is capable of going forward by going backwards; our "truth" is not eternal truth. Once they had got over their surprise, the intellectuals of Metropolis began developing new arguments to legitimize their new autocratic system and to sneer at what they saw as the "mob rule" of earlier times. They saw their autocratic system as aristocratic and morally superior to the plebian system of democracy to which they had formerly been shackled. They wanted to impose their wonderful aristocratic system on the rest of the world – just as our democratic forefathers had done with theirs. Metropolitan armies are most persuasive in this type of political debate.

The strategic elite, of course, was attempting to justify their oppressive system of survival and prosperity to themselves as well as the rest of the world. Just as the beneficiaries of all strategic systems have done in the past. The apologists for liberalism at the turn of the twenty-first century were no different in kind to those for autocracy in 2044. Ideological justification is a reflection of whatever dynamic strategy – technological change then, conquest now – is being pursued by Metropolis. And if, by some happy chance, our dynamic strategy shall become technological change once more, we will surely extol the virtues of liberalism and democracy again. Our changing perception of truth reflects the sequence of dynamic strategies we pursue. It is a response to the strategic *logos*.

****

Why publish Frederick Herac's writings at this time? It is both as a defiant gesture and a much-needed antidote to the lies generated by the New Order of Metropolis. Herac's writings show the self-proclaimed "truth" of the New Order for what it is – vicious, totalitarian propaganda.

Publication of this work will, for obvious reasons, be an underground affair. In 2044 all electronic books – the only type published through the normal channels – have to be approved by the state, which has total control over this medium. This book is being published in the old-fashioned, pre-twenty-first century way – on paper. Perhaps this is fortuitous, and I know Herac would have been delighted. Not only did he draw considerable pleasure from writing with pen and ink and reading with a real book in his hands, but he was also convinced that the new electronic medium encouraged metaphysical thinking. Perhaps another of his eccentricities!

While publication will be easy enough, distribution of Herac's books may pose difficulties. We will distribute Herac's books secretly among the freedom fighters and those Metropolitans known to be sympathetic to the cause. We will fight the Great Lie of the New Order using Herac's strategic truth, as well as modern weapons. Herac would be the first to remind us of what Zarathustra said about the ancient Persians in a similarly difficult time: "To tell the truth and *to shoot well with arrows*: that is Persian virtue". It will be our virtue as well. Zarathustra also drew our attention to the words of Ralph Waldo Emerson:

> Beware when the great God lets loose a thinker on this planet. Then all things are at risk. It is as when a conflagration has broken out in a great city, and no man knows what is safe, or where it will end.

The time for a great intellectual fire in Metropolis has surely arrived.

****

Frederick Herac's writings first came to my attention through an article published by one of his earliest disciples. It was, as I said earlier, while I was researching my doctoral thesis. The article included a footnote about a collection of notebooks, letters, and other manuscript papers belonging to F.S.S. Herac that had come into the author's possession after his master's death, owing to the disinterest of the National Library of Metropolis (NLM). Being unable to locate the author, probably because he too had died, I contacted all the used-book dealers and auction houses in Metropolis requesting they inform me if this collection ever came onto the market.

Only when I had virtually given up hope of finding Herac's papers did an email arrive from one of the city's more obscure auction houses. It announced that they were about to conduct a public auction that included materials that might be of interest to me. Early the following Saturday morning I arrived at the auction room, which was part of an old factory building in the formerly prosperous industrial center of Metropolis. After a brief survey of the auctioneer's unlikely looking offerings I found what I was looking for: lot 22/7/44, consisting of a total of twenty-two boxes of assorted notebooks and papers, surrounded by piles of dusty books tied with heavy twine into stacks of about a dozen books each. Once the bidding began, I was relieved to find that lot 22/7/44 attracted only token interest from the small crowd. Within a few minutes I became the delighted owner of Frederick Herac's intellectual legacy.

Editor's Introduction

Once I had taken possession Herac's papers and books, my life's work could finally begin. After a few months I had sorted the papers and notebooks into a number of subject areas – truth, good and evil, ethics, and the death of God – which I realized could form the basis of a series of books. Then I turned my attention to Herac's personal library of about 3,000 books, which are an excellent source of information about his ideas on their subject matter. Almost every book is heavily annotated in the margins of the text and on yellow "Post-it®" notes which protrude from most books like jaundiced porcupine quills.

All edited books that I might publish from these papers will begin with the allegorical sketches that Herac wrote not long before his death. Had he found a publisher, it is quite clear that this is the style of presentation he would have adopted. The reasons Herac preferred this form of rhetoric – which can be found in his handwritten letters (he kept *carbon* copies!) – are twofold. First, he wanted to draw a distinction between his realist philosophy, which is grounded in a general dynamic theory of life and human society, and the formal academic philosophy of his critics, which has no such grounding. Herac compared academic philosophy to castles built in the sky, which come crashing down to earth once the real dynamic mechanism of life is revealed. Second, and perhaps more importantly, Herac adopted an allegorical style because of the playful interaction between truth and lies that it affords. The truth of his teaching, which was derived from a systematic analysis of the patterns of human experience, is embodied in fictional form – a form of lies. In contrast, philosophy books generally take on a scientific appearance that masks their metaphysical nature – a body of lies presented in the form of truth. Truth, Herac maintained, may take the form but not the substance of a lie.

****

In this volume, Frederick Herac's writings have been organized into a prologue and four parts. Each part begins with an "editor's preamble", in which information about Herac's background and objectives are briefly outlined.

Part I – Truth in Metropolis – consists of extracts from Herac's notebooks on the following topics: the state, the people, the intellectuals, the business people, and the clergy of Metropolis. The purpose of these essays was to show how all sections of Metropolitan society were (and still are) riddled with lies, despite the insistence of those involved that they are devoted to the truth. Although Herac wrote essays on many issues, I have selected only those that deal with the so-called "war on terrorism" that was the dominant political issue in the early years of the twenty-first century. This issue provides an integrating theme for Herac's disparate essays written in the first decade of the twenty-first century.

Part II – Truth and the strategic *logos* – presents a series of extracts from Herac's notebooks about the everyday life of Metropolis. Here we find his existential theories about strategic man and the strategic *logos*. Truth and lies,

Herac argues, do not arise from the nature of man as Zarathustra claims, but are both equally valid responses to a changing strategic or logosian demand as the dynamic strategy of Metropolis unfolds. There is, in other words, no general "will to truth" as most philosophers appear to believe; and that tiny minority of the population who can claim to be truth-seekers are actually intellectual deviants rather than "higher" men. We are also introduced to the idea that what men call God is merely the strategic *logos*.

Part III – Truth the double-edged sword – focuses on truth as a sharp instrument. While truth can be a useful tool to understand both the world and ourselves – provided there is a logosian demand for this truth – it can also undermine the life-supporting illusions we hold about our real nature. As these illusions, which constitute what Herac calls **existential schizophrenia**, are essential to our successful strategic pursuit, their undermining can lead to mental disorders of both a neurotic and psychotic kind. Once again this part of the book consists of extracts from a large number of Herac's notebooks. Finally, Part IV – Does truth have a future? – comprises a few fragmented notebook jottings about the future of truth and truth-seekers in Metropolis. In particular we read about the precarious survival of truth as an extreme sport! It should be realized that these notebook essays were written over a period of almost twenty years. Accordingly there will be a degree of repetition and a slight change of emphasis on issues revisited.

****

To assist in the understanding of Frederick Herac's ideas, I have provided endnotes, a glossary, and a list of references. The endnotes, which have been compiled from the notebooks, letters, and book annotations, help to throw light on the more obscure passages in the text of this work. They also reveal what he thought about the work and lives of academic philosophers in this field. The glossary briefly explains the specialist language that Herac found it necessary to employ in developing his new theory about strategic man and the strategic *logos*. And, finally, the list of references contains the books Herac appears to have employed in writing the essays presented in this book. Needless to say, this is only a partial list, as some books from his library were lost after his death. Unfortunately, Herac did not always footnote his reading material in his notebooks. No attempt has been made to update the books in this field from the late twentieth century to the present (2044). While Herac's thought is specific to its time, it is also timeless.

****

Finally, it is worth repeating what Frederick Herac had to say about the reception of his work. He had no illusions that it would receive immediate attention.

Editor's Introduction

While that might have been pleasing, Herac realized that his ideas would appeal only to later generations as they gradually tuned in to his little-used frequency. His ideas were far too challenging to be acceptable to his own generation. He recognized that he stood outside the mainstream of life in Metropolis. Yet, despite this realization, Herac was shocked by the superficiality of the reception to his published work, particularly from Engle Land. "The ancient universities of that decayed society," he wrote in a letter to one of his closest friends, "merely turn out arrogant young men, who, incapable of original thought themselves, haven't the wit to recognize great ideas in others." But following each shock of this nature, Herac would comfort himself in the oft-quoted words of both of earlier thinkers: "My time has not yet come, some are born posthumously" (Zarathustra); and "My work is not a piece of writing designed to meet the taste of an immediate public, but was done to last forever" (Thucydides). This work, therefore, constitutes notes on truth from an outsider and a risk-taker.

PART I

TRUTH IN METROPOLIS

Editor's Preamble I

> Ever considered why there is an endless public debate on every conceivable issue, no matter how trivial? Why there are so many points of view on issues that seem so uncomplicated? Why we can't agree about the causes and consequences of things? Why we are so skillful at defending a large number of unlikely interpretations, and yet so inept at finding the correct solutions? Why we invariably take the moral high ground in these matters? Why, in short, the truth always appears to elude us?

This complex question was found on the opening page of one of the notebooks that Herac used to explore the nature and role of truth in the everyday life of Metropolis. These are the type of questions that Herac addressed repeatedly in his notebooks. Clearly, the total lack of truth and honesty with which the public debates in Metropolis were (and are) conducted was an ever-present source of irritation: self-interest and self-promotion everywhere parading as objective truth. Herac often claimed that the truth of an argument is inversely related to the passion and conviction with which it is conducted. Truth, he insisted, needs no embellishment, no righteous indignation. These things are merely a cover for self-interest.

Why raise these issues in this book? Surely perceptive thinkers have always been aware of the scarcity of truth in public affairs and daily life. At least as early as Thucydides (c. 455 – c. 401 BC) the real motives underlying affairs of state were laid bare. The main reason it is worth revisiting these issues is that most people, including many philosophers, continue to maintain that they are motivated by some sort of will to truth. And, of course, it is the background from which Herac's ideas about social values emerged.

Herac's writings on the untruthfulness of public and everyday life are scattered throughout the notebooks he maintained, almost on a daily basis. He had a fascination with truth and truthfulness throughout his life. Not only was he always passionate about understanding the truth about life, he found it difficult to understand how most people were able to be untruthful to both themselves and others. His jottings show that as a young boy he was shocked that his peers found no difficulty in lying to their parents and teachers if, by doing so, they were able to avoid unpleasant complications. In the beginning, this naive attitude led Herac to receiving minor punishments that his peers deftly side-stepped. Accordingly, he soon realized that his attitude to truth and truthfulness was not the norm. He soon realized that truth-seeking and truth-telling were deviant occupations in the society of Metropolis.

Because of the sheer volume and variety of context for Herac's writings on truth and truthfulness, I have focused on the single issue that reverberated throughout all quarters of Metropolis at the beginning of the twenty-first century – the so-called "war on terrorism". This issue illustrates most clearly how both truth and lies are employed for strategic ends. In addition, in our own time there is a growing interest in the struggle between strategic and antistrategic forces, which underpinned the earlier war on terror.

In reorganizing material from Herac's notebooks I have employed the following headings:

- the state
- the people
- the intellectuals
- the businesspeople
- the clergy.

Under these headings I have gathered together a large number of Herac's essays. The order in which they have been arranged is mine, not Herac's. I hope that this classification will not discourage readers from following a different reading scheme, particularly as I suspect Herac would find this system a trifle limiting himself. He always appreciated eccentricity in people, life, and literature.

When reading the work that follows, it is important to keep in mind that Herac was very close to the events and people he was discussing. Clearly there are times when his views are less than objective. Some four decades later we have the advantage of greater insight. Accordingly, we may have a different perspective on the truth of the issues with which Herac was concerned. Yet, despite this minor blemish, one cannot but be impressed by the systematic way he subjects every question he discusses to an empirically grounded theory of life and human society.

The State

1.

Without doubt the most fascinating global event coinciding with the opening of the twenty-first century is the "war on terrorism". Fascinating because it explodes the eternal myth about the "will to truth" in human society. While this event has attracted an unprecedented amount of recent intellectual and media attention, the best commentary by far is that by the Roman historian Thucydides, written some 2,400 years ago! That commentary is part of his *History of the Peloponnesian War* – a war between Athens and Sparta in which he had participated – concerning a critical debate between representatives of Athens and Melos in the war's sixteenth year. It is well worth considering this commentary for the insights it provides not only into historical circumstances but also concerning the contemporary debate. In doing so it should be realized that while Sparta had the upper-hand on land, Athens was supreme at sea.

In 415 BC, the leaders of Athens resolved to send a military force, consisting of thirty-eight ships, 2,700 hoplites, 300 archers, and twenty mounted archers, against the neutral Spartan colony of Melos in the Aegean's south-west, about 150 kilometers distant. Before commencing hostilities, the Athenians, led by the generals Cleomedes and Tisias, sent representatives to negotiate with the Melians. While the Athenian representatives proposed to address the entire community of Melos, they were permitted to talk only with the governing body. In their opening statement the Athenians made it clear they realized that the Melian leaders did not want their people to learn the truth in case they "be led astray".[1] One could confide in one's enemies but not in one's subjects. It was all about telling the truth to outsiders and lies to insiders.

The Athenians told the Melians they intended to be brutally honest in the hope of persuading their neighbor to make it easy for everyone by accepting Athens as overlord without war. Their logic was simple, and compelling. As they were more powerful, it was perfectly reasonable that Athens should rule over Melos. It was not a matter of who was right, but who was strongest and most determined. The gods always favor those who adopted this basic law of nature. Melos could not look to Sparta for support, because the Spartans, who always pursued their own self-interest (which they rationalized as being "honorable and just"), would not risk challenging Athens at sea, even to save their own colony.

The Athenian representatives even admitted they were less concerned about the possibility of Spartan attack than losing control of their own empire. Melos had to be absorbed into the Athenian empire or either they, the military leaders, would lose power in Athens, or their subject peoples would rise up against them. This is why one could tell the truth to outsiders but had to lie to insiders. It would be a mistake, therefore, for Melos to take an idealistic stand – to have "surrendered to an idea" about what was right – in the face of overwhelming power. The Athenians said that they were too realistic to make the error of lying to themselves. They claimed to follow the "safe rule" of never challenging those who are "superior", while displaying "moderation" to those who are inferior after they had exerted power over them.

It is fascinating to reflect on the words that Thucydides places in the mouths of the Athenian negotiators. They show his great insight into the minds of strategic leaders not only in ancient Greece but in all times and places. Including our own. The Athenians begin with refreshing honesty:

> Then we on our side will use no fine phrases saying, for example, that we have a right to our empire because we defeated the Persians, or that we have come against you now because of the injuries you have done us – a great mass of words that nobody would believe. And we ask you on your side not to imagine that you will influence us by saying that you, though a colony of Sparta, have not joined Sparta in the war, or that you have never done us any harm. Instead we recommend that you should try to get what is possible for you to get, *taking into consideration what we both really do think*; since you know as well as we do that, when these matters are discussed by practical people, the standard of justice depends on the equality of power to compel and that *in fact the strong do what they have power to do and the weak accept what they have to accept*.[2]

The Athenians also made clear their real motives in this military action:

> As for us, even assuming that our empire does come to an end, we are not despondent about what would happen next. One is not so much frightened of being conquered by a power which rules over others, as Sparta does (not that we are concerned with Sparta now), as of what would happen if a ruling power is attacked and defeated by its own subjects … We do not want any trouble in bringing you into our empire, and we want you to be spared for the good both of yourselves and of ourselves.

When the Melians protested that they would be happy to be "neutral, friends instead of enemies, but allies of neither side", the Athenians spelled out exactly why they were in Melos:

> It is not so much your hostility that injures us; it is rather the case that, if we were on friendly terms with you, our subjects would regard that as a sign of weakness in us, whereas your hatred is evidence of our power.

In other words, by failing to provide strategic leadership in strong societies like Athens, the threat from one's own subjects is more to be feared than that from aggressive neighbors. And in weak societies like Melos, the decision of its leaders to opt for "hope" – which "is by nature an expensive commodity" – rather than geopolitical realities, will lead to disaster.

When told by the defiant Melians that they "trust … the gods will give us fortune as good as yours, because we are standing for what is right against what is wrong", the Athenians replied:

> Our opinion of the gods and our knowledge of men lead us to conclude that it is a general and necessary law of nature to rule wherever one can ... and we know that you or anybody else with the same power as ours would be acting in precisely the same way.

Might, in other words, is right!

When the Melians suggest that Sparta will surely come to their aid for "honor's sake" owing to the existing bond of kinship, the Athenians reply cynically:

> Of all people we know the Spartans are most conspicuous for believing that what they are doing is honourable and what suits their interests is just. And this kind of attitude is not going to be of much help to you in your absurd quest for safety at the moment.

When the Melians counter by arguing that it is in Sparta's self-interest to come to the aid of Melos, because to refuse assistance "would mean losing the confidence of their friends among the Hellenes and doing good to their enemies", the Athenians reply:

> You seem to forget that if one follows one's self-interest one wants to be safe, whereas the path of justice and honour involves one in danger. And, where danger is concerned, the Spartans are not, as a rule, very venturesome.

After further Melian arguments about the possibility of the Athenians not detecting the rescuing Spartans on open waters, the Athenians concede a small chance of Spartan good fortune, but stress that the most likely outcome would be disaster for both the Spartans and the Melians. The only way to avoid this is for the Melians to accept realities rather than idealities.

> Do not be lead astray by a false sense of honour – a thing that often brings men to ruin when they are faced with an obvious danger that somehow affects their pride. For in many cases men have still been able to see the dangers ahead of them, but this thing called dishonour, this *word*, by its own force of seduction, has drawn them into a state where they have surrendered to an idea.[3]

The Athenians go on to argue that "there is nothing disgraceful in giving way to the greatest city in Hellas when she is offering you such reasonable terms – alliance on a tribute-paying basis and liberty to enjoy your own property ... This is the safe rule – to stand up to one's equals, to behave with deference to one's superiors, and to treat one's inferiors with moderation. Think it over again."

When the Melians did reconsider the Athenian proposal, they decided to pursue idealities rather than realities. The response was dramatic and final. The Athenians immediately placed Melos under siege, inducing starvation and, eventually, unconditional surrender. Sparta did not attempt to rescue Melos. All Melian men of military age were put to death, all the women and children were sold into slavery, and Melos was colonized by Athenians. The Athenians, therefore, spoke truly about the triumph of reality over ideality, of desire over ideas; but, despite all protestations to the contrary, they lied about treating "inferiors with moderation". In the end, strategic leaders lie to their enemies as well as their subjects.

2.

Thucydides' commentary is fascinating not only for what he says, but also for what he leaves unsaid. While he tells us what the Athenian leaders revealed to the Melians, he says nothing about what they told their own subjects. He merely implies they would be told a different story. Instead of the "truth", Athenian subjects would be told lies about the invasion of Melos. Why? To prevent them losing confidence in their military leaders and overlords and, subsequently, deposing them. We are left with the impression that the subjects of Athens were to be told the very opposite of what had been revealed to the Melian leaders.

Subjects of the Athenian empire would have been presented with "fine phrases" about the right of Athens to empire owing to their defeat of the Persians. In the specific case of the invasion of Melos, it would have been claimed by the military leaders to have been in compensation for the "injuries" the Melians had inflicted upon Athens by threatening to join forces with Sparta. They would have denied that it had anything to do with an attitude as crude and gross as "might is right" or with the "natural law" of the domination of the weak by the strong. Instead they would have announced that the Melians had been offered the role of a friendly neutral, but that they had refused this honor and had called upon their kinsmen in Sparta to intervene. In addition, they would have stressed the dangers of Sparta landing on Melos in force and using the island as a base for the conduct of sea warfare against Athens and its empire.

The Athenian military leaders would have explained to their subjects that their policies were honorable and just, rather than self-interested. At all times they made every attempt to pursue the right course of action. Theirs was a struggle of good against evil. They would have claimed that only when all their conciliatory offers had been rejected and a Spartan invasion appeared certain, did they reluctantly lay siege to Melos. And their harsh treatment of the Melians was due to the latter's intransigence. The subsequent colonization of Melos from Athens, of course, was necessary to prevent Sparta using the island as a future base for sea warfare. The military leaders were just as reluctant to sanction this invasion as were the Athenian people to participate in the spoils. Neither the leaders nor the people of Athens were driven in this by base material motives. Certainly the Athenians who did gain from this genocide and colonization would have been quick to agree. Only those with nothing to gain would have voiced their dissent. The purpose of these lies, of course, was to protect the finer sensibilities of the good citizens of Athens; ... oh, yes, ... and to protect the military leaders from attack from within. What a contemporary ring these lies have!

3.

It is becoming clearer how Thucydides' *History* could provide an insightful commentary on the contemporary war on terrorism. But before drawing out the implications, we need to consider this phenomenon, which has dominated the global activities of Metropolis over the past two years.

As I write, the second, more muted anniversary of the explosive event that launched the war on terrorism has just been mourned. Two years ago on November 9 the unthinkable happened. A terrorist organization claiming to be the radical activist arm of the Spirit-is-Supreme religion detonated a massive bomb in the basement of the skyscraper housing the stock exchange of Metropolis. The explosion and subsequent fire were so intense that the city's tallest building eventually imploded. Clearly the explosion was timed – mid-morning during the busiest period of the business year – to create maximum damage and loss of life. Total casualties, which included office workers, shoppers, and tourists, amounted to just less than 6,000 people, making it the largest single disaster ever to occur in our capital.

The people of Metropolis were shocked to their very core. It was the first time hostilities had ever reached our homeland. Owing to the military might of Metropolis, it was universally believed that our people would never experience the terror that we have been able to impose on others. The political reaction was predictable. Our great leaders competed among themselves to devise devastating ways of striking back at this new enemy. President Blushard of the Conservative Party was the chief amongst these. He declared a "war on terrorism" to prevent such an attack on Metropolis ever happening again. November 9 – popularly called 11/9 (or is that 9/11?) – would go down in the annals of infamy. The terrorists were to be tracked down and ruthlessly eliminated; and any country offering them material support would be swiftly brought to its knees. B.B.H. Blushard thundered to the rest of the world: "you are our friends or you are our enemies". Those countries thought to be protecting terrorists or providing them with weapons of mass destruction (WMDs) of a nuclear, chemical, or biological nature were theoretically branded as part of the "gang of evil". This was a clever way of targeting old enemies who may have had no contact with the Spirit-is-Supreme (SIS) terrorists.

Initially the people of Metropolis, who were united in a blend of grief, defiance, outrage, and revenge, stood firmly behind our President. But as the terrorists were hunted down and their alleged protectors were invaded and overthrown, Blushard's support began to decline. Committed to his war on terror, our President became more inventive in devising reasons for invading those countries included in his gang of evil. At the tope of this list was Babylon, a large oil-producing country, controlled by a particularly evil dictator, that had, ironically, been supported militarily by us in its earlier war against Persia. Persia at that time was our enemy of choice in the Middle East. As it transpired, the cure was worse than the disease. Babylon was nurturing conquest ambitions that threatened to destabilize this critically important oil-producing region and to disrupt the flow of oil essential for the continued prosperity of Metropolis. Blushard was determined that our great country would not be held to ransom by Middle-East bullies manipulating oil prices.

When the President announced his plan to present the Dictator of Babylon with an ultimatum to abandon his military ambitions or be invaded, the people of Metropolis were divided. While some supported this direct action, the majority preferred a policy of appeasement. Large demonstrations were organized by the opponents of war, including left-wing groups, students, opposition politicians, the clergy, and fearful citizens who were convinced that invasion of Babylon would lead to world war. In the main, they employed "moral" arguments to support their stand. Opinion polls published in the *Metropolitan Times* suggested that some 75 percent of the people opposed the war, and more than a million protestors marched through the centre of Metropolis' capital on a number of occasions, bringing the traffic to a standstill.

Once the war began, however, and Metropolitan troops experienced spectacular successes, opposition to the war fell dramatically to 44 percent, suggesting that many had not been committed to the moral arguments employed by their spokesmen. Part of the reason organized opposition to the war in Babylon fell apart so quickly was that it consisted of an uneasy coalition of a large number of groups with very different interests. They included opposition politicians who wanted to undermine the Blushard government; clergy who desperately wanted to be seen as relevant to contemporary society that has little need for religion; students who wanted to challenge the world of their parents in order to gain more power; and the fearful citizens, who were just unable to assess the real nature of the terrorism crisis but worried they would lose materially.

Undaunted by this early opposition, the President, who has staked his career on a war against terrorism, attempted energetically and imaginatively to sell his policy to the people of Metropolis. He had to keep the financial–industrial community on side. Blushard's argument for eliminating the Dictator of Babylon was threefold: the Dictator possessed an arsenal of weapons of mass destruction that could be unleashed on Metropolis with a lead time of merely 45 minutes; he was supplying terrorists with military aid; and he had developed an evil and dictatorial regime in Babylon. We were told in respect of the third of these issues, that "the basic values of Metropolis are good values: democracy, freedom, tolerance, justice; whereas those of Babylon are evil values: dictatorship, servitude, intolerance, injustice". Nothing, of course, was said about the desire to stabilize the main oil-producing region of the world or about the determination to force oil producers to maintain supplies at consistently low prices. Memories of the 1970s, when the oil producers' cartel dramatically increased the price of this strategic material, were paramount in Blushard's thinking. But the people of Metropolis were not ready for the truth.

****

The Dictator of Babylon was told a different story. Through Metropolis's diplomatic service, the Dictator was told that he might be an absolute ruler, but only of a very weak country. The armies of Metropolis would crush Babylon within weeks, and he and his vicious sons would either be killed in the invasion or tried as murderers and executed. He was told: "We know what you intend to do even before you do it, and we will be there before you to defeat your attempts to defend Babylon."

Make no mistake, the Dictator was told, Metropolis is vitally concerned to exercise effective influence, if not direct control, over the oil-producing countries, in order to achieve long-term, low-level oil prices. A strategic resource as important as oil must be secured by Metropolis to ensure our prosperity over the long run. Even massive short-run costs can be endured by a wealthy country like Metropolis to ensure long-run survival. Further, we intend to turn your dictatorship into a democracy, not because we believe that democracy is "noble" as our intelligentsia naively proclaim, but because democracy will reduce terrorism by reducing disaffection, and it will keep the other autocratic oil-producing countries in your region on their toes.

Do not be misled by the noisy but ineffectual left-wing intellectuals in Metropolis. The industrialists and financial interests, who are adamant that oil prices must be predictably low in the long run, constitute the real driving force in our country. The rest don't know what's in their best interests. While the ineffectual intellectuals criticize the strategic policies and interests in Metropolis, they are happy to consume the surpluses that the resulting dynamic process generates. They refuse to recognize that there is an iron relationship between the two: no dynamic process, no surplus. Instead they tell lies to themselves and each other, and are quick to take the moral high ground. What you must realize is that they have no effective power. They always make the mistake of believing that ideas can change the world. What they don't understand is that while desires drive, ideas merely facilitate, and, then, only when called upon to do so. The majority of Metropolitans will come around to our point of view once they understand where their best interests lie. It is our duty to educate them, even if we have to tell lies to do so.

Predictably, the Dictator responded by saying that as leader of the weaker society he is in the right and, hence, God will deliver him from the infidel. His exact words were: "God is disappointed with the enemy and He will support us. We pledge before God that we will pay them with all we have so that the enemy will go into the abyss." He was convinced that his "brave soldiers" would fight to the death to save him rather than surrender to the armies of Metropolis: "If Metropolis attacks Babylon, it will find under every rock and behind every tree or wall Babylonian fighters ready to fight and die as martyrs in the defense of Babylon." In any case, Babylon's old allies amongst the advanced countries to the north would never allow Metropolis to take sole control of the oil-producing region. Even if they did, all the Spirit-is-Supreme countries would unite and come to the aid of a brother in faith. Metropolis will greatly regret any attempt to invade Babylon.

Being clever fellows, the diplomats from Metropolis were quick to point out the fallacies in the Dictator's arguments. First, history shows that the most powerful countries invariably win the important wars. Hence, God clearly favors those societies able to help themselves. It is foolhardy for a weak society to rely on the favor of God. Second, Babylon's "brave soldiers" will not fight against overwhelming odds for a hated tyrant who has always treated them cruelly. Third, Babylon's old allies from the advanced countries to the north will not come to the Dictator's aid because, in their current reduced circumstances (arising from an unsuccessful struggle against Metropolis throughout the second half of the twentieth century), they need our financial assistance. And, last of all, some of the other Spirit-is-Supreme countries may be sympathetic to your cause, but none will endanger their own material development in the cause of religion. As always, desires drive and ideas, including religious ideas, merely facilitate.

At the end of these discussions, the President gave the Dictator a week to consider his decision. If the Dictator did not surrender his WMDs in that time, Metropolis would invade Babylon at a time of its choosing. The whole world counted down each day. While the world was distracted, the Metropolitan government passed the Patriotic Act, which gave it unprecedented powers over domestic surveillance, arrest, and incarceration without trial on the mere suspicion of being associated with terrorists. The people were told the lie that it was necessary to trade civil liberties for security. Intent on making Babylon more democratic, President Blushard made Metropolis less so.

Incredibly, the Dictator made no attempt to comply with the President's ultimatum. What could he be thinking? No country could stand against the military might of Metropolis, let alone a country as weak as Babylon. True to his word, the President mobilized his military forces and invaded Babylon, where not even token resistance was encountered. The Dictator's "brave soldiers", supposedly making a last stand on the outskirts of the capital Akkad, abandoned their military equipment and uniforms and melted into the civilian population; the "allies" from the north failed to act; and the other Spirit-is-Supreme countries merely looked the other way.

Within three weeks Babylon the Great had fallen. The Dictator and his sons were killed fleeing at the head of a vast train of trucks laden with the wealth they had plundered from their own countrymen during the previous twenty-five years. Babylon's Dictator had died for a paltry idea – the lie that he was a man of destiny and would succeed no matter what the odds against him. He had been instructed in the realities of geopolitical power by the diplomats of Metropolis, but preferred the idealities – the lies – of his own imagining. The Dictator could have retained both his power and life had he accepted these realities and surrendered his remaining military arsenal. The irony is that the

Dictator had already destroyed his WMDs. All he had to do, therefore, was to allow the weapon inspectors from Metropolis to confirm this. The Dictator lost both power and life because he had "surrendered to an idea" – and that idea was a lie.

****

With the end of a quick and successful war, the President expected to be lionized by the people of Metropolis. Instead, after an awed silence from his usual critics – the intellectuals, the press, and his political opponents – Blushard was subjected to a barrage of criticism. The intellectuals were determined to undermine the President's credibility by exposing the public lie on which the war on terrorism was based. Unlike the government, they were going to tell the truth. They began by questioning why the invading armies were not subjected to biological and chemical attack. If the Dictator had these WMDs, why hadn't he used them? It was most unlike him. Could it be that they didn't exist and that the "evidence" about them had been concocted? Surely the fact that after months of occupation no WMDs had been found confirmed this hypothesis about government deception.

The intellectuals also pointed out that, rather than abating, as the President had promised, the terrorists attacks, usually on "soft" tourist targets, actually increased after Babylon had fallen. If there were no WMDs, and as terrorism increased rather than declined, then the invasion of Babylon had been based on a series of lies. This criticism was repeated endlessly like a mantra in the press of Metropolis.

A breakthrough was made by the President's critics with the discovery that the intelligence on which Metropolis went to war was known to be false by the President and his advisors. This became clear when a weapons' scientist leaked information to the press, showing that the President had been warned that some of the intelligence about Babylon that he intended to make public was incorrect. These deliberate untruths included claims that a country to the south was supplying yellow cake to Babylon for weapons production; that Babylon had strong links to terrorist organizations; and that the Dictator of Babylon could, with 45 minutes notice, launch a nuclear attack. Yet, so anxious were intellectuals in the Metropolitan Broadcasting Commission (MBC) to expose these government lies, they not only told a series of lies themselves, but also caused so much pressure to be placed on the whistle-blowing scientist that he committed suicide. Both sides in this struggle over material self-interest dispensed with the truth and had blood on their hands; and thereafter both sides were quick to wash their hands of the affair.

This entire debate, therefore, is a lie. The intellectuals, press, and political opposition know why the President went to war in Babylon. They know it had nothing to do with terrorism or WMDs. They know it had everything to do with securing long-term supplies of oil at an acceptably low price. They know it was all about meeting the demands of the profit-seekers and keeping the dynamic strategy of Metropolis on course. In Blushard's place, the more robust amongst them would have done the same. Their aim is to advance their own material interests, not to arrive at the truth. So, instead of debating the real reason Metropolis went to war, they play games about the extent of the President's knowledge of Babylon's role in promoting terrorism and developing WMDs. Endless, boring games to deflect the truth.

The war in Babylon demonstrated that it was possible, even essential, to tell the truth to one's enemies while at the same time telling lies to one's citizens and allies. Truth and lies, as Thucydides noted 2,400 years ago, are merely part of the armory a leader requires to persuade the people to support what has to be done to ensure long-term strategic success. This, the President believed, involved securing strategic resources and eliminating antistrategists – whether they be terrorist groups or hostile societies – who are dedicated to disrupting the strategic pursuit of Metropolis. The President was prepared to let the intelligentsia take the moral high ground, because he believed it was the only thing they were good at; certainly they had no real interest in the truth itself, only in manipulating it to advance their position in society. "Who," the President is reported to have exclaimed in private to his closest advisors, "are the real hypocrites: the industrialists and their leaders who tell lies in the interests of Metropolis, or the intellectuals who claim that truth is sacrosanct and they its sole interpreters, yet use it for their own material purposes? The real debate in universities and the media," the President insisted, "should not be about the transcendent value of truth, but how to generate greater prosperity and security for Metropolis. After the war I will consider how this can be achieved."

4.

Clearly little in the moral domain has changed in the 2,400 years separating ancient Greece from modern Metropolis. Truth and lies are merely instruments employed by society's leaders to retain power and promote the strategic pursuit. Our leaders, as we have seen, are more likely to tell the truth to other weaker societies (although not to stronger societies) that they intend invading than to our own people. They tell the truth to weaker nations in order to reduce the costs of compliance, and they lie to their own citizens to gain support for their strategic policies and to retain power. The people are more concerned with survival and prosperity in the short run rather than the long run. But, of course, even weaker combatants, should not depend on consistently being told the truth. There is usually a sting in the tail: in the case of Melos it was their complete destruction; and in the case of Babylon it was the lie that democracy would be introduced. As my dynamic-strategy theory shows, democracy is a response to strategic demand, not political decree. And in a Third-World country, there is no strategic demand for democratic institutions. To rigidly impose advanced democracy would be to ensure the total collapse of Babylon.

The State

No *successful* leadership ever acts on the basis of idealism. Idealism merely leads to chaos, as we saw in Metropolis a generation ago. In the Presidential elections following a notorious case of Presidential deceit and thuggery, which was too blatant to be ignored, a naive born-again Christian unexpectedly surfed the wave of moral outrage (an outcome of **existential schizophrenia**) from the rural back-blocks to the Presidency. A man so unsuited to office that he was unable to suppress the truth that he had carnal thoughts about women other than his wife. Compare that with a later president who was unable to suppress the lie that he "never had sex with that woman". This born-again President was so out of his depth in the moral twilight of Metropolitan government that he had no chance of re-election.

The interests of more typical political leaders are not with moral values or other ideals, but with successful engagement in the **strategic pursuit**. By providing **strategic leadership** to facilitate the objectives and ambitions of the strategists they represent, societal leaders attempt to realize their own material ambitions. Thucydides had no illusions about the central role of material self-interest. Those leaders making the mistake of pursuing an ideal rather than the prevailing material realities, destroy either themselves, their societies, or both. All ideals are ruinous, whether they take the form of religion (Akhenaten), race (Hitler), political extremism (Lenin-Stalin, Pol Pot, Mao) or economic rationalism (Metropolis), because they are always antistrategic. They undermine rather than facilitate the strategic pursuit. *One should always beware intellectuals bearing ideals.*

5.

There is great confusion among the intelligentsia of Metropolis about the role of the state. This became particularly marked during the last quarter of the twentieth century when governments of the Western World lost their way. I call this the **fatal forgetfulness** because, for the first time in the history of civilization, governments on a global basis appeared to forget the role that society's leaders have always played in the strategic pursuit.

Since the early 1980s Western governments have largely abandoned their strategic leadership role. Metropolis was a leader in this respect. At that time it became fashionable to believe, under the influence of neoliberal economic experts, that the best of all worlds could be achieved simply by dismantling the organizations of strategic leadership and selling, with indecent haste and at bargain prices, the associated publicly owned infrastructure to private interests. The resulting funds were merely used as a "war chest" to fight subsequent elections by pork barreling on a massive scale. Since the early 1980s it has become fashionable in intellectual circles to believe that the strategists of Metropolis can, and should, lead themselves. This is curious fashion, because it flies in the face of human experience over the past 10,000 years. In essence, it involves abandoning the universal role of strategic leadership.

The State

What do I mean by the "universal role of strategic leadership"? Throughout the history of civilization, a close relationship has existed between those individuals – the dynamic **strategists** – who drive the material progress of society, and their leaders. It is a relationship essential to the prosperity of civilization. Indeed, the primary reason for the emergence of government at the dawn of civilization, and for its expensive maintenance ever since, was, and is, to facilitate the strategic pursuit of its people. This has been discussed at length elsewhere.[4]

Successful strategic leadership is achieved by coordinating the efforts of the strategists, directly through government directives and incentives, and indirectly through cultural institutions such as religion, ideology, and the arts. In pursuing this role the state provides basic infrastructure that is beyond the financial resources of individual and corporations, it negotiates economic and political deals with other societies, it protects the **dynamic strategy** at home and abroad from terrorists and hostile nations, it encourages the emergence of new dynamic strategies during recessions and depressions, and it provides basic facilities for the education, training, and research required to nourish the prevailing dynamic strategy. At its best, this is a proactive rather than a passive role, and it is provided by representatives of the strategists for the benefit of the strategists. Accordingly, if you wish to prosper, it is best to be among their ranks. Yet, to be successful, the strategic leaders must listen carefully to what the strategists say they require. Those that forget this requirement are always swept away, even in the most autocratic societies.

Hence, it is strategic reality and not metaphysical ideality that governs the nature and role of the state. Truth is never the objective, although it, together with its opposite, will be employed from time to time as strategic instruments in the relentless pursuit of survival and prosperity.

6.

An excellent example of the failure of governments to listen to the strategists, concerns the critical issue of climate mitigation. At the end of the first decade of the twenty-first century, the Social Democrat government of Metropolis has decided to listen to the priestly philosophers – the metaphysicians – rather than the strategists. The issue regarding the impact of climate change on the future of Metropolis and the world is one of faith. Natural scientists claiming there is irrefutable evidence that current climate change is the outcome of human activity have effectively disqualified themselves as experts on the future course of climate change and of its impact on human society. Why? because, these matters will, on their insistence, be determined by the dynamics of human society, *a subject about which they have no expert knowledge*. If they were really interested in the truth, these natural scientists would withdraw from the debate and leave it to those who do have this expertise. As they refuse to do this, their conclusions regarding the outcome of future climate change are a matter of faith, not science.

But then, the whole approach of government in Metropolis is based on faith rather than objective analysis. Take for example the recent establishment by the Social Democrats of a so-called "independent" Climate Commission, which is tasked with promoting "greater understanding and consensus about reducing Metropolis' carbon pollution". In effect, the Commission's role is not to establish the truth concerning climate mitigation and its impact on our future survival and prosperity (as natural scientists have no expertise in the dynamics of human society), but to explain and promote the government's proposed carbon tax. It will be an instrument to persuade the people of Metropolis to the "truth" of government policies on climate mitigation.

To achieve this, the government has appointed a well-known natural scientist, Professor Flim Flammery to head the Commission, and has provided him with $5.6 million to achieve this task. Professor Flammery is well known for his Malthusian approach to societal change, first propounded in *The Future Bleaters*. Despite the fact that Malthusian population dynamics has been totally discredited, Flammery argues that under certain "favorable" conditions, population growth outstrips resources, eventually leading to the collapse of the species or human society. Such a theory, however, defies real world evidence, in which population is not an independent variable, but responds to logosian demand. No viable strategic society, as I show in *The Dynamic Society* (1996), has ever collapsed as the result of Malthusian forces. Despite this, Flammery advocated that if we are to avoid crisis, the population of Metropolis should be halved. How this was to be achieved, we were not told, but in the real world, rather than the virtual one that radical ecologists inhabit, there are only two ways in the shorter-term – forced emigration or death camps! But times change, and if crisis from uncontrolled population growth and societal collapse did not prove to be a winner, then why not advocate collapse from climate change as an exciting alternative? ("Have crisis, will travel", seems to be his motto!) When interviewed about his role as Chief Commissioner, Flammery said that "I'm a scientist and I don't believe anything – we are great skeptics". But how can this be true, when natural scientists, by their own admission, have no expertise as scientists in predicting the future of human society, only as believers? Clearly, being a totally unrealistic believer does not disqualify one to head the Climate Commission. And why should it, when the objective is persuasion rather than truth?

If natural scientists have disqualified themselves, who are the experts on the future of climate change and its impact on human society? Certainly not those orthodox economists who claim to be able to measure the impact of a comprehensive climate mitigation program on the economy of Metropolis over the next one to two centuries. Why? because orthodox economic theory is only suitable for the analysis of marginal (small), short-run, and static (equilibrium) issues. Such as the determinants of the price of a cup of tea! In contrast, climate change and its impact over the next century, or so, is a non-marginal (actually

The State

it is a huge!), long-run, and dynamic (disequilibria) issue. This is a complete mismatch.

What then is required to successfully analyze climate change and the role of climate mitigation policies? The answer is as straightforward as it is difficult. It is necessary to develop and employ a realist general dynamic theory. This is a theory based not on deductive, or metaphysical, reasoning, but one based on systematic observation and strategic (inductive) thinking. A theory that can make realist predictions about the likely significant structural changes that will take place in the economy of Metropolis over the next century or so. Astoundingly, the orthodox mitigationists employing their comparative-static cost-benefit analysis, have *assumed* that here will be no significant structural change in Metropolitan or global economies over the next century or so. Can you imagine the policy failure that this prediction would have involved had it been made in the mid eighteenth century, just prior to the huge structural change known as the Industrial Revolution. And the pace of the conditions underlying paradigm change have increased exponentially since then! It is for this reason they are able to assure us that a comprehensive climate mitigation program will cost no more that 1-2 percent of world GDP each year from its inception.

In contrast, I have developed a realist general dynamic theory, based on four decades of observation and strategic thinking. As I show in detail in my book *The Coming Eclipse* (2010), there will be massive structural change occurring in the twenty-first century, on a par with that we call the Industrial Revolution. My general dynamic theory suggests that the resulting Solar Revolution will begin in the middle decades of this century and will, in the space of a few decades, transform the nature of energy use, technological change, and even the strategic *logos*. Provided, only, that Metropolis and the rest of the world resist the temptation to heed the call of the priestly philosophers of climate mitigation to establish a command climate-mitigation system. This would turn the strategic *logos* into an antistrategic society, just like that constructed by the society of Muscovy. And the end would be the same – the perversion of the normal dynamic system and collapse within the space of a few generations.

In *The Coming Eclipse* (2010) I show that the cost to the world by 2100 of derailing the Solar Revolution would amount, in 2007 prices, to 28 quadrillion dollars – or 28 million, billion dollars. To put this in a way that can be more easily understood: if the world devoted its entire GDP each year to paying off this massive sum, it would take 422 years to do so! So, a fully-fledged climate mitigation program would, by 2100, cost the world as much as 90 percent of its GDP each and every year. Even by 2050 this cost would amount to 12 percent of WGDP, and it would increase exponentially each year thereafter. So much for the calculation of orthodox economists that the total cost of climate mitigation would amount to merely 1-2 percent of GDP!

No doubt, these same economists, transported back to the mid-eighteenth century, would claim that a coercive environmental protection program would also cost a mere 1-2 percent of GDP! A coercive environmental program designed to prevent the use of timber for fuel and construction, and of horses for motive power and transport, through the imposition of the alternative power sources of water mills and wind mills, and of coolie labor. But then such a calculation would have failed to take into account the cost of legislating the Industrial Revolution out of existence. Try to imagine a world without the Industrial Revolution and its aftermath.

Interestingly, my old colleague Professor Nic Serious has thrown in his lot with the priestly philosophers. This came as a complete surprise. In the past we have had interesting discussions about the wealth and progress of nations. Admittedly, we did not agree often, but he always took an empirical approach. It is disappointing to see him sell out to this metaphysical lobby group. Why he did so I prefer not to speculate. The upshot is that he, like all born-again environmentalists, wants to eliminate unplanned societal dynamics; to conserve natural resources; to usher in "sustainability" ("equilibrium" or the "stationary state" by another name). But my realist dynamic-strategy theory shows that the sooner we exhaust the present technological paradigm and use-up fossil fuels, the sooner we will begin the new technological paradigm – the Solar Revolution. This technological paradigm shift will not only generate an exponential increase in global living standards but will release us from the current problem of increasing pollution and climate change. Mitigationists, therefore, are enemies not only of the strategic *logos* but also of the planet!

The People

1.

Are the people interested in truth? Do we embrace tertiary education so comprehensively today in order to understand reality? Do we buy books to gain insight about ourselves and life? Do we purchase television to devour educational programs, and computers to seek out the accumulated knowledge of humanity? Do we follow developments in medical science so avidly from a love of science and research? Do we consume the news of wars, terrorist attacks, serial murders, bushfires and other disaster so closely to help the victims and prevent such happenings in the future? The answer to each of these questions is a simple no. We, the people, have little interest in the truth for its own sake. Our main interest is in surviving and prospering, *and* being diverted from the consequences of our actions in doing so.

The people want and need to be entertained. We want to be told lies, entertaining lies, not the harsh, unbearable truth about ourselves and about life. We want it so badly that we have been willing to transform entertainers into a new class of the super wealthy. Who are the new super-rich groups in Metropolis? They are, as everyone knows, the film and TV stars, the pop idols, sports stars, and writers of popular books. These famous entertainers have become the new aristocracy. They are the ones wealthy enough to buy the manorial houses and estates originally created by the ancient warrior class of Metropolis during its highly successful conquest strategy, and which were subsequently taken over by the wealthy representatives of the succeeding commerce and industrial-technology strategies.

The recent surge to prominence of the entertainers is due to the revolution in electronic technology, and to the acceleration of the process of globalization. Instead of playing to local audiences numbered in the hundreds or thousands, they are seen, heard, and read by billions of people around the globe. In terms of wealth, the entertainers are second only to the entrepreneurs who own and control the media, through which their diversionary antics have been brought to the entire world. But, of course, in terms of fame, they are second to none. They are central to the illusions we need to have about life and about ourselves. Illusion is absolutely essential if we are to live with the horror of the life force within us. We cannot survive and prosper unless we can be diverted from the truth.

To what extent do the people recognize this reality? Some insight is provided by a recent survey commissioned by the *Metropolis Times*. A random sample of Metropolitans was asked to name the occupation they "most admired". The results were instructive. The three leading occupations by far were nurses, doctors (medical), and teachers; while at the other extreme were accountants, politicians, real estate agents, customs officers, and judges. Between these two extremes, the good citizens of Metropolis ranked artists, entertainers, and sportspersons – but they fell much closer to the bottom than the top of this range. The irony is obvious. While teachers and nurses are among the most admired, they are also among the most lowly paid professionals in Metropolis; and while entertainers and sportspeople are not high in the "most admired" rankings (with a mere 15 percent of the votes of the top three occupations), the elite among them are paid multi-millions of dollars by the same public. Nurses and teachers are among the "most admired", but not the most valued. Where lies the truth?

It would, for reasons to emerge shortly, be interesting to know how much Metropolitans admire the writers of children's books in comparison with nurses and teachers. Unfortunately, the survey commissioned by the *Metropolis Times* doesn't tell us. Except by implication. No one bothered to nominate the writing of children's books as a most-admired occupation. Perhaps no one thought it was an occupation, admired or not. Yet, during the past year, a children's author sold a record number of books in any classification on the first day of publication. It was the fifth book in a popular series written by this author – Jake Roulin – over the past few years. The subject matter was magic and alchemy, something that had been purged in serious literature by the scientific revolution that began with Galileo at the beginning of the seventeenth century. This form of escapism has plunged the child and adult readers of this author back into a world of lies and illusion that hasn't existed in serious literature for four centuries.

On the first day of publication, the fifth volume in this travesty of reality sold almost 2 million copies in Metropolis. And over the last calendar year (2003) its author has received $300 million from the sale of all books in this series, more than half from the last of these, which had been on sale for only seven months. Roulin's earning power during the past year has placed her – she uses a male pseudonym – fifth on the list of Metropolis's highest earners, far outpacing even our greatest football player who came in at 34th with an income of $50 million. Even though she has been publishing books for only a few years, and comes from a poor background, her accumulated wealth of $1.3 billion places her at 122nd on the "rich list" of Metropolis (and 552nd in the world), some eleven places ahead of our Queen. Where on that "rich list", I wonder, are the architects of the twenty-first-century science that has displaced magic and alchemy? Also, it is interesting that immature readers, whatever their age, seem more in need of lies and illusion than most. Perhaps the shock of discovering the truth about life is just too much for them.

****

What do the *Metropolis Times* surveys have to tell us about the importance of truth in the daily life of our society? When asked whether it was "acceptable" for politicians to lie, 60 percent said "no", and only 28 percent said "yes", with 12 percent saying "maybe". When the same respondents were categorized according to age, only 5 percent of those under 20 years thought it was acceptable for politicians to lie; but this rose rapidly to 30 percent for those 21 to 35 years, and to 40 percent for those 36 to 55 years. But it fell to 23 percent for those over 55 years.

There are a number of conclusions we can draw from this survey date. First, there is a clear majority who believe it is not acceptable for our political leaders to lie to us. This contrasts with our earlier observation of the preferences that Metropolitans have for lies over truth in their daily lives. Clearly we say one thing, while acting out its negation. Hence, we lie to ourselves and others about the real choices we make in life. This is a double lie. Second, we are more tolerant of political lies when we are battling to make our way in the world. No doubt our own lies make us more tolerant of the lies of others. In contrast, the under 21s and the over 55s are forced less often to make the choice between truth and material prosperity and, hence, they are able to be more idealistic and less realistic.

The double standards we juggle so expertly were further exposed in this survey when the same respondents were asked to rank the "truthfulness" and the "effectiveness" of four of our leading politicians. While only 26 percent ranked President Blushard as the "most honest" of the four, 60 percent believed him to be the "most effective". The least truthful leader was considered to be the best. The inconsistency here is highlighted by responses to the question: "What do you look for in a political leader?": 34 percent said honesty; 18 percent, strength; 17 percent, fairness; 17 percent, effectiveness; 7 percent, personality; 7 percent, other. Hence, while these respondents claimed that honesty as a desirable attribute was twice as important as effectiveness, they rated the popularly elected President Blushard as more than twice as effective as he was honest (relative to other major leaders). This inconsistency was also reinforced by a separate survey undertaken at the same time by the government-funded MBC (Metropolis Broadcasting Commission), which found that while two-thirds of the respondents believed that President Blushard had lied to them over the war on terrorism, more than 50 percent said they would re-elect him. Truth is clearly not taken as seriously by the public as they claim it should be. This makes the government's task of telling truth to one's weaker enemies, but lies to one's electorate, so much easier.

****

The good citizens of Metropolis, according to the same survey conducted by the *Metropolis Times*, also believe that we have become "less honest" at work and in the home. When asked "have Metropolitans become less honest

The People

in business and work?," 63 percent said "yes", 16 percent said "maybe", and only 21 percent said "no". And when asked if we had become less honest in our "everyday lives", only 44 percent said "yes", 16 percent said "maybe", and 40 percent said "no".

Once again there are a number of interesting conclusions to be drawn. First, we appear to be getting progressively less honest! That standards of honesty are slipping has probably been the impression of every generation since the dawn of civilization. Of course, had this been true, we would all be lying to each other all the time, which would make any form of social interaction completely impossible. Probably what our respondents really mean is not that Metropolis is becoming progressively less honest, but that they, as individuals, have become less honest since they abandoned the naive idealism of youth supported by the income of their parents in order to survive and prosper in the wider world. This occurs generation after generation against the background of a relatively stable degree of honesty/dishonesty in society as a whole. In other words, honesty/dishonesty is stable for society and cyclical for individuals. Only when a society's dynamic strategy has been terminally exhausted, and it is headed for collapse, will the degree of honesty decline significantly from the norm. The implication is that we are lying to ourselves and the surveyor by projecting our own "maturing" dishonesty onto society.

Second, the willingness to blame others rather than ourselves for our own "maturing" dishonesty can be seen reflected in this survey's differential evaluation of dishonesty at work and in the home. We see business as more dishonest than the family. The "no" vote for declining honesty was twice as high for our "everyday lives" (40 percent) as for "business and work" (21 percent). Clearly our perception of a growing dishonesty in Metropolis is regarded as more the fault of business ("them") than the family ("us"). Someone else is always to blame. Further, a higher proportion of females than males thought that Metropolitans at work (55 percent compared to 45 percent) and in the family (57 percent to 43 percent) had "become less honest". As males dominate both spheres of life, females are saying, in effect, that they are more honest than males. Men are to blame for the decline in honesty. Our lives, quite clearly, are a tissue of lies.

2.

The people of Metropolis want to be entertained not informed. They want to be diverted from reality, not reminded of their role in its darker side. Our demands are well catered for by both the electronic and print entertainment providers. My preference is for books rather than the Internet and I'm pleased to note that we Metropolitans are still great readers. But exactly what do we read? To answer this question in a fairly impressionistic way, I have, over the past twelve months, taken a close interest in the book offerings of the main bookshops in Metropolis.

The "new releases" section of all our bookshops consist of hundreds of would-be bestsellers that all look the same in their florid covers. On closer inspection there are a varying mixture of romances, political thrillers, detective stories, horror stories, historical novels, biographies of sports heroes and other entertainers, quirky real-life stories, travel books, and cooking books. All to satisfy the senses. From the lurid cover illustrations it would seem that sex plays a central role in most of them. It is curious how we celebrate what we have in common with the rest of nature rather than what sets us apart. Books on more cerebral matters rarely find their way onto the new releases shelves – with the sole exception of a breathless history of science written by a very popular travel writer – but are tucked away on more specialized and obscure shelves usually found at the rear of the bookshop.

Of late, even the new releases are beginning to look jaded and less confident. With good reason. Their former readers are turning away in increasing numbers from this printed gruel, despite the expensive promotion provided by the popular presses. The fortunes made by the pioneers of these popular books led to a vast wave of hopeful imitators that eventually swamped the market for this form of entertainment and escapism. Popular publishers, initially enjoying supernormal profits, are now finding it difficult to cover their extravagant marketing expenditures and authors' advances. Even the pioneering popular authors are currently experiencing falling sales. Diversion from reality appears to require constant change to refresh jaded palates.

Against this background of growing reader boredom, a number of major new departures have occurred to revitalize reader interest in "literary" diversion. During the second half of 2003, a few new forms of publishing successes have emerged. The first and most phenomenal was the publication of a children's book about magic and alchemy that also appealed to many adults. As mentioned elsewhere, it broke all sales records and remained at number one in our leading bookshops for about five months, and was only finally pushed aside by a book detailing the sexual preferences of a not-so-anonymous housewife. Children's magic and housewives' sexual exploits promise to be the new form of popular entertainment over the next few years as the imitators begin turning to these topics and looking for all-too-willing publishers. A few hopefuls are already appearing prominently on the new-releases shelves, with titles like "How I Left Hubby at Home and Had an Affair in Italy"!

While other "literary" forms are unlikely to seriously challenge this type of entertainment for a number of years, a few have found their way into the minor placings. These include the memoirs of a former First Lady of Metropolis, who had been publicly embarrassed by the sexual exploits of her husband, a former President, together with the surprising and heroic attempt by a popular travel writer to make the history of science entertaining to the people. And, of course, there are the old faithfuls: travel adventures and cooking delights. What better way of diverting us from the unappetizing realities of life.

3.

I thought it might be instructive to read some of the new popular writers to establish what the ingredients are for diverting the people from reality. Try as I might, the only one I could open was a history of science and scientists written by a highly successful travel writer called William Byson.[1] Byson, for obvious reasons, is usually referred to as "Buffalo" Bill. One irreverent critic even suggested that just as William Cody, the original Buffalo Bill, turned the Wild West into a traveling sideshow, so William Byson, the new Buffalo Bill, has turned the scientific world into a freak show. That will be worth following up.

Even popular travel writers probably become bored making large amounts of money by writing to a formula. But who would have expected the doyen of these to attempt to transform science into popular entertainment? Clearly the challenge of doing so must have been considerable, because the people of Metropolis prefer fantasy to reality, and lies to truth. It would take a very clever writer to meet this challenge.

Bill Byson is a very clever popular writer. Indeed, one has the impression that he only blundered into travel writing by accident and, finding he could make a very nice living from it, was unable to escape. Perhaps this new book is Byson's attempt to do so. Certainly it is a very considerable literary achievement. It tells a comprehensive story about the beginning of both the Universe and Earth, the rise and fall of life, together with the part played by science in enabling this story to be told. It comprises a fusion of a history of science and of scientists on the one hand, with a history of the "evolution" of inorganic and organic structures. Inevitably, important parts of the story get left out – such as the first great scientist Galileo Galilei (1564–1642) among many others – but what is included has been shaped into an entertaining account of this unlikely subject for popular readership. Yet, while this story exudes sensationalism, it lacks the excitement of real discovery and genius, which can only be found in books that the people of Metropolis fail to find entertaining – works of truth rather than illusion.

Byson takes a schoolmasterly approach to his subject. He is determined to make us interested in all these arcane facts about the Universe, Earth, life, and all that. There is a "golly, gosh" tone to it all. He labors matters like the *enormous* distances in space, the *immense* number of stars in the heavens, the *vast* number of species – and he repeats it all, just in case we were looking out the window, or stuffing Sally's long blond plaits in the inkwell. And in good show-business style, Byson tries to keep us on the edge of our seats by scaring the life out of us. We are warned about the very real possibility of collision with *gigantic* asteroids; the outbreak of *massive* earthquakes, *huge* volcanoes (Yellowstone, we are told is a "supervolcano" 65 kilometers wide just waiting for a record number of tourists to arrive before exploding), and *scalding* hydrothermal explosions; of being swept away by *massive* rock falls and landslides; of being *swamped* by the effects of global warming or, alternatively, being left high and dry and *frozen* by the sudden onset of a new, much overdue, ice age; and of the high likelihood of bacterial and viruses running out of control and *eating* us all from the inside out! In concluding he reassures us that "only one thing is certain: we live on a knife edge". And we thought it was only death and taxes!

This schoolmasterly seriousness is, however, leavened with humor, usually at the expense of the scientists whose work he lifts from simple textbooks. Scientists – or at least a highly selective sample – are characterized as "eccentric", "odd and crazed-looking", "unstable", "peculiar", "foolish", "buffoons", and as possessing "charming oddity", and even "interestingly willful hair". We are told engaging stories about their amusing forgetfulness, and of gentleman geologists going into the field in top hats and academic gowns, as if this were more unusual in earlier centuries than people dressed in tee-shirts and jeans today. Byson drags out all the old stereotypes of academics that can be relied upon to appeal to the self-defensive prejudices of the good people of Metropolis.

Like the omniscient schoolmaster he probably should have been (except that this would not have been very remunerative), Byson treats history's most innovative thinkers as wayward, but amusing, schoolboys. Yet he is careful not to treat any female, or any prominent scientist who is still alive, in this untruthful way. While this is a good survival technique, it also betrays a widely held view that people in earlier times were more child-like and simple than we are. We can afford to indulge, therefore, in gentle, even affectionate, ridicule, owing to our superior level of knowledge and intellectual sophistication. There is no recognition here of average intellects today seeing further than scientists in the past merely because they stand (with considerable assistance from others) on the shoulders of giants.

Byson has attempted to keep the unruly schoolchildren of Metropolis entertained throughout this lower-form science lesson by turning the story of science into a modern-day sideshow. Through entertainment the hard-won truths of science are turned into diverting lies. This raises the issue not only of motives, but also of property rights. The overwhelming majority of the scientists in Byson's story – and the many who were omitted – failed to profit from the new ideas they discovered and developed. Indeed, because new ideas tend to undermine the reputations and careers of one's academic peers, these ideas and their originators are ignored, boycotted, and savagely attacked by other more orthodox scientists. A tragic outcome was that many highly innovative scientists suffered severely from depression and physical illnesses, and not a few actually committed suicide.[2] Only after – often long after – their deaths, were they recognized for their important achievements, not only in helping us understand our world but also profiting from this understanding.

Those who turn truth into entertainment are the ones who reap the personal and financial rewards that have been denied to the world's scientific geniuses.

The People

There is an excellent case here for the granting of intellectual property rights in ideas, as well as in the form in which these ideas are communicated. This would at least grant benefits to the families of genius, if not to the individual scientists. But, of course, that would be to acknowledge that truth is as important as entertainment.

4.

What of truth and terrorism? Terrorism has been a major episode in the recent history of Metropolis. It was a great shock to the people. For the first time in living memory, war had been brought to the homeland. Throughout the nineteenth and twentieth centuries, the wars in which Metropolis participated occurred in the backyards of others. Not ours. It came as a massive shock that terrorists from the Third World could penetrate our defenses. After all, Metropolis is the most powerful country the world has ever known.

We were shocked, but also fascinated. We couldn't tear ourselves away from our TVs, as the disaster was shown over and over again. We were shocked but, more significantly, we were also entertained. For our diversion, the media of Metropolis turned this real but minor tragedy into the greatest, most brazen, cowardly, and life-threatening outrage in the entire history of human civilization. We were told by the President, who linked arms with the heroic firemen at the "outrage site", that these terrorists are the most important threat to our survival, and that they must be pursued relentlessly until they are all rooted out and utterly destroyed. The good people of Metropolis had been viciously and unpremeditatedly attacked by forces of evil. We need to realize, he told us, that we are now involved in a desperate struggle between good and evil, between the truth and the lie. We must not rest until the struggle has been won and evil vanquished. It was nothing less than a new holy crusade. We were shocked but also secretly thrilled. This was the best entertainment in town.

Our leader is right, we exclaimed: we must win this struggle between good and evil. We must pursue these evil terrorists no matter where they hide, no matter what the financial cost. We must stand behind the President as he leads us in this great crusade. We were no longer shocked. We were consumed by righteous indignation and desire for revenge. Only a few confused souls protested weakly that the pursuit of revenge would merely make things worse – make us even more tempting targets for terrorists. We treated them with contempt.

The highly effective secret service of Metropolis (MSS) discovered that the base employed by the terrorists was in Media, a poverty-stricken Middle-Eastern nation dominated by a ruthless class of religious fundamentalists. Here the terrorists were trained in their evil ways, and here they were developing plans for further attacks into the very heart of Metropolis. Excitement mounted when the Medes refused our demands to surrender the terrorist leaders to our assembling forces. Our gallant leader on hearing this shocking news called a special meeting of the People's Palace and informed the assembled members and, through national television, the entire people of Metropolis that he has declaring war on Media in order to destroy not only the terrorists but also the uncooperative and, hence, evil fundamentalist Median regime. The people of Metropolis as one (with the exception of those mindless pacifists) rose, briefly, from their TV sofas to cheer and offer our heroic President their full support. This war was going to be a TV event not to be missed. Entertainment at its very best.

With the collapse of the evil Medes – presented in color on television – our great leader became convinced that the focus of global terrorism had shifted to Babylon. The people of Metropolis, however, were not so sure. After the government announced its plans to invade Babylon in the name of democracy and freedom, a growing proportion of the people began to whisper among themselves that Babylon had no obvious links to the Spirit-is-Supreme fanatics. Some even began to accuse the President of hypocrisy – of concealing imperialist aims behind the rhetoric of a crusade for freedom against the evil forces of terrorism. Can you image that: accusing the President of lying to the people!

Quick to realize that this rapidly growing opposition from the people of Metropolis could derail his strategic plans, the President initiated an "information drive" – "propaganda program" the more cynical called it – to demonstrate that Babylon was an immediate threat to our security. The people were well-meaning, he told his advisors, but, because their immediate welfare was not linked to the invasion of Babylon, they failed to understand what was in their long-term interests. They had to be persuaded to support this extended war on terrorism – the name he applied to anyone threatening the strategic resources as well as the population of Metropolis – even if it was necessary to be "somewhat liberal with the truth". Sometimes, our great leader argued in private, it is necessary to tell strategic lies in order to arrive at a greater truth. This is how our President, a practicing Christian, attempted to justify his actions to himself and his closest supporters. I know, because one of his aids is a former student of mine.

I have already rehearsed, elsewhere in my notebooks, the arguments employed by the government of Metropolis to persuade the people of the justice of the Babylonian war. It was highly successful. The President achieved the support from the public and their political representatives that he required to wage war. Yet, not everyone was convinced. While this war was going to rest heavily on the taxpayers, it would not contribute directly to their prosperity, nor even to their survival as it was likely to provoke further terrorist attacks in the short run. Only the industrialists and financiers of Metropolis, who could supply the equipment requirements of the military or would receive contracts for the post-war reconstruction of Babylon, would gain directly from this war. This is why our leaders felt it necessary to exaggerate the threat posed by the Dictator of Babylon.

Once the invasion began, the proportion of people supporting the war surged. Once gain the war on terrorism became the best show in town. The people followed every airborne attack on Akkad, the Babylonian capital, every massive explosion, every burst of tracer bullets arcing across the night sky. After all, the government had promised them a great display of "shock and awe". Without doubt, this was the President's most successful sales pitch – bread and circuses.

Modern wars are the ultimate in "reality" television. Not that reality TV is about reality, it is about diversion from reality – about lies, illusions, and entertainment. In the ancient world dominated by the dynamic strategy of conquest, the people benefited materially from war through plunder, whereas in the modern world dominated by the dynamic strategy of technological change, the people benefit psychically from war through diversionary entertainment. War today is the modern equivalent of the Colosseum in Rome. War as reality has been replaced by war as fantasy, where truth rather than troops are the main casualties.

Only after the war had been rapidly concluded by the invading armies of Metropolis, and the entertainment had ceased, did the people again begin to question the wisdom of this "extended" war on terrorism. They became particularly concerned about the failure of Metropolitan forces to uncover the WMDs that the President had assured us all were being stockpiled by the Beast of Babylon, and later, by the growing casualties among our occupying forces. It became clear to most of the people that the government had lied to them about the reasons for going to war. And yet, as we have seen, a majority of the people still support our President. Quite clearly, strategic interests and diversionary entertainment are more important to the people of Metropolis than the truth. Only the growing casualties sustained in policing Babylon may shift the political balance.

5.

Truth and participation in terrorism. This is not an easy subject to explore, because few participants in terrorism are willing to talk about their involvement. When challenged, most ex-terrorists strenuously deny any involvement at all. Those willing to admit any participation are convinced their actions were justified by the evil forces that threatened to destroy them and their society. Truth is an extremely scarce commodity among terrorists.

The most appalling act of terrorism in the modern world was that committed by the Nazis against the Jews and other minorities in Europe. Some six million people were victimized, had all their property confiscated, were placed in concentration camps under inhuman conditions, and were finally slaughtered. All of this is well known, except, it would seem, by the greatest of all liars who continue to deny it. What I want to explore here is how individuals in the Nazi regime were able to justify their participation, either directly or indirectly, in this systematic process of genocide. What lies did they have to tell themselves in order to remain sane in the midst of this unjustifiable brutality and degradation? There are two interesting cases with which I am familiar – Albert Speer and Bruno Manz – that can be used to explore this issue. While Albert Speer was Hitler's architect and, later, overlord of the entire Nazi war economy and Hitler's hopeful heir, Bruno Manz was merely a young man who grew to maturity in the Third Reich, entering the army and participating in Hitler's war on leaving school. These two men were at the opposite ends of a whole society implicated in this monumental tragedy – a whole society that was effectively able to look the other way, to accept and act out lies rather than the truth.

Albert Speer made a Faustian contract with the forces of evil. He was taken up to the mountain top and shown the whole of Europe transformed both politically and architecturally under his ultimate leadership. Rather than telling Hitler, a modern personification of the devil, to get behind him, he accepted all that was offered, albeit after a mighty struggle with his conscience. Because Speer was the only organizational genius in the Third Reich, and because he was the only one in the Nazi Party that Hitler could really trust, in 1942 he became the supreme authority over the Nazi war economy, and appeared likely to become Hitler's successor.

Speer always claimed never to have known about the Holocaust. Clearly this was the greatest of all lies. A lie told by a man who regarded himself as an educated and civilized European, a lie necessary to retain his own sanity and sense of dignity as he participated in the most inhuman act that any society could ever perpetrate. Despite his protestations to the contrary, Speer as Reich Minister for Armaments and War Production employed slave labor under appalling conditions in his factories, which he regularly visited; and he was a keynote speaker at the infamous meeting in Posen on 6 October 1943 when Himmler announced, to the Nazi hierarchy, Hitler's plans to systematically exterminate the Jews in Europe. Speer always claimed he didn't know he was working slaves to their deaths in his factories, or that the Jews and other minorities of Europe were being systematically exterminated. This beggars belief. Even Bruno Manz, a junior NCO sent to fight the Soviets in the Arctic Circle had heard rumors about the death camps. How much more would the second most important person in the Third Reich from 1942 have known about a vast undertaking that locked up a substantial proportion of transport and organizational (including a major network of Global Business Machines (GBM) punch-card machines) resources that otherwise would have been available to Speer's Ministry.

Clearly the Holocaust was so offensive to Speer's civilized sensibilities that he found it impossible to face the truth of his complicity in this unthinkable crime against humanity. Only the most evil of men – men like Hitler and Himmler – could contemplate it openly. But, of course, they too had defensive arguments concerning the need to exterminate "vermin" that were destroying the Third Reich from within. Even Speer, revolted as he was by this genocide, was not going to let it derail his destiny of transforming Europe. As he could not accept Hitler's arguments about the socially corrosive nature of the Jews, Speer's only way forward was to lie to himself and others about his knowledge of the death camps. Speer's case shows what a powerful strategic instrument is **existential schizophrenia.**

Nevertheless, for a cultured man like Speer, this self-deception was not easily achieved. This struggle between ambition and conscience led to a complete nervous and physical breakdown from late January to early February 1944, just three months after the Posen meeting. Initially Speer seemed to be seeking death – which came very close – as a solution to this enormous moral dilemma, but gradually his Napoleonic ambition gained the upper hand. Once he had embraced his Faustian contract, Speer quickly regained his health, returned to his Ministry, and swept aside his rivals (Bormann, Himmler, Göring, and Ley) who, in the Reich Minister's absence, were attempting to assume his role as heir apparent. By this time, Speer had expunged all knowledge of the Holocaust from his conscious mind. There would be no further repetition of this crisis of conscience. The truth had been denied once and for all. Even after the war – during his long imprisonment and final release – Speer was unable to admit that he knew anything about the Holocaust, even under the brilliant questioning of his biographer.[3]

****

Bruno Manz played a very different part in the crimes of the Third Reich. He was, according to his own account, brought up by a loving father, who was a committed Nazi and anti-Semite.[4] Manz was an early member of the Hitler Youth, enthusiastically accepted Nazi propaganda, was a moderate anti-Semite, and believed that Hitler was the world's greatest human being. On leaving school, he joined the army of the Third Reich and was part of the force that occupied Finland and fought the Soviets in the Arctic Circle.

Manz's autobiography is a frank account of his acceptance of Nazi doctrine and of the numerous times he was confronted by the truth from which he turned away lest his whole world unravel. Hitler only fell from the pedestal on which Manz had placed him when it became clear that the war had been lost. Yet, even then he failed to realize that his former idol had been guilty of crimes against humanity. Although he had heard rumors of the concentration camps, his initial reaction to post-war news of the Holocaust was total disbelief and a determination to prove the critics wrong. But Manz's research led him to the opposite conclusion.

Once convinced of the truth of the charges made by the Allies at Nuremberg (a conviction not shared by his father), Manz's life changed forever. In the early fifties he and his wife left Tutonia (where, after the war, he had earned a PhD in physics) for Metropolis to work on missile technology and, where later in life, he wrote a frank autobiography to atone for his involvement in Hitler's crimes. Of this turning point in his life, Manz said: "It was as harrowing as Judgement Day, but it was the truth, the sacred truth".[5] This truth had been withheld from him in his youth, and had been rejected on many occasions when it arose to confront him. But in the end he was honest enough to admit his participation, albeit unknowingly, in these crimes, and decent enough to use his autobiography to "apologize" to the victims and to "ask for forgiveness".

Of course, it was easier for Manz to face the truth than it was for Speer, because Manz's moral failings were minor in comparison, and his responsibility, which he shared with the vast majority of his countrymen, was indirect. True, Manz had been rude to Jewish acquaintances and had refused to investigate the warning signs as some of his more scrupulous comrades had done (leading to the death of at least one of them), but he had not entered into a Faustian contract with the forces of evil as Speer had done. Of course, he had never been offered such a contract! Interestingly, of the mighty Reich Minister, Manz writes:

> With regard to Speer, I still believe he knew more than he admitted. If word of the concentration camps had reached me at the Arctic front, then surely it must have reached Speer in Berlin. As engaging a personality as he was, I believe he deserved his long sentence in Spandau.[6]

What, I wonder, would Manz, or anyone else, have done in Speer's place? It is revealing that on migrating to Metropolis in the 1950s, Manz embraced what he calls the "Metropolis spirit" – a love of democracy, freedom, and toleration. Indeed, he is convinced that had the Metropolitans been in Tutonia's situation in the interwar period, they would, owing to this Metropolis spirit, not have acted as the Tutonians had done.

Unfortunately, for all his introspection, Manz has failed to realize that the "Metropolis spirit" is merely an institutional and attitudinal response to the requirements of a highly successful dynamic strategy generated in Metropolis. Had the Metropolitans, with all their democratic traditions, been miraculously transported to Tutonia in the immediate post-World War 1 era – where they would have experienced the collapse of their dynamic strategy – it is highly likely that they too would have responded by placing their faith in the promises of the radical right. National "spirit" cannot be divorced from the material circumstances that give rise to it. Even in Metropolis today, there are a number of influential intellectuals who see no reason to trust the "Metropolis spirit". In the end, one is left with the impression that Manz was able to transfer his faith from the "spirit" of the Third Reich to the "Metropolis spirit" a little too easily. National ideology, whether fascist or democratic, should always be viewed with a healthy skepticism.

****

The People

Many people in World War 2 had experiences that fell between these two extremes. Caught up in extraordinary events, very ordinary people committed horrific crimes against humanity. There are many examples, not just those confined to the Axis powers. But the difference between Axis and Allied atrocities was that the former were condoned or encouraged by military and political authorities, right to the top of the chain of command. Axis atrocities, therefore, were more systematic and were undertaken on a larger scale.

I have recently seen televised interviews with two engineers from the Rising-Sun Society who were amongst those ordered by their high command to construct the Burma railway as quickly as possible with slave labor consisting of allied POWs and Asian indentured workers. Hundreds of thousands of men (and, in the case of the former indentured workers, also women and children) were worked to death on this amazing engineering project. The interviewed responses of the two Rising-Sun engineers, who were responsible for thousands of deaths, were quite different but essentially the same. One denied that any deaths had occurred on his section of the line, while the other agreed that many had died, but claimed it was due, not to overwork, brutality, and criminal neglect, but to the inability of POWs to adapt to a rice diet! Even half a century later, neither man was able to admit to the interviewer, nor to himself, that he was a brutal mass murderer.

****

Since World War 2 there have been many outbreaks of terrorism throughout the world by terrorist groups and terrorist states. As we have come to expect, the participants on both sides of these brutal acts had no difficulty justifying the atrocities they committed. Take the case of Algeria, fighting for its independence against the imperial Frankish power. The Algerian "freedom fighters" enlisted attractive young women to plant bombs in crowded cafes that exploded, killing large numbers of civilians, after the bombers had left. (This was the time before the popularity of suicide bombings.) One of these female bombers, now a successful lawyer, told a television interviewer that she had no regrets because "the imperialists were oppressive and brutal". On the Frankish side, a retired senior army officer admitted to torturing and killing Algerian rebels. His excuse, which appears sufficiently effective to enable him to sleep at night, was that he had "a great responsibility" to obtain information about Algerian insurgents.

Rebel leaders in other independence movements – in Judaea, Cape Colony, and Setting-Sun Island for example – were also able to justify the violence and killing they sanctioned and were involved in, by their conviction regarding the importance of their causes. Two such leaders were even granted the Nobel Peace Prize many years later. Needless to say their opposite numbers were just as ruthless and just as adept in justifying their crimes to themselves. Truth and terrorism do not walk the same path.

What of terrorism today? Terrorists still lie to themselves and others so as to destroy the lives of their fellow human beings and, at the same time, to think of themselves as heroic and decent people. Today, only the type of justification they employ has changed. Increasingly, terrorists are invoking the name of a divinity to justify their actions. The most extreme of these are even convinced that their god not only approves the atrocities they are committing but will even reward it in what they like to think of as the afterlife. Hence, suicide bombers – the latest terrorist fashion – lie to themselves that, when they die a martyr's death, they will go instantly to "paradise". The clergy who persuade young impressionable people to take this insane course of action are, according even to the mainstream of their own religion, evil men who distort the words of their own prophets for their own ends. Their lies feed their own ambitions. Truth would destroy their antistrategic cause – their crusade against life.

Yet, as we now know, the terrorists do not have a monopoly on callous brutality and untruth. The military forces of Metropolis are also guilty of systematic breaches of the Geneva Convention in the treatment of prisoners in Babylon. Our great President has never ceased to tell us that we are a force for good in the world, and that an important reason for our invasion of Babylon was to overthrow a tyrant who tortured and killed large numbers of his own people. Yet, only a year after the war, graphic images from inside the old tyrant's prison in Akkad show that our own security forces are also guilty of systematic brutality, sexual crimes, and religious humiliation. The initial response at all levels, of course, was denial. Our great and worthy government declared it the random work of degenerate individuals, and these "degenerate" individuals claimed they were only acting on orders from their superior officers. Obviously they were also ordered to enjoy themselves in the process, as the photographs leaked to the media show some very happy jailers in the presence of many frightened and humiliated prisoners. Once again, no one was willing to accept responsibility or to tell the truth.

The Intellectuals

1.

There is a great deal of confusion in both educated and general circles about the role of intellectuals in society. Owing to the highly specialized and inaccessible nature of cerebral pursuits, intellectuals are regarded with considerable suspicion by the general public. They are distrusted and resented by the people, largely because they possess the potential to embarrass non-intellectuals concerning their own cerebral capabilities.

Curiously, most people are more sensitive to intellectual than physical shortcomings. We are happy to lionize an "elite" sportsperson but become very defensive about intellectual giants. I suppose we feel we understand what sport is about and can participate in it, if only at a basic level. That an "elite" sportsperson is physically superior to us is not a matter of concern. We are, in fact, prepared to exaggerate sporting achievements and regard our best sportspeople as "heroes" or even "gods".

On the retirement recently of a famous ballplayer, for example, the *Metropolis Times*, under the bold heading "Twilight of a god among gods" (Zarathustra's substitution of "idols" for "gods" would be more apt), trumpeted:

> Our hero, who has assured himself a place among the elite of the elite, belongs in the Pantheon reserved for our sporting gods ... The Pantheon – a domed temple of the gods erected by the Roman emperor Hadrian – is a particularly apt term ... He is more than a sportsman – he is a gladiator. He has taken sporting combat to a new level.

All this purple prose about a man in his late thirties who plays a game – striking a hard leather ball with a piece of wood – that most of us abandoned once we left school. About a man who participates in a very simple and intellectually undemanding form of entertainment. Needless to say, he was that year's recipient of the award for "Metropolitan of the Year", rather than the medical scientist who had developed the "bionic ear" that has already restored hearing to tens of thousands of people. And to compound this insult, the bionic-ear man, who is in his prime, was offered "*Senior* Metropolitan of the Year" in the following year! It is unthinkable that such superlatives ever be attached to an intellectual genius, even though he might be responsible for an idea that fundamentally changes the lives of all of us for the better. In fact it is virtually forbidden to even talk about intellectual "elites". To be accused of intellectual elitism is the most wounding indictment imaginable by the people. They suffer a huge intellectual inferiority complex.

At a deeper level, the people feel threatened by intellectual elitism because, as shown in *The Collapse of Darwinism* (2003), finesse rather than force has long been the successful dynamic strategy of the mammal dynasty in general and of mankind in particular. It was the pursuit of finesse rather than force that generated the Intellectual Revolution (2 myrs to 0.15 myrs BP), which transformed the size and complexity of hominid brains. In this remarkable process of genetic change through **strategic selection**, those individuals with greater intelligence eliminated those with less in the struggle to survive and prosper. So important was this cerebral transformation to what we are today that the people still fear intellectual elites will eclipse them as they did in our deep past.

Intellectuals, on the other hand, usually overrate their importance in contemporary human society. They like to think they play a driving role in the progress of human civilization. After all, innovative ideas of all types are closely associated with advances in human society today. Many intellectuals, therefore, find it difficult to understand why those who gain most from the progress of civilization are those who own or manage physical capital rather than those responsible for creating ideas. They find it difficult to answer the defensive quip: "If you're so smart, why aren't you rich?" But all of this washes over those intellectuals of patrician demeanor, who believe, contrary to all evidence, that their caste can actually reshape the world just by thinking about it. Perhaps they are the reason that many people hate intellectuals.

When considering the role of intellectuals, we should always remember the dictum that "desires drive and ideas facilitate".[1] I have demonstrated at length elsewhere that the force driving both human society and life is strategic desire, and that the resulting strategic demand is responsible for eliciting the provision of a variety of strategic inputs ranging from factors of production (land, labor, and capital), institutions (societal rules), organizations, and, last but not least, ideas.[2] These ideas are wide ranging, encompassing those that inform technology, science, music, the arts, and culture generally. This supply-response to strategic demand is, of course, mediated by local conditions and history. All of this will become clearer when I discuss the strategic *logos*.[3]

While it is true that not all ideas generated at any given time are a direct response to strategic demand, they can only take place within the space defined by the dynamic strategies we pursue, and they are only absorbed into human society (or life) when they facilitate our desires. Although intellectuals – except those in antistrategic societies – have a degree of freedom to generate ideas, this freedom is severely constrained. Intellectual freedom is a function of the material surplus, either public or private, that is devoted by a society to research and scholarship. This surplus is required to fund the living requirements of research staff and thinkers, as well as to provide the equipment, materials and facilities necessary to undertake the work they are engaged on. Also the objectives of most research, particularly in the natural sciences, are determined by those individuals or organizations granting research funds. Even in the social sciences and humanities, intellectual freedom is tightly constrained. The less orthodox a researcher becomes, the less financial support he can expect to receive, the less public exposure he will achieve through the conservative publishing outlets, and the less secure his research job will become. Thinkers generating radical ideas are ignored, boycotted, made redundant, and often hounded into ill-health, both physical and mental, leading even to suicide.

Intellectual history is scarred by such tragedies. These include Socrates' forced death by hemlock in 399 BC; Galileo's house arrest in 1634 and induced heart palpitations; Isaac Newton's nervous breakdown in 1693 at age 50 years; David Hume's well-known nervous breakdown in the 1730s while in his early twenties; Michael Faraday's nervous breakdown in the late 1830s when in his forties; Julius Robert von Mayer's depression and attempted suicide in 1850 at 36 years; Charles Darwin's nervous stomach, suffered all his adult life and implicated in his death in 1882 at 73 years; John Waterston's depression and suicide in 1883 at 71 years; George Fitzgerald's death from stomach ulcers in 1901 at 50 years; and Ludwig Boltzman's depression and suicide in 1906 at 62 years.[4] And this is only the tip of the iceberg of those who suffered for their ideas in a scholarly world constrained by logosian demand.

In contrast, those researchers generating ideas directly in response to logosian demand are lavished with resources, prizes (including the Nobel Prize), career promotion, "merit" allowances, and academic and social honors. These are the crumbs from the table of material success that many intellectuals are prepared to fight over. And in their rush to monopolize these strategic rewards, the worldly intellectuals are prepared to employ conquest tactics – plundering resources and positions in their own institutions – against their more innovative and, hence, exposed "colleagues". But none of these intellectual conquistadores will be ultimately recognized as the geniuses of their era. The geniuses of today are not yet known by name.

It is not recognized in intellectual circles that a tension exists between the quest for truth and the strategic pursuit. Naturally it is essential to survive and prosper if one is to pursue truth, but once prosperity becomes the prime objective, the quest for truth becomes a sham. The attempt to improve and maintain a higher material standard of living requires the systematic use of deception and lies. Truth is sacrificed on the altar of the strategic pursuit. Even philosophers who claim to understand the nature of truth fall into this trap. Even philosophers have blood on their hands, as a knowledge of Nazi Germany makes clear.

2.

What interests do intellectuals have in exposing and telling the truth? This will appear to be a redundant question to those who believe that the primary focus of intellectuals is the truth. Why, they might exclaim, does our society invest so much in universities and public research organizations if this were not so? Why indeed.

Intellectuals, of course, are no different to any other group of professionally trained people in Metropolis. Their primary concern is to survive and prosper. While they become researchers, writers, and thinkers because they posses the necessary interest and skills, the underlying objective is to make a comfortable living. The best test of this proposition would be to significantly lower the relative remuneration of researchers and observe what occupations young people with intellectual abilities select. Such an "experiment" was actually undertaken during the last quarter of the twentieth century in Metropolis and most of the Western world. Owing to the greater proportion of the population electing to go to university, together with an inability of governments to draw a distinction between the quality of institutions when granting funds for salaries, education budgets threatened to blow out. As expenditure on staff is the largest component of these budgets, the government allowed university salaries to decline substantially relative to those of other professional and managerial groups. Not surprisingly, existing academics able to find alternative employment did so, and many of the brighter students, who in earlier generations would have become academic researchers, took up employment opportunities elsewhere, particularly in the legal and financial arena. It was a triumph of strategic desire over the quest for truth.

Like all other professionals, scholars and researchers take their work seriously. But this is not the same as saying they will be successful in exposing, let alone telling, the truth. There are a number of reasons for this. First, most scholars don't have the imagination and originality to discover more than trivial aspects of reality, either in historical documents, ecosociopolitical data, or in laboratory experiments. Second, the wider implications of these minor discoveries are usually not understood, owing to the adoption of flawed theories, such as those held by Marxists, Freudians, or Darwinists.

Third, the view of the world held by scholars is usually conditioned by their metaphysical beliefs. Many natural scientists in the nineteenth and early twentieth centuries found it difficult to accept Darwin's theory of natural selection because of their Christian beliefs; just as many Muslims today have the same difficulty. As it turns out they were right, but for the wrong reasons: in my *The Collapse of Darwinism* (2003), I show that Darwinism is fatally flawed on scientific grounds. There are many other examples of ideology, especially in antistrategic societies such as the former USSR and communist China, distorting their scientists' perception of the truth.

Fourth, some intellectuals claim that the truth is unknowable, at least to them personally. It is always difficult to accept this postmodern stance as sincere, because the intellectuals holding it usually have strong views about what is right and wrong in their own specialist disciplines. And most of them have views about the way the world works, and what needs to be done to improve it. How, we might ask, is this possible if the truth is unknowable. At best, intellectuals holding this position are badly self-deceived and, at worst, they are highly disingenuous.

While the great majority of intellectuals are concerned to make their way in the world, there are some for whom it assumes particular importance. First, there are those who, in the words of a ballad recorded in the 1970s, "are just trying to keep my customers satisfied, satisfied". They tell their clients – whether government, military or business – exactly what they want to hear, in order to get repeat business and, thereby, a steady income. They tell their clients, in technical mumbo-jumbo of course, that their activities, policies, or wars are righteous and just and will be successful. Truth is bad for business in academia.

Second, there are intellectuals for whom winning is everything. Truth is not even considered by those people in their rush to acquire research funds, "merit" allowances, prizes, and academic and societal honors. Some are prepared to go to any lengths to achieve their material objectives. They lie, engage in corrupt practices, and have no compunction about destroying the departments and careers of serious scholars to gain access to their resources. This predatory activity usually increases when resources in academic institutions become relatively scarce, as occurred in the National University of Metropolis (NUM) in the late 1990s. Yet, these same "intellectuals" are quick to deny, to themselves as well as others, their involvement in untruthful activities. When their motives are questioned they indignantly take the moral high ground.

The number of intellectuals who possess the desire and ability to expose the truth of a non-trivial kind are very few indeed. They are deviants in normal human society. These few, however, are consumed by a desire to understand how the world works and what their role in it might be. They are willing to pursue this quest beyond the point where it begins to endanger their health and prosperity. While they possess considerable intellectual ability, it is their willingness to subject themselves to the long, lonely struggle to discover the truth that sets them apart from their more orthodox materialist fellows. In the process, they expose themselves not only to rejection and ridicule at the hands of their less imaginative and less scrupulous "colleagues", but also to dangerous forms of self-knowledge. Truth, as Zarathustra discovered, is a sharp instrument – an instrument of self-vivisection. Truth, therefore, is not much in demand, and few are willing or able to supply it. Even among the intelligentsia.

3.

The people appear to believe that the intelligentsia constitute a homogenous caste. Even insiders, who make the distinction between the "secular priesthood" and the principled few, appear not to understand the true divisions within intellectual ranks.[5] It will be useful to sort out this issue before focusing on the ideas of a number of leading intellectuals in Metropolis. I'm going to suggest that there are three broad categories – with a number of lesser subdivisions –

within the intelligentsia today. These categories, which are determined by the way intellectuals respond to a society's unfolding dynamic strategy, including strategic, antistrategic, and nonstrategic intellectuals. Intellectuals are not necessarily **truth-seekers**.

Strategic intellectuals are concerned to understand reality. They are the empiricists who gather and examine data about the real world, and who employ the inductive method to construct their theories. They are under no illusion that the ideas they, or anyone else, generate, drive human society. Their aim isn't to tell the dynamic strategists how to conduct the strategic pursuit, merely to advise on the removal of strategic barriers, and on matters of policy detail. They know that it is impossible to "reshape" societal institutions unless this is required by strategic demand, in which case it will happen without the "assistance" of intellectuals. The main role of strategic intellectuals, therefore, is to expose false ideas that could retard the unfolding of the existing dynamic strategy. They realize that the role of ideas in human society is to facilitate rather than drive the strategic pursuit.

Yet, while strategic intellectuals facilitate the existing dynamic strategy, they are not necessarily supporters of existing institutions. They realize that institutions can be perverted by antistrategic groups if the latter gain the necessary power to hijack the political system. Strategic intellectuals, therefore, are prepared to make critical attacks on any wayward power structure or any flawed policy stance by governments.[6] Their loyalty is to strategic truth and strategic success, not to the powers that be. They are the fewest of the few.

In contrast, **antistrategic intellectuals** see their role as attacking and destroying strategic organizations in the public and corporate sectors. Why? Because the materialistic objectives of strategic organizations, such as big business and big government, run counter to their prescriptive views about the way the world *should* work. The main antistrategic philosophy is moral idealism.

Moral idealists believe that moral principles, which are either god-given or gene-given, should be the primary basis for all individual and group action. As "moral" action systematically pursued will always cut across the strategic pursuit of any society, the idealists are determined to "overthrow power" of what they see as immoral strategic organizations in the public and corporate sectors. These idealists include some surprising bedfellows: religious fundamentalists, whether Islamic, Christian, Jewish, Hindi, or Buddhist; radical ecologists; climate mitigationists; and philosophical fundamentalists, such as Maon Linguisky (discussed elsewhere). While their methods may differ, their objectives are the same: to, in Linguisky's words, "overthrow power" – to destroy strategic institutions – and to encourage or impose the adoption of their brand of idealism on human society. This is an attempt to impose ideas on desires and, thereby, to reverse the dynamic mechanism in life.

Proactive idealists of this type are clearly antistrategists, but they are more – they are also terrorists. Everyone accepts that those religious fundamentalists who destroy individuals and their survival organizations by violent means are terrorists. But what about those who encourage the overthrow of strategic organizations, such as the government and the corporations of Metropolis, from within, all in the name of freedom, or of the ecology? If they are successful we will witness the collapse of our existing dynamic strategy of technological change, and the emergence of warlords pursuing the conquest strategy as the only viable alternative. In turn this would result in the death of many people as well as the immiserization of the survivors who are not part of the new warrior elite. Terrorists employ rhetoric as well as bombs – seductive lies as well as violence.

Finally, there are the **nonstrategic intellectuals** – the largest of the three categories – who are not interested either in supporting or undermining the strategic pursuit. Their aim is merely to live successful or comfortable lives. In the process they will give their support to whatever political or other organizational faction that happens to be in power and that provides research and salary funding. They are the "intellectuals" who happily support even antistrategic organizations as long as they provide the necessary finance. They never criticize existing governments either to keep them on the correct strategic path as do the strategic intellectuals, or to deflect them from it as do the antistrategic intellectuals. The nonstrategic intellectuals are driven not by principle but by self-interest. And they justify their position by claiming that the violence committed by their society is done for the noblest reasons and is in the world's best interests. They embrace lies rather than truths.

4.

The "war on terrorism" is society's litmus test for truth and untruth today, just as the war in Vietnam was during the late 1960s and early 1970s. It is fascinating to see how Metropolis's intellectuals have lined up on this key issue. Their public statements on this problematic issue can best be sorted out using my strategic classification.

As expected, the majority intellectual response can be pigeon-holed in the nonstrategic category. They are the ones who, either overtly or covertly, support the government stance on the way in which terrorists and their "supporters" should be treated. From this group come the "media stars", who offer commentary and predictions on each "crisis" as it arises, taking care never to criticize the authorities in a fundamental way. Elsewhere I have called them the prosperity-seekers. As they are keen to maximize their research funding, these intellectuals take on any project offering substantial financial grants, and they deliver the results that the granting organizations expect to receive. Even when funds are not involved, the nonstrategic intellectual recognizes that to get published in the right places and to be invited to join committees of inquiry, it is necessary to accept that governmental actions are always good and those of its enemies always evil. They accept the President's claim that "those who are with us are on the side of truth, and those against us are on the side of untruth". What is done to us, therefore, is terrorism, and what we do to others is liberation.

Strategic intellectuals are more discerning. They recognize the need to remove antistrategic (terrorist) forces in the world by massive military action if necessary, but they also reserve the right to criticize powerful organizations (including governments) that stray from facilitating their society's strategic pursuit to indulge in gratuitous terrorism of their own. In contrast, antistrategic intellectuals reject the need for strategic leadership and focus largely on the destructive force employed by their own governments and military, and provide support for the very terrorist forces attempting to bring their country down. They do this, as we have seen, for ideological reasons, believing that their anti-materialist objectives can be achieved only through the destruction of those forces underlying the success of the strategic pursuit.

To illustrate the thinking of our most influential antistrategic and nonstrategic intellectuals, I will focus on three of Metropolis's celebrities: Maon Linguisky, N.M. Novalis, and Seth Duckwitton.[7] While Linguisky is a radical antistrategic intellectual, Novalis is a conservative antistrategic intellectual, and Duckwitton is a conservative nonstrategic intellectual. I will explore the recent writings of each in three separate essays.[8]

5.

Maon Linguisky, a philosopher of language and the mind, came to widespread attention in Metropolis and the world during the Vietnam War, owing to his outspoken criticism of government aggression in Southeast Asia. From that time he became the intellectual leader of dissent against the abuse of power by the government of Metropolis. When the war on terrorism was declared, following the terrorist attack on Metropolis's stock exchange on November 9, 2001 (popularly called 11/9), many readers familiar with his earlier books and lectures looked to Linguisky again for intellectual leadership. They were not disappointed. What I will consider here is whether Linguisky really is the "voice of reason and conscience" in Metropolis, as claimed by his supporters, and whether this role is consistent with discovering and telling the truth.

Linguisky portrays life as a struggle between "the people", who act from innate moral principles, and state/corporate organizations that exercise arbitrary power, particularly in the Third World. He claims that the pursuit of power is an exercise in terrorism, far more terrifying that that conducted by the Spirit-is-Supreme fundamentalists. Although the state and big corporations of Metropolis possess or control most of its wealth and power, the people possess the numbers and a monopoly over moral truth. The people constitute the "second superpower".

Linguisky appears confident that the people – the "popular forces" – once they are informed of the real state of affairs by the "principled" intellectuals like himself, will be able to "overthrow power". Rather than "speaking truth to power" as the Quakers advise, Linguisky wants to "speak truth to the people who will dismantle, and overthrow, and constrain power". Unlike the people, the powerful never listen to reason.[9] For that reason they are to be ignored.

Linguisky even claims to have detected a real advance in the "civilized" attitude of the people of Metropolis since beginning his campaign. In his own words: "The population of Metropolis is a lot more civilized than it was forty years ago, and this increases." He also detects a shift in government attitudes regarding its exercise of violence in the Third World, "as a result of plenty of popular struggle". Eventually, he believes, power in Metropolis will be overthrown and the people will usher in a new form of socialism based not on power but on moral principles. I will call Linguisky's utopia a "moralarchy".

What is the basis of the utopia of moralarchy? The true foundation of decision-making and value-setting in human society is, according to Linguisky, a moral module implanted in the brain. This module, possessed by every normal human being, is "uniform" – by which he means universal – throughout our species. It is also independent of the materialist struggle of organisms for power, and thus is an alternative basis for action. Hence, the active principle in human society is what we might call "moral man", a very different creature from the **materialist man** of reality. All that is required to activate it and to reform society, we are told, is knowledge about the abuse of power by the state and big corporations of Metropolis. The provision of this knowledge is, according to Linguisky, the proper role of the intellectual. The reformed institutions of the moralarchy of Metropolis will flow quite naturally from these liberated moral values (or moral faculty).

Of course, there is nothing really novel about a supply-side approach of this type. Even Linguisky draws our attention to David Hume's claim that moral values are a function of human nature, rather than some imagined divinity. And, as we are aware, Zarathustra employed a slightly different supply-side model – in which moral values are an outcome of the entire physiology of different classes of mankind – with very different sociopolitical outcomes. Zarathustra claimed that mankind's stronger types generated "master" values (of "good and bad"), while its weaker types generated "slave" values (of "evil and good") owing to their *ressentiment*. Presumably it was to avoid the classist and racist implications of Zarathustra's model, that Linguisky insisted, without any evidence, that the alleged moral module is "uniform" throughout our species.

What is the basis for Linguisky's supply-side model of value formation? Essentially it is derived by analogy from his story about language that has been so influential in the discipline of linguistics in both Metropolis and the rest of the world. Linguisky is famous for his theory in which language is generated by "a dedicated language module" in the brain.[10] This language module is "a common human possession", which we bring with us into the world at birth. It is, in effect, a system of universal principles, which is characterized by "parameters", or "choice points", that can be set (or "fixed") by reference to "incoming linguistic data" to produce a specific language, such as Chinese, English, Italian, or French. In the words of a Linguisky disciple: "acquiring a language thus means selecting, among the options generated by the mind, those which match experience, and discarding the other options". Linguisky even claims that this language module in the brain is an "optimally designed system", at least in the sense of its interaction with other modules in the same brain.

It should be realized that there is no evidence to support this modular theory of language. But this doesn't worry Linguisky a great deal. He subscribes to something called "the Galilean style" of science, which pertains to Galileo Galilei, not to Jesus Christ as some might have thought! It is, however, a delightful ambiguity. The Galilean style, we are told, involves

> the recognition that it is the abstract systems that you are constructing that are really the truth; the array of phenomenon is some distortion of the truth because of too many factors ... And so it often makes good sense to disregard phenomena and search for principles that really seem to give some deep insight into why some of them are that way, recognizing that there are others that you can't pay attention to.

He goes on to say that

> Newton essentially showed that the world itself is not intelligible ... and the best you can do is to construct theories that are intelligible ... our minds and the nature of the world are not compatible.

Here Linguisky rejects the concept of Popperian falsification, claiming, like the most fundamental deductivist, that if the evidence does not support the theory, then it is the evidence that is wrong. Actually, this metaphysical conception would appear to owe more to that other Galilean style.

This modular theory of language, Linguisky claims, receives support from the "important discovery" that natural languages are far more uniform than traditionally believed. It has certainly seriously challenged the traditional focus on language-specific rule systems and constructions. But, like all supply-side theories, it is wrong. The brain, as shown elsewhere, is not "massively modular" – consisting of a large number of dedicated modules, including one for language and another for moral values – as claimed by the evolutionary psychologists.[11] Rather the human brain has emerged as a general pattern-recognizing, rule-creating system, and language is just one of many rule systems, or "institutions", developed in response to the strategic demand generated by an unfolding dynamic strategy. Language, therefore, is not the "holy grail" that many linguists believe it to be.

The reason there is both a basic structural uniformity in natural languages, together with a degree of superficial variation, is that the strategic brain provides a broadly similar approach to rule making within the context of a dynamic system offering a limited number of distinct dynamic strategies. If the number of dynamic strategies were infinite, there would be little uniformity in our natural languages. The same is true of all human institutions, which are designed to facilitate a particular dynamic strategy or strategic sequence. They are not just extruded unaided from the human brain as Linguisky and his followers argue.

How, one might ask, would Linguisky attempt to explain the larger number of human institutions of a social, political, and economic kind. With a large number of dedicated modules in the human brain? How could "evolution" – which neo-Darwinists tell us takes hundreds of thousands, even millions, of years to generate genetic adaptations – possibly have anticipated the nature and diversity of modern institutions? Even a sociobiologists of the stature of E.O. Wilson – who says that "the great mystery of human evolution [is] how to account for calculus and Mozart" – recognizes that it could not. Linguisky, however, supports a constrained form of neo-Darwinian natural selection – constrained by *physical* laws: "everybody believes Darwin is basically right, there is no question about that".[12] (Not everyone as my *The Collapse of Darwinism* demonstrates.) In reality the strategic brain emerged as a general instrument to cope both flexibly and imaginatively with novel and unexpected changes in strategic demand by creating a large range of social institutions, including language. Hence, Linguisky's concept of a language module in the brain falls to the ground, taking with it the idea of a moral module.

****

If it were true that mankind possessed a moral module in the brain, how would Linguisky explain the common occurrence of war? In the case of the war on terrorism in general and the wars against Media and Babylon in particular, Linguisky places the blame squarely on the government of Metropolis. Metropolis, he claims, has a long history of unjustifiable terrorist acts against largely defenseless Third-World countries, and an equally long history of telling lies to its own people about the nobility of fighting just wars. Strangely, individuals who enter government appear to suffer spontaneous moral-module malfunction.

Acts of "state terror", which the propaganda machinery of Metropolis proclaims are undertaken for "noble" and "idealistic" reasons, usually in the name of democracy and freedom, have created much resentment throughout the Third World. This resentment, which has been compounded by Metropolitan support for ruthless dictators employing terror "on our behalf", has accelerated since we emerged from the Cold War as the world's new "hyperpower". Is it any wonder, Linguisky asks, that religious fundamentalists from the world's poorest countries have struck back. What is the solution? Linguisky believes it is quite simple: "Everyone's worried about stopping terrorism. Well, there's a really easy way: Stop participating in it."

Linguisky, however, is under no illusion that the government of Metropolis can be persuaded to stop their "acts of terrorism". Instead he is attempting to persuade "the people" to force the President to abandon terrorism and to pursue global peace. Left to themselves, he tells us, the government and its corporate backers will continue to use taxpayers funds to gain control of essential resources in the Third World to increase their own wealth and power. Linguisky is realistic in this if nothing else. The wars against Media and Babylon were, he claims quite correctly, all about controlling oil, an essential requirement for the capitalist machine.

Linguisky also recognizes that he has a great deal of competition in "speaking truth to the people" from what he calls the "secular priesthood". His concern is that his "truth" may not be noticed over all the "flag-waving" propaganda and lies being told by the secular priesthood. While Isaiah Berlin had coined the term in reference to communist intellectuals ministering to the dark religion of Stalinism, Linguisky uses it in reference to Metropolitan intellectuals who support the terrorism – by a different name – of our government. It is their role to seduce the people to the cause of Metropolitan terrorism and dominance, as well as to protect them from the "unpleasant experience" of realizing their acquiescence in this process.

The secular priests are the intellectual warriors of the Western world. They target dissident intellectuals, such as Linguisky, to prevent them "talking truth to the people" and, thereby, "overthrowing power". In a free country like Metropolis, is isn't possible to act illegally against dissidents, but it is possible to ignore, boycott, harass, and reject them.[13] There are some ideas which, and some thinkers who, are unable to gain access to mainstream journals, publishers, or media. Even their most profound ideas, which are of great significance to human society, are treated with total silence. So Linguisky tells us. In contrast, the secular priests are forever featured in the media and granted the status of "genius" for their support of state terrorism. Of course, as we have seen in other contexts, there is nothing surprising in this. Unpopular ideas always receive a rough reception.

Zarathustra also used the term "priests" in reference to certain intellectuals. But in a very different context. He used the term to apply to all intellectuals adopting the deductive – or, in his words, "dogmatic" – method of scientific analysis. The intellectual priests in Zarathustra's world are the distorters of reality, the purveyors of metaphysical ideas, the "idealists" who encourage the "herd" to attack and destroy the "master" class, just as he thought Christian priests did. Ironically, in Zarathustra's terms, Linguisky is an intellectual priest, as he exhorts the "principled" people – the idealists – to overthrow the holders of power.

****

We have seen what Linguisky says about his relationship to the truth, but does he live up to this ideal? No doubt he would protest about the nature of this question. I recall he once denied knowing what truth is. When discussing the Quaker determination to "speak truth to power", Linguisky claimed, as we have already noted, that it was better to "speak truth to the people", and then, almost as an afterthought, he said something like: "Furthermore, I don't like the phrase 'speak truth to'. We don't know the truth. At least I don't."

After reading some of Linguisky's work, both on language and politics, I find it difficult to take this statement at face value. In his professional work, which he obviously takes very seriously, Linguisky has had a major impact on the thinking of his peers. Clearly he recognizes this, because he regards the developments in linguistics from the early 1980s, which he inspired, as a "radical change" in a discipline that hadn't changed much in the preceding two thousand years. If Linguisky really believed that the modular theory wasn't true – "we don't know the truth ... I don't" – why does he permit his peers to lionize him? How could this possibly be consistent with his openly stated moral principles. Similarly, if Linguisky doesn't believe that his analysis of moral man, or of state involvement in terrorism, is true why does he continue to persuade "the people" to act "morally" and to "overthrow power"? and how is he able to conclude that the situation in this respect is better today than it was in the 1950s? Could it be that Linguisky is not telling the truth when he says that he doesn't know what truth is?

Or is he? In the light cast by the realist dynamic-strategy theory, Linguisky is definitely *not* telling the truth about reality. As shown in *The Selfcreating Mind*, the idea of the modular mind is not supported by the physiological evidence, nor is it consistent with any realist theory of biological dynamics. Hence, Linguisky's theories about both the language module underlying his work in linguistics, and the moral-principles model underlying his political analysis, do not ring true. He is telling the wrong stories about both the acquisition of language and the nature of international politics. In other words, he is telling untruths about the nature of the real world and how it can be reshaped. Presumably these lies are unintentional and are the outcome of misplaced intellectual confidence. As he probably believes he is telling the truth about the real world, he must also recognize that he is lying to his trusting audience when he tells them he doesn't know what truth is. And, ironically, if I'm telling the truth about the falseness of Linguisky's theories of reality, then he is doubly wrong, because, unknowingly, he is actually telling the truth when, disingenuously, he says he doesn't know the truth. As Walter Scott (in Marmion) truthfully said: "What a tangled web we weave, when first we practice to deceive".

Linguisky also tells an incomplete and misleading story about the role of other intellectuals. He makes a simple division in intellectual ranks between those who support government policy and those, like himself, who attempt to expose the excesses of power. It is a distinction between the bad and the good among intellectuals. Reality, however, is more complex and interesting than this. It is just not true that all intellectuals who, at some time or another, support government policy are also supporting unwarranted state violence. While it is true that nonstrategic intellectuals – the committed prosperity-seekers – consistently support powerful organizations including the state, strategic intellectuals only do so when the state is providing effective strategic leadership. At other times, strategic thinkers are highly critical of their political leaders. But, being realists, they are critical of different aspects of government policy to Linguisky, who is an idealist.

Because of his false theory of the way the world works, Linguisky usually ends up undermining the strategic pursuit of Metropolis. Like all successful societies in the history of mankind – and all successful species in the history of life – Metropolis is attempting to survive and prosper. Because of this, it competes aggressively in the global community for strategic resources and strategic bases. While excessive and misguided force must, and will, be criticized by strategic intellectuals – here they are at one with Linguisky and his valuable expose of gratuitous state violence – they will support aggressive but humane force deployed by Metropolis if it can be shown to be essential to the strategic pursuit. This includes taking prompt military action against all global antistrategists who seriously attempt to derail Metropolis's strategic pursuit. But they will not support external aggression based on untruths.

"**Antistrategists**" is a more appropriate word than "terrorists", because it discriminates between acts of aggression conducted by strategic societies on the one hand, and those of antistrategic societies, groups, or individuals attempting to undermine humanity's strategic pursuit. What is wrong with the antistrategists? Essentially that antistrategists are anti-life. Take the example of the former USSR, which oppressed its own dynamic strategists, plundered their surpluses, and, accordingly, drove their society into the ground. The Cold War, therefore, was a very real struggle for survival between strategic societies and antistrategic societies. In the long run, strategic societies that take up the challenge of life will always triumph over antistrategic societies, because they are better at generating economic growth and individual freedom. The reason that strategic intellectuals support appropriate leadership in strategic societies is that, in the long run, this promotes the survival and prosperity of all peoples throughout the world. Leadership in antistrategic societies, in contrast, is anti-life as it leads to repression, poverty, and death. Those intellectual, like Linguisky, who consistently and indiscriminately attack the strategic leadership of Metropolis, are playing out an antistrategic rather than a principled role. The ideal leads inevitably, if circuitously, to the antistrategic.

It is true, as Linguisky points out, that intellectuals often attempt to protect the citizens of Metropolis from "unpleasant experiences". But the reasons for this are complex. Linguisky is not correct when he claims that this is undertaken by "secular priests" solely in order to disguise government "terrorism". Rather, it involves an implicit contract between strategic intellectuals and the people. In order to survive and prosper, most of us need to divorce what we (and our governments) do on a daily basis from the rational image we have of ourselves. This is the survival mechanism that I call **existential schizophrenia**. It is, as shown in *The Selfcreating Mind*, an outcome of **strategic dualism**: consisting of **strategic desire** that dominates the organism, and reason that dominates the **strategic cerebrum**. Without existential schizophrenia, we are all highly vulnerable to psychotic disorders, which progress from voluntary (normal) to involuntary (pathological) schizophrenic states. We are, in other words, forced to lie to ourselves (and each other) in order to survive.

By playing an antistrategic role and exposing the terror that we commit as a society through our participation in the strategic pursuit – the pursuit of life – Linguisky is actually undermining the protective existential schizophrenia of the people of Metropolis. As this is a very powerful protective mechanism – otherwise a much higher proportion of the population would submit to pathological psychosis – the people are not easily persuaded. Owing to the strong strategic desire implanted in all of us, the people know what is in their best material and psychological interests. Only a small minority of people, in whom the strategic cerebrum has triumphed over the strategic organism, are tempted to heed Linguisky's "principled" arguments. These people are always on the edge of existence. In a crisis, they are always the first to be swept away and their vulnerable genes are eliminated from the human genome. They are also highly susceptible to mental disorders, precisely because they allow their protective existential-schizophrenia shield to deteriorate. Only the more robust among them, like Linguisky – can survive crises, and they do so by holding the moral high ground. While these idealists attack the moral standing of those they regard as being implicated, either directly or indirectly, in terrorism, they consider themselves absolved from the moral guilt associated with the atrocities their society commits.

While existential schizophrenia clearly is a lie told by the individual to himself to enable survival – to prevent drug addiction, mental disorders, and suicide – taking the moral high ground is merely an even more devious form of the same mechanism. *All* the citizens of Metropolis are implicated in the process and outcome of our strategic pursuit, whether they like it or not. Linguisky, for example, enjoys the freedom offered by an advanced strategic society; he accepts a good salary from the prestigious International University of Metropolis; he accepts royalties from the extensive sales of his books published in Metropolis; he receives fees for public lectures and media appearances; and he pays taxes that are used, in part, to finance the military "terrorism" of our nation. Yes, I know. He failed to pay any taxes for about a decade before the state just confiscated it from the sources of his gross income. But this was a rather hollow gesture, for which no criminal punishment was required or offered. Only by abandoning the freedom and affluence he enjoys in Metropolis by living as an oppressed citizen of the Third World could Linguisky take the moral high ground in good conscience. Anything less involves living a lie.

Of course, by remaining in Metropolis, the only way Linguisky and his fellow travelers can face what they see as the horrors of "state terrorism", which are a normal part of our successful strategic pursuit, is by taking a self-righteous stance. They say, in effect: "we can acknowledge the horrors that the rest of you are determined to ignore, because we are 'principled' people and, therefore, are not responsible for these actions, even though we enjoy the very substantial fruits of these actions". The moral high ground, therefore, is Linguisky's existential schizophrenia. Needless to say, the idealist's response involves a double lie – they are self-deceived about being self-deceived.

****

In the light of this analysis of motivation, what can be said about Linguisky's political role? How realistic is his analysis of the political situation, and how effective is his crusade? Linguisky claims it is possible to reduce, even eliminate, "state terrorism" if Metropolis just ceases to participate in it, and it is our current ruthless stance that "threatens survival". How is this to be achieved? Linguisky tells us in a recent (2003) book that global peace can be achieved

> if we are willing to enter the moral arena in a serious way, going beyond the merest truisms and recognizing the obligation to help suffering people as best we can, a responsibility that naturally accrues to privilege.[14]

Terrorism in the Third World will evaporate if these nations are faced with a truly benevolent rather than a ruthless Metropolis. But is this possible? Is there any hope? Linguisky, at least, is hopeful, owing to what he detects as a slow rise since the 1960s of the strength of "popular forces" over issues such as civil rights, freedom, and peace in Metropolis.

But is he right? Is Linguisky telling the truth about reality? What he fails to realize, because he has no realist general dynamic theory, is that these "popular forces" – a growing democratization – in Metropolis and the rest of the First World are a response to the unfolding technological strategy pursued by Metropolis and facilitated by our government's strategic leadership. In other words, both strategic leadership and "popular forces" are responses to the same fundamental dynamic mechanism, and are not incompatible at all. Linguisky's argument, therefore, is self-contradictory. Further, it is not a matter of hegemony *or* survival as suggested in his latest book, but hegemony *and* survival as Metropolis struggles against antistrategic forces to secure strategic resources. And, what is involved is the survival not just of Metropolis and the First World, but of the entire Third World as these nations are gradually drawn into the **global strategic transition** of world economic development and democracy.[15] In the final analysis, it is clear that Linguisky has been telling lies to himself and his followers about the nature of political reality.

How effective is Linguisky's crusade to change the political face of Metropolis? Just as he regards Quakers as being deceived about "speaking truth to power", so Linguisky is deceived about "speaking truth to the people". Very few are really listening, except those willing and able to take shelter on the moral high ground. The only way that the political structure of Metropolis will be transformed is if our unfolding dynamic strategy generates a demand for such a change. Linguisky's political role, therefore, is merely that of entertainer to those who feel comfortable on the ideological heights, and who enjoy abstract moral stories. As these people will always remain a small minority among the worldly citizens of Metropolis, Linguisky's political influence will be negligible.[16]

6.

N.M. Novalis, who has similar concerns to Linguisky, is of a more conservative nature and comes from a very different intellectual tradition. His intellectual background is literary rather than scientific, and it was forged in war rather than academia. Novalis's intellectual interests focus on the borderlands between fiction and political reality. While he has written novels, political history, and popular biography, his impact has been greatest as a commentator on the wars in which Metropolis has been engaged during the past sixty years.

Currently, Novalis is concerned with the struggle between freedom-loving individuals and state/corporate power, within the context of the war on terrorism.[17] It is this concern that invites comparison with the work of Linguisky. Novalis has become a prophet of the demise of democracy in Metropolis, and of its present and future quest for a conquest empire. In this role he sees himself as a critic who loves his country: "When you have a great country, its your duty to be critical of it so it can become even greater." This romantic declaration contrasts sharply with Linguisky's colder, more cerebral relationship with Metropolis. Novalis's warm embrace of our country is what we might expect of a strategic intellectual, but his failure to understand the dynamics of Metropolis leads him to conclusions that are similar to the antistrategic stance of Linguisky. Intellectually I see him as a conservative antistrategist.

Novalis's primary concern is with the future of democracy and freedom in Metropolis. He views democracy as the outcome of a "noble" idea pursued relentlessly by "good" men in the face of the corrosive forces of materialism driven by large and powerful corporations. In his mind democracy is eternally vulnerable.

Democracy, according to Novalis, arises from an idea – a "notion" that is both "exquisite and dangerous". This idea is that when freedom is granted to "the populace", "more good than bad will result". He is under the curious impression that when Metropolis initially explored this political experiment, it was for "the first time in the history of civilization", and it was based on the "daring" premise that there is "more good than bad in people". Why was this experiment so daring? Because "we all know that any man or woman can go from being a relatively good person to a bad one – we can all become corrupted or embittered". Consequently, while more authoritarian political systems, such as a monarchy or a fascist state, can be taken "for granted" – regarded as a "given" – "democracy changes all the time". Herein, we are told, lies its vulnerability. As in Plato's republic, the ideal state can be lost merely because of change.

Democracy, Novalis claims, is something "noble" and "beautiful" that is constructed by basically "good" individuals struggling to achieve and maintain freedom in the face of materialist power. And as it is built by man it can be demolished by man. Only "traditions" established over long periods of time can really protect this "delicate structure", and if these traditions are ignored, this "noble and delicate structure" will become endangered. Somewhat mystically Novalis concludes: "Because democracy is noble, it is always endangered, Nobility ... is always in danger."

Democracy is noble because it is atypical. It arises, Novalis claims, from "a state of grace attained only by those countries that have a host of individuals not only ready to enjoy freedom but to undergo the heavy labor of maintaining it". Fascism, we are told, is a more "natural" form of government for humanity "given the uglier depths of human nature". Because this "state of grace" is so rare, so atypical, it is pointless for Metropolis to export democracy to other countries, such as Media and Babylon.

It will be clear by now what system of thought underlies Novalis's concept of freedom and democracy – indeed, of his approach to values and institutions generally. Like Linguisky, Novalis has developed a simple supply-side theory in which values and institutions emerge from the nature of human nature. But, in contrast to Linguisky, he believes that the characteristics of human nature that he calls "good" and "bad" are not fixed uniformly by our genetic structure, but are free to differ between individuals and to change within a given individual over time. Humans, therefore, must possess a *changing* balance of both "good" and "bad" characteristics. When the good characteristics are in the ascendancy, noble values dominate and democracy and freedom prevail; but when bad characteristics outweigh the good, then ignoble, even "evil", values dominate, and fascism and oppression prevail. Because this balance between good and evil in human nature is always changing, so too is the nature and stability of democracy. Herein, according to Novalis, lies the vulnerability of democracy – formerly good men and women can be "corrupted and embittered", and this will turn democracy into fascism.

What then is the future of democracy in Metropolis according to Novalis? He claims that, owing to the relatively short history of democratic institutions in Metropolis – in comparison to those in Engle Land – our system of democracy is in ever-present danger. This danger owes its existence to the "crass patriotism" that surged up following the terrorism of November 9 (11/9 – or 9/11?), when the citizens of Metropolis faced a massive "identity crisis". Prior to 11/9, the people of Metropolis had thought of themselves as a force for good in the world; but suddenly they were forced to ask themselves: "Why are we so hated, if we are so good?" Such a naive question, of course, could only be asked by a people addicted to **existential schizophrenia**. And, of course, the abuses perpetrated recently (early 2004) by the security forces of Metropolis – which postdate the published work to which I refer – against the Babylonian prisoners in Akkad, answer the second part of that question.

According to Novalis, the President of Metropolis, who sees himself as a force for good, is determined to solve this identity crisis at home by going on the offensive overseas, to create a "world empire". Blushard hopes to do this, we are told, by exploiting the fear and uncertainty arising from 11/9. The President believes that conquest would have psychological benefits through the imposition of "military discipline" and "moral reform" on the people of Metropolis. While there would be important economic advantages resulting from a world empire, the President's real motive is associated with a maladjusted man's "dream" of global glory. Novalis is certain that President Blushard is so maladjusted that he told the leaders of the Great-Wall Civilization – which is struggling to catch-up technologically with Metropolis – in effect that:

> You can have your technology; may it be great! But you had better understand: We still have the military power. Your best bet, therefore, is to become Greek slaves to us Romans.

In his dream of empire the President has the support of the "flag-waving conservatives" and big-corporation leaders. Owing to the corruption of human nature through great wealth, these powerful people prefer empire to democracy. And they have an influence on the government that is disproportionate to their numbers. Novalis believes that:

> Corporate power is running the country now ... I think we have a pre-totalitarian situation here now ... the situation is serious. If we ... fall into desperate economic times, I don't know what's going to hold this country together ... Fascism ... is not going to come with a political party. Nor with black shirts or brown shirts. Homeland security has put the machinery in place ...

Crass materialism, Novalis tells us, is the fundamental problem for Metropolis: "money leaches out all other values". Unlike Linguisky, he is highly pessimistic about the future of democracy and freedom in Metropolis. And the reason for this pessimism is his supply-side theory about the changeable nature of human nature.

****

What is Novalis's relationship to the truth? To tell the truth about life, it is necessary to ensure that one's story and underlying theory about human actions, values, and institutions are correct. It is not a valid defense to assert, as some intellectuals are inclined to do, that their fiction (or lies) contains a larger truth. That is merely a double lie.

Novalis got it wrong. First, his supply-side theory of human nature as the source of all values and institutions is untrue. It is a necessary but not a sufficient condition. Values and institutions, as I argue elsewhere, are generated within the **strategic *logos*** as an outcome of the interaction between strategic desire and strategic demand. They do not arise spontaneously from the nature of man as many intellectuals, from David Hume onward, have claimed. Not only is this theory untrue, it is also dangerous. It can be used to support unsavory views about class and race. If values and institutions reflect the balance of characteristics in human nature, and some societies can be shown to have evil, perverted, or second-rate values and institutions, then it is but a short, logical step to conclude that this is because the people in those societies are evil, perverted, or second rate. **To put it bluntly, *all* supply-side theories about human society are inherently racist, whether their supporters understand this (and generally they don't) or not.**

As mentioned earlier, this is probably why Linguisky insists that the modules in the human brain allegedly responsible for language, moral principles, and so on, are "uniform" for all normal people in all societies. Even if I have guessed correctly in this, Linguisky is still left with the puzzle of why, if all people have the same moral module, some, but not all, exercise power over others. Further, the cost to Linguisky of this supply-side constraint is that it becomes more difficult to explain how values and institutions change through time and space. If we are all the same morally, how is it that our values and institutions differ at a point in time as well as throughout time? The dynamic-strategy theory in contrast has no difficulty here: changing values and institutions are a response to a changing strategic demand, as a society's dynamic strategy unfolds, is exhausted, and is replaced; and different values and institutions are due to differences in strategic demand generated by different dynamic strategies, or even the same dynamic strategies at different phases of their unfolding. Hence, only realist demand-side theories are free from the major defect of racism.

Second, it is impossible to accept the *truth* of Novalis's analysis of democracy, freedom, and institutional change. To begin with, institutions – whether democratic, monarchist, or fascist – are just not based on ideas, noble or otherwise. As shown elsewhere, different dynamic strategies, and different phases of a given dynamic strategy, require different facilitating institutions and values. Democracy, for example, is the outcome of logosian demand generated by the mature commerce (ancient Greece) and technological (Metropolis) strategies. It is not, as Novalis claims, the outcome of a "state of grace"! Further, democracy is only as vulnerable as the dynamic strategy that spawned it. Traditions of democracy, no matter how venerable, can't maintain this political system once a society's technological strategy has collapsed. Ancient Greece clearly demonstrates this. And the only way the technological strategy will collapse is if it is assaulted by a determined and persistent government policy that permanently frustrates the ambitious of its dynamic strategists. This could happen if growth-inducing technological change were banned by an ecological dictatorship pursuing a fully-fledged climate mitigation program, or by neoliberal policies that target strategic inflation and continually disrupt the dynamic process. The first possibility is discussed in *The Dynamic Society* (1996) and *the Coming Eclipse* (2010), and the second in *The Global Crisis Makers* (2000).[18] The way the current Social Democratic government is proceeding, in proposing a carbon tax, the first of these calamities may overtake us soon.

We need to tidy up a few other misconceptions about democracy contributed by Novalis. First, institutional change is not to be feared. It is a normal outcome, as we have seen, of any unfolding dynamic strategy. In a society possessing a viable dynamic strategy, therefore, democracy is not in peril. Second, democracy is not a "noble" institution. It is merely the political institution required to facilitate a particular phase of the unfolding process of its strategic sequence. In this fundamental sense – rather than in the sense of what is likely to maximize the well-being of all of the people – democracy is no more noble than any other political system. It is a common characteristic of human psychology to regard one's own values and institutions as superior in all respects to all others. Even the citizens of conquest societies like Rome or the Aztecs regarded their autocratic political systems as "noble", and as the model that all societies should aspire to. Nobility is merely in the eye of the beholder – it is a reflection of the way ruling strategists view their own societies. A Roman patrician would have regarded democracy as a most ignoble and unaesthetic institution, dominated as it was in Athenian society by the vulgar common man.

There is, therefore, not much in the analysis of Novalis that is true. As in Linguisky's case, it would be a dangerous basis for serious action. In the end, Novalis, like Linguisky, is telling a fictional story – a novel perhaps – about the real world. It is, of course, the time-honored and romantic story about the epic struggle between good and evil. No doubt his usual readers find the story entertaining, but no one should take it seriously. Owing to the lies we tell each other, it is indeed fortunate that desires drive and ideas, filtered through the realistic apparatus of trial and error, merely facilitate those desires. Otherwise, human civilization would be in a hopeless mess. Indeed, it would never have begun.

The Intellectuals

7.

Seth Duckwitton is a leading political scientist at the Metropolitan Institute of Technology, and was part of the administration of an earlier Presidency. In the mid-1990s he published a bestseller about a predicted forthcoming "conflict of cultures", which appears to have been taken seriously by some academic and government figures, as well as by the general public. It is, of course, a great responsibility to be taken seriously in this way, because one might just have an influence on national policy. Accordingly, it is essential that one's analysis and predictions be correct – we need to be able to detect and tell the truth about reality. Duckwitton, as we shall see, doesn't even come close on either counts.

Duckwitton's hypothesis is that culture is the fundamental shaping force in the creation and operation of civilizations. Culture, we are told, determines national identities and "shapes" their economic and political development. In his own words:

> Cultures can change, and the nature of their impact on politics and economics can very from one period to another. Yet the major differences in political and economic development among civilizations are clearly rooted in their different cultures. East Asia economic success has its source in East Asian culture, as do the difficulties East Asian societies have had in achieving stable democratic political systems. Islamic culture explains in large part the failure of democracy to emerge in much of the Muslim world. Development in the postcommunist societies of Eastern Europe and the former Soviet Union are shaped by their civilizational identities. Those with Western Christian heritages are making progress toward economic development and democratic politics; the prospects for economic and political development in the Orthodox countries are uncertain; the prospects in the Muslim republics are bleak.[20]

By applying this simple cultural model to local and global politics since the Cold War, Duckwitton arrives at what he likes to think as a "new paradigm" in the field of political science. He sums up his argument as follows:

> In this new [post-Cold War] world, local politics is the politics of civilizations. The rivalry of the superpowers is replaced by the clash of civilizations ... [In this new era] the most pervasive, important, and dangerous conflicts will not be between social classes, rich and poor, or other economically defined groups, but between peoples belonging to different cultural entities ... Violence between states and groups from different civilizations, however, carries with it the potential for escalation as other states and groups from these civilizations rally to the support of their 'kin countries'.

Here we are provided with a direct prediction that arises from Duckwitton's simple cultural model. I will return to it later, when discussing the war on terrorism.

Duckwitton also employs this cultural model to explain why certain societies are subjected to tension, from which some even disintegrate. We are told that "societies united by ideology or historical circumstance but divided by civilization [i.e. culture] either come apart, as did the Soviet Union, Yugoslavia, and Bosnia, or are subjected to intense strain, as is the case with Ukraine, Nigeria, Sudan, India, Sri Lanka, and many others". On the other hand, "countries with cultural affinities cooperate economically and politically".

****

This is hardly a "new paradigm". Culture has always been the most popular explanation among historians and social scientists of differences in the economic and political performance of nations. The only problem is that this "theory" suffers from a number of very serious flaws. The first and most unfortunate flaw is – usually unknown to the scholar presenting the argument – its racist nature. To say that culture determines economic and political performance merely begs the question: and what determines culture? Clearly it can't be economics or politics as culture is supposed to explain these. It can only be the outcome of differences in the innate mental qualities of the different peoples that constitute each society or each group of societies (which Duckwitton calls "civilizations"), and presumably this has some sort of genetic basis (the basis of his statement about "kin countries"?). This is admitted by many, who argue that values and institutions are determined by human nature.

This cultural model tells us, for example, that the reason for the "European miracle" – the generation of the first Industrial Revolution and high rates of sustained economic growth – is the superiority of the European race. If you believe in the cultural model – and Duckwitton has this in common not only with Linguisky and Novalis, but almost all historians and social scientists – there is no avoiding this most unfortunate conclusion. Yet, it is also a totally unnecessary conclusion. If one adopts the dynamic-strategy theory – a demand-side model – this racist problem just disappears.

The second fatal flaw is that the cultural model is wrong. Not only is a society's economic and political performance shaped by logosian demand driven by the unfolding dynamic strategy, so is its culture. To put it more clearly, culture is a response to the type of dynamic strategy pursued by a society, together with the way it unfolds. Naturally, a society's cultural response is conditioned by its degree of isolation, physical environment, and historical background, but these supply-side forces influence only the superficial differences between cultures and not their underlying structural similarities. The essential thing to realize is that culture is driven by logosian demand, rather than being an independent driving force of economic and political change. A well-known example of this is the Rising-Sun Society which, having adopted the industrial technological strategy in the mid-to-late nineteenth century, quickly abandoned its old culture and adopted one required to facilitate industrialization: Today, Rising-Sun youth know virtually nothing of their traditional culture.[21]

The third problem is that one cannot validly employ culture to explain the disintegration of the former societies of the USSR and "Yugoslavia". These societies did not "come apart" because they were multicultural, but because the **antistrategy** they employed – of suppressing strategists, replacing a market with a command system and diverting the national surplus to rent seekers – eventually and inevitably ground to a halt. Owing to inefficiencies and ignorance of market requirements – or **strategic blindness** – these societies could not compete with the strategic West. While **antistrategic countries** are good at oppressing their strategists and expropriating surpluses, they are bad at economic growth. And as history shows repeatedly, societies that fall behind in long-run economic growth always collapse, under competitive pressure from more successful societies. On the other hand, if societies were to disintegrate because of their multicultural nature, the leading Western nations, which are profoundly multicultural, would not exist today. Multiculturalism, therefore, is not the cause of economic and political crisis. Duckwitton is just *not* telling the truth about reality.

The fourth problem with Duckwitton's cultural model is that its predictions are hopelessly wrong. War on terrorism is a case in point. If his predictions had been correct, the other Spirit-is-Supreme societies in the Middle East would have come to the aid of the Medes and Babylonians, just as Sparta would have come to the aid of its colony Melos. They did not, and the "civilizational" hypothesis is in tatters. In contrast, the dynamic-strategy model predicts this non-civilizational outcome. Under-developed nations aspiring to become **strategic countries** (SCs) will not offer military assistance to antistrategic countries (ASCs) with similar cultural backgrounds if it is clear that by doing so they will endanger their own strategic progress. They will, however, offer assistance to other strategic countries – a category that cuts across cultural definitions – particularly when they are not at risk in doing so. As history has shown, none of the other Spirit-is-Supreme nations came to the assistance of either Media or Babylon when they were invaded by Metropolis, and some even offered us their military assistance. History also shows that the most bitter wars are fought between countries in the same "civilization"; such as those of Europe and its off-shoots during the First and Second World wars. This should have been obvious to Duckwitton.

Finally, Duckwitton's concepts of civilization and culture are confused. He regards a "civilization" as a group of nations possessing similar religions and associated cultural institutions. This concept is both *ad hoc* and vague, requiring him to redraw his cultural world map three times for the twentieth century. Duckwitton also claims that these cultural groups, or "civilizations", have causal effects on global politics, and that they can be used to make predictions about world conflict in the future. In making such claims, he ignores the historicist fallacy involved in extrapolating patterns of historical experience into the future. Prediction must be based on theory not history.

In reality, civilizational groups are merely historical artifacts, which have no causal role in world affairs. They are the outcome, perceived at a point in time, of the way different **technological paradigms** have impacted on the world.[22] Currently, the world exhibits cultural artifacts arising from three historical technological paradigms: the palaeolithic (hunting/gathering), with remnants in the Kalahari and the outback of Terra Australis; the neolithic (agriculture), which encompasses the Third World; and the modern (industrial), which involves the First World. Most societies are in transition between these three technological paradigms. Societies operating in the same technological paradigm possess very similar structural characteristics (basic institutions and organizations) concerning their cultures, even when the superficial characteristics (religious form, language, dress, art, architecture) appear to vary considerably.

The different "civilizations" identified by Duckwitton, therefore, are merely the artifacts of these historical technological paradigms, which in turn have been fragmented by different degrees of isolation. Hence, while the Middle East, India, and China are in transition from the neolithic to the modern technological paradigm, their superficial cultural differences largely reflect the degree of their historical isolation from each other. Deep structural differences only exist between societies located in different technological paradigms. Duckwitton, as well as most other writers on "civilizations", fail to realize this.[23] Global transition, as I discuss in a book of the same name, will eventually remove all structural and many superficial differences concerning world cultures. In the longer term we should not regard "the prospects of the Muslim republics" as "bleak".

While "civilizations" are merely historical artifacts, societies (what Duckwitton calls "cultures") are strategic vehicles that do indeed play a causal role on the world stage. Societies, through their individual strategists and strategic leaders, adopt dynamic strategies in order to survive and prosper; "civilizations" do not. Societies have meaningful cultures that are required to facilitate the strategic pursuit; "civilizations" do not. Societies change the face of the world; "civilizations" do not.

The implication of this dynamic-strategy argument is that once all nations in the world have successfully adopted the industrial technological strategy, there will be only one "civilization" – at least until the next **technological paradigm shift**, which should occur during the second half of the twenty-first century.[24] But the outcome of global politics will be determined by a number of megastates – North America, the European Union, the Moscovian Union, the Middle East, the Hindustan subcontinent, Australasia, Africa, etc.[25] While there will be superficial cultural differences reflecting the different historical backgrounds of societies both within and between these megastates, their structural (strategic) characteristics will be the same. Only once the present industrial technological paradigm has been exhausted will a new paradigm generate a strategic demand for fundamentally new cultural institutions.

****

The Intellectuals

While Duckwitton has, I'm sure, acted in good faith like all serious scholars, he has still been telling lies to himself and others about the way the world works. This is fine, provided his listeners are interested only in a good story, well told. There is, as we have seen, a place for diversionary entertainment. The danger is, however, that policymakers may take him seriously, and be led into grievous error.

The Businesspeople

1.

No one expects to find the words "truth" and "business" in the same sentence – except this one. Which is not to say that there are no truthful businesspeople, just that they are not numerous nor very wealthy. The stakes are just too high, it would seem, for businesspeople to afford the luxury of systematically telling the truth. What is more, they don't even need to know the truth about reality in order to become wealthy; they merely need to imitate the successful businesspeople around them.

Businesspeople come in many shapes and sizes, ranging from small local types to the CEOs of large global corporations. Each of these types is involved in a fairly intense struggle to maximize the returns from their business activities. In the dynamic-strategy theory these strategists, driven by strategic desire, are trying to maximize the probability of survival and prosperity.

CEOs of large corporations possessing great market power are the conquistadors of the modern world. On behalf of their shareholders and, particularly, themselves, they plunder the people of Metropolis and the rest of the world. Their rewards are salaries and share options that are so large they are difficult for the rest of us to comprehend. Our highest-paid CEOs receive more in a single year than the average salary worker could earn in 400 years – perhaps even double that amount of time in the most extreme cases. Needless to say, such enormous salaries bear no relationship whatsoever to the productivity of these CEOs, who are employed by shareholders, not to generate productivity and profits, but merely to increase the value of the corporation's shares that can be sold for a handsome return. Shareholders and their CEOs are rent-seekers not profit-seekers.

CEO salaries are the outcome of mutual greed and lies. Neither the board of directors nor the shareholders have any real interest in the commodities or services produced by their corporation. Nor are they interested in providing the best service to the consumer. Their only interest is in increasing their joint wealth. It is well known in the business circles of Metropolis that a conspiracy exists among the interlocking networks of directors of large companies, who vote for high salaries for chief executives on the understanding they will receive high salaries in return. The majority of shareholders appear unconcerned about this corruption and deceit, for as long as the value of their shares continues to increase rapidly. This vast conspiracy between owners and managers of our largest corporations is hidden beneath an array of lies told at public shareholders' meetings and published in glossy annual reports.

For some CEOs this largely legal conspiracy is not enough to satisfy their greed. A surprisingly large number of CEOs in the 1990s began diverting very large amounts of corporation resources into their own bank accounts and disguising their theft by falsifying the company accounts. This could only be achieved by making substantial payments to the auditors whose job it is to uncover CEO theft and company fraud. The private guardians of our Platonic republic are just as corrupt as the conquistadors they were established to monitor. Of course there are always exceptions, but, in the main, untruth prevails in the world of business.

The losers from this conspiracy of lies are the consumers of the goods and services produced by these large corporations. This is particularly the case with banking and finance. There was a time in Metropolis when the government sought to protect the consumer of financial services from the would-be conquistadors of the corporate world. The former People's Bank of Metropolis set the standards that the commercial banks had to follow – standards of service, supply of a wide range of banking products, and fair rates of interest paid to and by small customers. But they were the days before all political parties, including those left of center, were ensnared by neoliberal cant about private enterprise and efficiency. Once neoliberal economists captured the commanding heights of government policymaking, the People's Bank was hastily sold off to private interests at scandalously low prices – "mates rates" – in order to allow the commercial banks to "compete" effectively.

The outcome of this "competition" – read "collusion" – was the redundancy of thousands of bank workers and their replacement with computers; the institution of endlessly long queues for those of us who have problems too complex for computers; a reduction in financial products available to small customers, together with increased costs of those still provided; and the abolition of interest payments on the deposits of small savers. So effective was this neoliberal "competition" that increased pressure was applied to the consumers of Metropolis simultaneously by the dwindling number of banks that grew larger through systematic mergers. This collusion between a handful of gigantic financial corporations yielded a high return for their shareholders and CEOs, through exploitation of the people of Metropolis, who were told that this neoliberal "competition" and these "efficiencies" were in their best interests. Truth and banking rarely go together. Lies are the true currency of the financial system.

2.

The highest salaries in Metropolis are paid to the managerial class, not to those who create the ideas on which this remuneration is based. Even the owners of capital, who are not part of the managerial class, receive much higher returns than the creators of ideas. I draw a distinction here between "owners" and "creators", because while there are property rights in perpetuity for physical property there are no such rights for intellectual property. Of course, patents are granted to inventors and copyright to authors, but these cover not the ideas involved, only the physical expression of those ideas, and only for a limited time. Hence, those who own physical property grow rich and get to pass it on to their offspring, while those who create the facilitating ideas, together with their descendants, remain poor.

An excellent illustration of particular interest to me is the book industry. It hardly needs to be said that without authors and illustrators the book industry wouldn't exist. Because of this fact one could be excused for thinking that these creators must receive a reasonable proportion of the total revenue generated by this industry. In fact, the royalties and fees paid to Metropolitan authors and illustrators in the financial year 2000–01 amounted to a scandalous 6.3 percent of total book sales. This is despite the fact that a few – a very few – popular authors were able to exploit global markets and to make huge personal fortunes. What it means, of course, is that the great majority of authors earn extremely little from their creative ideas, and are forced to support themselves by working in other industries. Usually the smallest payments – sometimes negative as some authors are forced to publish at their own expense – are received by those publishing unconventional and, hence, unpopular ideas that may ultimately fuel the future technological and social progress of society. In such cases, the creators of truth receive little, while the perpetuators of lies receive much of the material benefits of life.

Is there anything in this discussion of property rights in ideas that elevates it above the usual sectional argument for a greater share of society's wealth? Let's review some of the facts. The most relevant facts are that the dominant dynamic strategy in Metropolis and the rest of the West is technological change, and that the primary requirement for technological change is ideas. While ideas do not drive the strategic pursuit, they certainly facilitate it. Without a steady stream of ideas, the technological strategy will cease to unfold, and material progress will grind to a halt. Currently, the only incentive available to creative people to generate new ideas is the love of doing so. This is a rather fragile foundation on which to construct a modern strategic society. Imagine a world in which the only return to owners of capital was the love of collecting. If the creators of ideas are not granted equal rights in the future dynamic strategy of Metropolis, there may well be no future for any of us to enjoy.

The usual arguments for perpetuating the present system of property rights is that legal rights in ideas would be too complicated to be practical, and that such rights would increase the costs to entrepreneurs. Yet these same arguments could be applied to legal rights on physical property. It is interesting that those who hold these "objective" views, just happen to be the people who stand to part with a small proportion of their hard-won plunder. Similar arguments were marshaled against attempts in the nineteenth century to invest property rights in the novel forms (inventions, books, illustrations) in which ideas are embodied. Essentially, the owners of physical property want to have free access to the ideas of thinkers, writers, scientists, and inventors. I suspect that if owners of physical property were also creators of ideas, intellectual property rights would have existed long before now – probably at the dawn of civilization.[1] Where is the truth in the arguments of capitalists against intellectual property rights?

3.

While truth is violated daily – even hourly and minutely – in the business world, the most disturbing examples surface in industries that adversely affect the health, and significantly shorten the lives, of their workers and other members of the public. There is a long list of notorious offenders, including tobacco, asbestos, chemicals, nuclear energy, and weapons of mass destruction. Just to name a few of the worst. Large corporations involved in these industries deliberately lie about the safety of their products and processes, prevent information concerning health risks from reaching the public, and mount expensive legal cases against individuals and groups seeking compensation for ruined lives.

The classic case is the tobacco industry. Tobacco companies have long known of the causal connection between smoking and health problems such as lung and throat cancer, heart disease, and strokes, but they have, until recently, categorically denied any relationship and suppressed the evidence. They have also denied any link between nicotine in cigarettes and addiction to smoking, at the very time they were undertaking secret research into ways of delivering higher doses of nicotine so as to increase and secure their markets, particularly among youths and females. Any attempt made by individuals or groups to gain compensation for damaged health was always met by the tobacco industry with massively expensive legal cases aimed at keeping the litigants in court until they either died or exhausted their fighting funds. Recently, when it appeared likely that the High Court of Metropolis would take a more sympathetic view of consumers' cases, the tobacco corporations began systematically destroying all paperwork in their archives on these issues. Truth is the greatest enemy of the tobacco industry.

This is not to say that those campaigning against the tobacco industry have a monopoly on the truth. Indeed many in the anti-tobacco lobby appear more concerned with winning its campaign than with the truth. There are many benefits for those in a successful organization of this kind. Sometimes the motivating force is the prospect of exercising power over others by denying them something that the lobbyist doesn't enjoy. Hitler tried to ban smoking during the thirties because he didn't like it. Accordingly, the very real dangers of smoking are exaggerated (particularly in relation to secondary and tertiary "smoking") and contrary evidence is sometimes suppressed by zealots (particularly concerning pipe and cigar smoking, which doesn't involve inhaling). Neither the tobacco industry nor the anti-tobacco lobby are interested in the truth, only in pursuing their own personal and material interests.

Needless to say, the tobacco industry is not unique in this respect. Asbestos interests in the mining, manufacturing, and construction industries are equally notorious. It has to be admitted that asbestos possesses many useful qualities. Not only is it fireproof but, owing to its long fibers, asbestos can be woven into a flexible fabric and used to make clothing and blankets for firefighting. Asbestos has also been used in firebricks, fire-retardant paint, fire-proof seals, and fire-proof insulation. And, in conjunction with cement, it can be used to manufacture relatively inexpensive lightweight building panels and roofing sheets, thereby providing the basis for economic housing. Yet, while it is a highly useful material, it is also lethal. The problem is that when asbestos dust is inhaled, its long, sharp fibers lodge in the lungs, gradually destroying them through scarring (asbestosis) and giving rise to a formerly rare form of cancer (mesothelioma).

As early as the late nineteenth century, acute observers in Engle Land realized that asbestos caused lung problems, and as early as the 1930s in fascist Tutonia its cancer-causing properties were recognized. Interestingly, Hitler's Third Reich made the dangers of asbestos known to the public and introduced regulations for its manufacture and use designed to reduce the people's exposure to this dangerous material. In contrast, the state and businessmen of democratic Metropolis conspired to keep this information from the people. Reports of mid-twentieth-century investigations into health problems suffered by asbestos-industry workers were systematically suppressed. Hence, it was not until the early 1970s that rumors of the dangers of asbestos finally appeared in the *Metropolis Times*.

Truth will always surface, but it can take a long time owing to the lies told by businesspeople, politicians, and bureaucrats; and it leaves many lives ruined unnecessarily. The bottom line is that businesspeople, on average, are interested not in truth, or indeed the welfare of fellow citizens, only in maximizing their material returns. They will even protest that this evaluation is not true – another double lie. Not that anyone with any experience of the business world believes them.

4.

Corporations are capable of lying not only to consumers about the nature of their products and services, but also to the entire nation about the role they play in global politics. Some play the role of double agent. The most remarkable example of this is the part played by Global Business Machines (GBM) – a household name in Metropolis – in contributing to the war effort and Holocaust of the Third Reich. It has been revealed recently that Hitler was only able to exterminate such large numbers of Jews and other ethnic minorities because of GBM's punch-card technology.[2]

Using GBM technology, which was the computer system of the 1930s and 1940s, the Third Reich was able to record everything there was to be known about the Jews, not only in Tutonia but in every occupied country in Europe. Each time Tutonia invaded another country, GBM machines moved in with the army. Once information about the Jews in the newly occupied territories was entered on GBM cards, the victims could be "targeted for efficient asset confiscation, ghettoization, deportation, enslaved labor, and ultimately, annihilation".

What must be understood is that the CEO of GBM, Thomas J. Watson, not only knew what role his company's machines – which were leased, not sold to the Third Reich – were playing, but he retained remarkably effective control over their operation through loyal GBM agents in Tutonia, ensuring that they were serviced, supplied with spare parts, and provided with millions of special punch cards that could only be produced in Metropolis. The efficient machinery of the Holocaust was vital to the profitability of GBM and to the status of its CEO. But this could only take place under a shroud of lies.

It is telling that the Third Reich never felt the need to confiscate GBM machines, and while rental payments were frozen during the war they continued to accumulate in trust accounts for payment at the end of hostilities. Needless to say, Watson kept GBM's traitorous role secret throughout the war, misleading not only the public but also government agents who became suspicious of GBM's activities. As it turned out, the government of Metropolis didn't inquire too closely, because its war effort also depended heavily on the use of GBM-organizational technology. Hence, GBM was able to successfully pursue its role as double agent during the Second World War. This was the corporation that introduced computers – which some see as the facilitators of truth – into the world. A great facilitator of truth, therefore, had its origins in a morass of lies and an orgy of human genocide.

No doubt there are many examples of this type of double-dealing – of a network of lies that endanger us all. In a recent case, for example, a large iron and steel corporation, Broken Promise Mines (BPM) headquartered in Metropolis, was discovered to be doing business with an official state enemy. At the height of UN sanctions against Babylon, BPM was negotiating with leading Babylonian officials in Akkad over contracts for the development of Babylonian oil fields and for the supply of spare parts. Naturally, these talks were highly secret, and were only discovered because correspondence between BPM and the government of Babylon was found in the ransacked Foreign Ministry in Akkad after the invasion by Metropolis. There are even reports that representatives of BPM had explained to Babylonian officials that the people of Metropolis would never support the anti-Babylonian policies of President Blushard.

Needless to say, as soon as this story broke in the *Metropolis Times*, BPM denied that it was true; and when the documentary evidence was made public, the corporation placed the entire blame on an executive who had already left BPM to establish his own company to pursue oil-field contracts in the Middle

East. Even today, Metropolitan corporations are actively involved in secretly pursuing business interests contrary to, and destructive of, national policies. And one can be sure that they will lie about their activities once they are in danger of being uncovered. If the stakes are high enough, lies will always triumph over truth in the world of business. And those stakes don't have to be all that high.

5.

Not only is truth a major casualty of business, but businesspeople don't even have to know the truth about reality to succeed. Indeed, such knowledge may even reduce the likelihood of financial success – hence the businessperson's taunt to intellectuals: "If you're so smart, why aren't you rich?" The answer, of course, is that you don't have to be smart to be rich, just opportunistic. Smartness is the lion in this path.

It is clear from a lifetime of observation and analysis that it isn't necessary to understand how the world works to be successful in business, only to recognize success and to systematically imitate it. Within the context of the dynamic-strategy theory, I have called this important mechanism, which is central to the process by which the dominant dynamic strategy unfolds, **strategic imitation**.[3] Briefly, what is involved is a two-stage mechanism consisting of **strategic pioneers** and **strategic followers**. This encompasses the drive and ambition of imaginative risk-takers and the competitive process of exploiting successful ideas. The strategic pioneers are the imaginative risk-takers, who invest most of their time in developing new business ideas that they *believe* will bring them fame and fortune, rather than – as is usually argued – in collecting a mass of information about costs and benefits, developing conceptual models about reality, and computing optimal solutions. While these ideas are usually arrived at through some familiarity with the requirements of the unfolding technological strategy in their industry area, some come from out of leftfield through analogical thinking. Essentially, it is faith in their own "bright ideas" that drives new business projects into the marketplace.

While the faith of most of these strategic pioneers is misplaced, a few fortuitously achieve outstanding success. It is reality that sorts out winners and losers (rather than the other way around), and it is the strategic followers who recognize the success of the winners and who want to participate in the high material rewards it brings. What begins as a personal and esoteric exercise ends as an industry-wide – even nation-wide – activity. The only truth that matters in business, therefore, is material success. And this can be achieved without a complex understanding of the truth of reality.

The Clergy

1.

The historical role of institutionalized religion has been to support the strategic leadership of the state in both war and peace. In this role the church has attracted intellectually inclined men and women, and provided them with the opportunity to acquire learning and to philosophize about their place in society. Inevitably, the resulting deductive theology has little contact with the real purpose of religion.

While theologians, at least from the time of Zoroaster (seventh century BC), have claimed that religion is the outcome of a quest for ultimate truth – involving a great struggle between good and evil – in reality religion owes its existence to, and is shaped by, the strategic pursuit of its host society. As I have dealt with this issue in detail elsewhere, it can be treated briefly here.[1]

Religion emerged and developed in human society to facilitate the strategic pursuit. It can be shown that the gods adopted by any society in the past reflected the requirements of its dominant dynamic strategy. Subsistence societies worshiped gods of fertility (both organic and climatic), conquest societies followed gods of war, commerce societies looked to gods of the sea and desert, and technological societies pursued gods of science and technology. Significantly, as a given dynamic strategy unfolded, so the nature of the dominant religion was transformed; and when the strategy had been exhausted – leading either to the emergence of a new dynamic strategy, or to collapse – the old gods were either remodeled to reflect the new strategy, or just abandoned. This can be seen in the case of Rome: as the conquest strategy unfolded, the old Republican gods were replaced by emperor worship, and when conquest had been exhausted, the pagan gods of war fell from favor and were replaced by numerous eastern cults, the most "effective" of which turned out to be Christianity.

Worship of the gods was intended to bring both strategic guidance and strategic success, thereby enabling the people to maximize the probability of survival and prosperity. In effect, the great mystery of life that the gods were invented to explain, protect, and maintain was the unknown **strategic *logos***, an entity that has been discussed elsewhere.[2] Religion has been employed by ruling elites to achieve strategic cohesion in their society, by focusing the attention of the entire people – not just the core strategists who reap most of the material rewards – on the dominant dynamic strategy.

The clergy have not only facilitated the strategic pursuit, they have gained materially from it. Those strategists profiting from their society's dynamic strategy – warlords and merchants returning from successful campaigns and travels, and industrialists from their profitable factories and offices – have been generous patrons of their state religions. Gifts to the gods are seen as essential to maintaining the material success of their strategic pursuit. Accordingly, the church and, hence, leading members of the clergy have become rich and powerful, with some (in theocracies) even taking on the role of strategic leadership. In many societies, elite families usually directed their eldest sons into the strategic business – war, commerce, or industry – and at least one of their other sons (and even daughters) into the church. In medieval Europe, for example, the castle and cathedral – as in the old city of Durham in Engle Land – were just different sides of the same coin. The clergy, therefore, had much to gain and lose materially from the fluctuating fortunes of their society's strategic pursuit. In these circumstances, it is hardly surprising that tensions arose amongst the clergy between the pursuits of ultimate truth and strategic success.

If religion is a response to logosian demand, how do we account for the concept of ultimate truth? It is, in fact, a concept with very pragmatic origins. To exercise power over the people, the clergy, who were usually without military weapons, needed to possess psychological means of control. If they could claim that their gods had control not only over strategic success but also the afterlife, then the clergy, by virtue of their close relationship with the divinity, had a delegated power in this respect. They could provide the gateway to paradise (sometimes for an economic price) or the trapdoor to hell. Needless to say, intellectuals can never leave "good enough" alone. What began as an attempt to maximize their power and influence was further developed by cerebrally inclined members of the clergy into a complete theology. In the process, a simple strategic divinity was converted into a god who was responsible for the creation of the universe, for the great struggle between good and evil (a theological inflation of their society's conflict with its neighbor), and for ultimate truth.

It is somewhat ironical that the concept of ultimate truth has its origin in the materialist strategic pursuit. Ironical because the strategic pursuit is based at all levels – state, people, business – on the rejection of the truth whenever it acted as a constraint on material success. Ultimate truth, therefore, has the same origins as strategic lies. Whether they realize it or not, the clergy practice a profession that more than any other is based upon lies about both reality and their role in it.

Because of this threatening contradiction, it has been necessary for all state religions to facilitate the compatibility between strategic lies and ultimate truth. Necessary not only for the layperson but also for the clergy which created this tension. Typically this has been achieved by making it possible for the society (through the high priest), and even the individual, to confess their strategic lies and, thereby, gain forgiveness from god, the personification of ultimate truth. This has been a clever sleight of hand. Because the clergy has played a central role in this process of redemption, it has gained even greater control over the people and over their own material position. Ultimate truth, therefore, is a very useful weapon wielded by the clergy. But it involves them in the complex lie that ultimate truth exists, that the strategic pursuit violates this truth, and that the only way the strategists can experience redemption is through gifts and supplication to the church.

2.

In today's Metropolis, and much of the Western World, the church has lost its way. Since the Industrial Revolution it has ceased to play a strategic role. Metropolitans today place their faith not in the gods of the past – which have included gods of fertility, war, and commerce – but in modern science and technology. Now that we face a prosperous and secure future in this world, based on the highly successful dynamic strategy of industrial technological change, we have little real concern about an afterlife that grows increasingly less likely as our scientific knowledge of life and the universe develops, and as our control over the material foundations of societies expands. Our need for ultimate truth has diminished through a growing understanding of strategic truth. In Metropolis today, scientific truth has replaced religious truth as the societal focus. There is nothing mystical about this – it is the age-old institutional response to logosian demand that changes as the technological strategy unfolds. The old religious clergy has been effectively displaced by a new secular clergy – the natural and social scientists – who are the keepers of the mysteries of science and technology.

3.

The religious clergy of Metropolis are experiencing a crisis of both strategic and moral proportions. Rather than supporting the strategic purpose of the nation, they are increasingly opposing it. In past wars, the State Church of Metropolis supported and sanctioned our military involvement, whereas during the war on terror the clergy were prominent in public protests against hostilities against both the Medes and the Babylonians. Reflecting the confusion concerning their strategic role, the clergy joined with other antistrategists, such as the Linguiskians and environmentalists, who insist that our behavior should be based on "moral" principles rather than national self-interest. These antistrategists comprise a highly heterogeneous collection of social groups and individuals: the Linguiskians claim their moral principles are the outcome of a genetically determined module in the brain; the environmentalists that they are determined by nature; and the clergy that it emanates from the "Word of God". As the dynamic strategists command the plains of reality, the clergy and other idealists have been forced to take the moral high ground. Only with their heads in the clouds, do they feel comfortable.

An additional problem for the clergy in Metropolis today is that the moral high ground is shifting beneath them. After centuries of suppression emanating from on high in the church organization, the sexual abuse committed by a significant minority of the clergy against vulnerable parishioners and children in their care, is finally becoming public. A recent report published in the *Metropolis Times* shows that in the leading archdiocese of the State Church, 162 of its priests were accused of sexual abuse between 1950 and 2003, amounting to about 7 percent of all serving archdiocesan priests during that period. And this would have been just the tip of the iceberg. These clergymen, who claim to be dedicated to the love of mankind and to the ultimate truth, are guilty of transgressing against both. This is not only a cynical abuse of their "high" calling, but also a callous disregard of common decency. Rather than living in the light of truth, they are wallowing in the darkness of the lie.

Even worse, the church of which they are members was aware of their crimes and conspired with the guilty clergy against their defenseless victims to prevent it becoming common knowledge, and to allow these predators to remain in the church to repeat their crimes endlessly. Leading figures in the State Church of Metropolis not only knew of this terrible abuse, but some were actually participants, sometimes as part of a sinister web of abusers. Even when news of these crimes began to emerge in public, the State Church, rather than acknowledge the truth, paid large sums of money to victims in exchange for formal secrecy agreements. All of this from an institution that claims to seek and uphold ultimate truth, and from individuals who, these days, are quick to attack the state and the corporate sector for their double standards. Clearly, desire in man will always triumph over truth.

PART II

TRUTH AND THE STRATEGIC *LOGOS*

Editor's Preamble II

The keystone of Frederick Herac's system of thought is his concept of the strategic *logos*. This concept not only clarifies the work of a lifetime, it also provides the key to understanding the reality of life and the nature of religion. In these collected writings we witness Herac's thinking change focus from a general dynamic *theory* about the way life functions to the *reality* at the heart of life – to the strategic *logos*. It amounts to a transition from hypothesis to truth.

The strategic *logos* was a discovery of the greatest importance, which should have been celebrated by the citizens of Metropolis, or at least by its intellectuals. In fact, it was totally ignored, and these writings remained unpublished for four decades. At the time, they circulated only among Herac's closest friends, and even then only through photocopies of the original handwritten essays. It is high time they enjoyed a wider and more public circulation.

Herac's discovery of the strategic *logos* was an outcome of the strategic thinking that he championed throughout his lifetime. He began his philosophical career by exploring the recurring patterns embodied in existence. Formally this occupied Herac for more than two decades, and informally, while he was growing up, for almost as long. Only in his mid-forties did Herac make a sustained and comprehensive effort to explain these patterns by developing a general dynamic theory of human society and of life. And not until his sixtieth year did he finally understand where his theory was leading – to the strategic *logos*. The *logos* finally enabled Herac to make sense of man, God, and the universe – issues that had troubled him for as long as he could remember.

From childhood, Herac had been fascinated by the changing patterns of the natural and human worlds. Of the clockwork patterns in the night sky, which he would watch with his family from the front garden of their home in the northeastern suburbs of Metropolis, listening intently to the explanations of his parents and his young and enthusiastic maternal uncle. Of the perplexing patterns of life and death in his family, particularly the early deaths of his father (45 years) and his father's older brother (29 years). Of mysterious patterns in the world beyond Metropolis – particularly the ruins of ancient civilizations – described to him by his travel-experienced grandparents and great aunts, sheltering from a scorching summer sun in the shade of wide verandahs. Of other-worldly patterns in God's relationship with man, recorded in the Bible and interpreted by a kindly Sunday-school teacher (who earned a living from the building trades, just like his master, Jesus). Of more familiar patterns in recent history, taught with varying degrees of interest and expertise by public school teachers and university lecturers. And of thrilling patterns in new social relationships as he passed from childhood into youth. Herac had long been fascinated by patterns in life that were imprecise, fragmented, and difficult to reconcile.

Editor's Preamble II

Only after completing his university training did Herac have the opportunity to try and fashion some order from this primeval chaos. While he could do little about the fragmented nature of life's patterns at this time, Herac was able to render some of them more precisely, and he had some success in integrating some of the diverse elements on a small scale. From his early twenties to mid-forties, Herac embarked on a succession of detailed but highly varied historical studies of Metropolis. While many colleagues regarded these studies as disconnected and dilettantish, Herac single-mindedly focused his interests on the motivation of the main actors – whether statesmen, businessmen, professionals (mainly artists), or ordinary consumers – and on the dynamic process by which various organizations at the regional or national level rose and fell over time. On closer inspection, it is clear that, rather than working dilettantishly, Herac was taking a wide sample of historical patterns in order to understand what they had in common – what was driving them and what were the mechanisms by which they unfolded. Herac, like a young but serious artist, was preparing a large number of diverse and detailed sketches before embarking on a major work of art.

By his mid-forties, Herac felt he had learnt enough about the patterns of human society from these small detailed sketches to begin a series of large-scale canvasses on the dynamics of life. Right from the beginning of this new stage in his career, he had a clear idea of what needed to be done. Herac wanted to develop a general dynamic theory that could be used to draw together all the fragmented patterns of life he had been observing for more than four decades. He wanted to deliver order from apparent chaos. He wanted to fashion a theory that would account not only for the recurring patterns in life, but also for the nature and role of truth, good and evil, ethics, and religion. He wanted to be able to explain man, history, nature, and God using the same theoretical system. Here we have a man clearly undaunted by extreme intellectual challenges.

What Herac could not know at this early stage was what this general dynamic theory would look like or where it might lead. In particular he had no idea that it would give birth to the strategic *logos*. But it was the *logos* that finally enabled Herac to make sense of all those fascinating but confusing life patterns of his childhood, youth, and adulthood. At the same time, it was this paradigm-shifting work that caused Herac's academic competitors – who saw this as an excellent time to plunder his institutional resources – to attack and marginalize him. In the process, Herac's health deteriorated, and he resigned his university position. During this highly creative but difficult period of his life, Herac came to fully appreciate the words of Zarathustra that had intrigued him in his late twenties: "With my tears go into your loneliness, my brother, I love him who wants to create over and beyond himself and thus perishes."

The Strategic *Logos*

1.

The one issue that has fascinated thinkers and leaders alike is the mysterious system that generates the rise and fall of mighty dynasties. In the ancient world, kings and priests sought to understand how they could sustain the dynamic life system that had brought them wealth and power. The ruins of older dynasties and civilizations around them warned of the ephemeral nature of material success. With anxiety in their hearts, they were keen to propitiate the gods that ruled over the invisible mechanism of their dynastic system. Many of these gods demanded a high price in terms of animal and human blood – the elixir of life – as well as precious metals for doing so.

In the medieval world, while refining their concept of the god who presided over their dynastic system, priestly philosophers counseled kings who wanted assurances that their conquest or commerce strategies would continue to generate prosperity in a world of frightening uncertainty. Even in our contemporary world, secular intellectuals, or worldly philosophers, advise democratic leaders how to maintain the dynamic materialist systems that provide modern prosperity and liberty. Curiously, even today, thinkers and leaders are no closer to understanding this mystery of mysteries than were their ancient counterparts many thousands of years ago. Until now.

What, then, is this great creative system of life – this great pulsating heart of all living systems – that has preoccupied the attention of thinkers and leaders down through the millennia? Why have its secrets eluded us all this time?

****

I call this mystery of mysteries the **strategic *logos***. One of the first to write about the central importance of what the ancient Greeks called the *Logos* (λόγου), "from which all things follow", was Heraclitus of Ephesus.[1] Despite being centrally important to life, Heraclitus realized that the *Logos* was incomprehensible to most men:

> The *Logos* proves
> those first hearing it
> as numb to understanding
> as the ones who have not heard.

Instead, he reported disappointedly, the people and their leaders prefer the shallow explanations of "specialists", or experts:

> Although we need the *Logos*
> to keep things known in common,

The Strategic Logos

> people still treat specialists
> as if their nonsense
> were a form of wisdom.

Further, these "specialists", deluded by their popularity with the people, roundly attack those who seek to discover and explain the *Logos*:

> Dogs by this same logic,
> bark at what they cannot understand.

Unfortunately, we have no record of what Heraclitus understood the *Logos* to be. Indeed, his surviving writings only exist as quotations in the work's of others. Perhaps he never attempted to explain this mystery, because he wants us all to discover it for ourselves:

> For wisdom, listen
> not to me but to the *Logos*,
> and know that all is one.

What he does suggest is that the *Logos* is divine, a common error in the history of human civilization that turned the search for the *Logos* into a metaphysical expedition. In the hands of less scrupulous thinkers, who Heraclitus ridiculed, metaphysics became theology. Ignorance was the underlying reason. Unable to understand the *Logos* "from which all things follow", the priestly philosophers turned it into religion to be worshiped rather than a matter of science to be analyzed. The strategic *logos*, as we shall discover, is ephemeral rather than eternal, mortal rather than divine.

2.

The strategic *logos* is ephemeral because it exists only for as long as the society with which it is associated exists. While the *logos* accounts for the rise and fall of a particular society, it is in fact the creation of that society – or, at least, of all the individuals in that society, who are integrated by their common strategic pursuit. As will be shown, the *logos* is the outcome of, and the reason for, the creative interaction between the people and their society. The strategic *logos*, therefore, is born with the emergence of a particular society and it dies with that society. It is this close and essential relationship that has led human societies to worship the unknown *logos* and to call it God.[2]

As each society creates its own strategic *logos* – and in turn is created by it – many *logoi* exist at any point in time, both in the animal and human worlds. It is for this reason that early human societies in both the Old and New World had their own local gods. Each society had its own god or gods in order to sustain its own strategic *logos*. In ancient Mesopotamia, for example, each city-state had its own dominant god. When a city-state flourished, it was said to be because their god dwelt among, and smiled upon, them; and when that city experienced crisis, it was because their god had abandoned the city and no longer supported them. This is why invading armies from a rival city-state would "godnap" the statue of the captured city's god and install it in their own capital. Underlying this symbolism was the incorporation of the conquered strategic *logos* into that of the conquering society.

This early, simple connection between a city's god and its *logos* was eventually severed in the minds of both thinkers and leaders. This was the outcome of both empire building and deductive thinking. As increasingly powerful city-states in the Middle East built empires through conquest, an amalgamated hierarchy of gods emerged. In turn, this led newly emerging societies elsewhere to adopt the leading gods of successful empires. "Surely," they must have reasoned, "if these gods brought prosperity to the world's great empires, they will do the same for us." By adopting these powerful gods as their own, they were, it was no doubt thought, also adopting the successful strategic *logos* over which these gods presided. This is just another example of the powerful mechanism of **strategic imitation**.

The growing amalgamation of divinities was also reinforced by the priestly philosophers once they began developing theologies around these strategic gods. This is the inevitable and unfortunate outcome of deductive forms of thought. One particularly influential theology was that developed during the seventh century BC by the Persian prophet Zoroaster, who proposed the utterly outlandish idea that there was only one God called Ahura Mazda. Outlandish because it implied that the strategic *logos* (or rather the *Logos*) was eternal and divine, rather than ephemeral and mortal as all early civilizations were fully aware. Outlandish because Zoroaster shifted our focus from strategic success in this life to metaphysical success in an imagined afterlife. Zoroasterism had a remarkable impact on the subsequent theologians who shaped the world's great religious of Judaism, Christianity, and Islam.

Of course, pragmatic societies adapted these great religions to their own strategic ends. In medieval Europe, for example, each state adopted the same Christian God – the God of the Holy Trinity – as the divinity responsible for the success of their particular strategic *logos*. We see this reflected in the invocation of the "same" God by each European state for the success of their conquest strategy. Each state regarded the Christian God as their *own* God: just as the city-states of ancient Mesopotamia had regarded a particular god as their *own* god. In other words, they thought of God in strategic rather than theological terms. This implies that there was not just one Christian God in Europe, but many Christian gods – one for each state. It makes little strategic sense for two combatants in war asking the *same* god for victory over the other. In reality, each European state asked its *own* god (*logos* I) for victory over the *other* god (*logos* II). Only Europe's priestly philosophers were able to believe in a supreme God that transcended the host of strategic *logoi*.

In the contemporary world – at least in the most developed part of it – the relationship between the strategic *logos* and the traditional divinity is all but severed. Few national leaders in the First World believe that God is actually responsible for their strategic success. While the name of God might be invoked during a national crisis, and prayers intoned in the nation's churches, most leaders realize that strategic success depends on successful scientific and technological programs together with good economic management, and a strong military force. This is why they look for advice not to theologians but to "worldly philosophers" and technocrats. The days of the priestly philosophers are over, except in universities[3] and Third-World countries. Yet, despite this more pragmatic approach to life, neither our contemporary leaders nor our contemporary thinkers understand the nature of the strategic *logos*. It is time, then, to turn to this matter.

3.

In what sense does the strategic *logos* exist? To answer this question it may help to employ an analogy. Normally I avoid this approach, because of the difficulties it can generate. As I show in *The Collapse of Darwinism* (2003), Charles Darwin led both himself and some six generations of scholars astray by using analogy *as a form of reasoning*. By employing the "barnyard" analogy of artificial selection to solve the critical problem he was experiencing in explaining biotransition, Darwin introduced the analogous but completely flawed explanation of natural selection. As he was unable to unravel the Gordian knot, he merely slashed it apart. Natural selection was a short-hand method of trying to explain biotransition without developing and applying a general dynamic theory of life through the more difficult process of strategic thinking (pattern recognition and induction). In contrast to Darwin, I will use analogy here, not as a form of reasoning, but merely to suggest what the strategic *logos* – which has already been determined by strategic thinking – is like.

What, then, is the strategic *logos* like? In existential terms it is like the personality of an individual human being. How so? In the first place, an individual personality is the outcome of unseen interactions between the very large number (some 100 billion) of nerve cells in the human brain. This interaction is an outcome of the role played by the individual in its various social groupings. This is "like", but not the same as, the strategic *logos*, which is the outcome of unseen interactions between strategic demand and a very large number of individuals. In *The Selfcreating Mind* (2006), I suggested that a useful metaphor when thinking about the human brain is that of the "metropolis of the mind". The link between mind and metropolis is that both are shaped by the response to strategic demand.

Second, just as we "know" the hidden individual personality only by its actions in the wider world, so we "know" the hidden strategic *logos* only by what it achieves in the wider world. The individual personality is no more visible than is the *logos*. What do we actually "see" of the individual personality? We see facial expressions, we hear vocal utterances, and we observe various actions and reactions in a variety of situations. From these observations we make inferences about individual personality. We are unable to observe the individual personality directly. It is much the same with the strategic *logos*. While we can't detect the *logos* through the senses, we can observe the outcomes of its operation – the nature of its institutions and organizations, its cultural characteristics, and its economic performance. By recording and analyzing these patterns we can draw inferences about the existence and nature of the *logos*. What I am saying, is that the hidden *logos* exists in reality in the same sort of way that the individual personality exists.

Finally, just as the individual personality exists only as long as its host body, so the strategic *logos* exists only as long as its host society. In both cases the visible vehicle is the carrier of the invisible life force. In both cases this life force is ephemeral. One moment it exists, and the next moment it is gone, forever. And with its passing it leaves behind either a formerly viable society in dysfunctional chaos, or a formerly viable human body in a state of disintegration. Both are swept away by life.

4.

The strategic logos *is an invisible circular process of interaction between man and his society. It can be thought of as the dynamic mandala of life – the pulsating heart of human society. It is a self-generating and self-maintaining mechanism that, in the absence of overwhelming external shocks, continues to pulsate until the entire sequence of dynamic strategies available to a given society is completely exhausted. In the case of the world's most successful societies, such as ancient Rome and ancient Egypt, this can last for between one and three millennia. Ultimately, however, the strategically exhausted society collapses, because the* logos *runs down – the heart of society throbs no more.*

The Strategic Logos

Figure 1 **The Strategic *Logos***

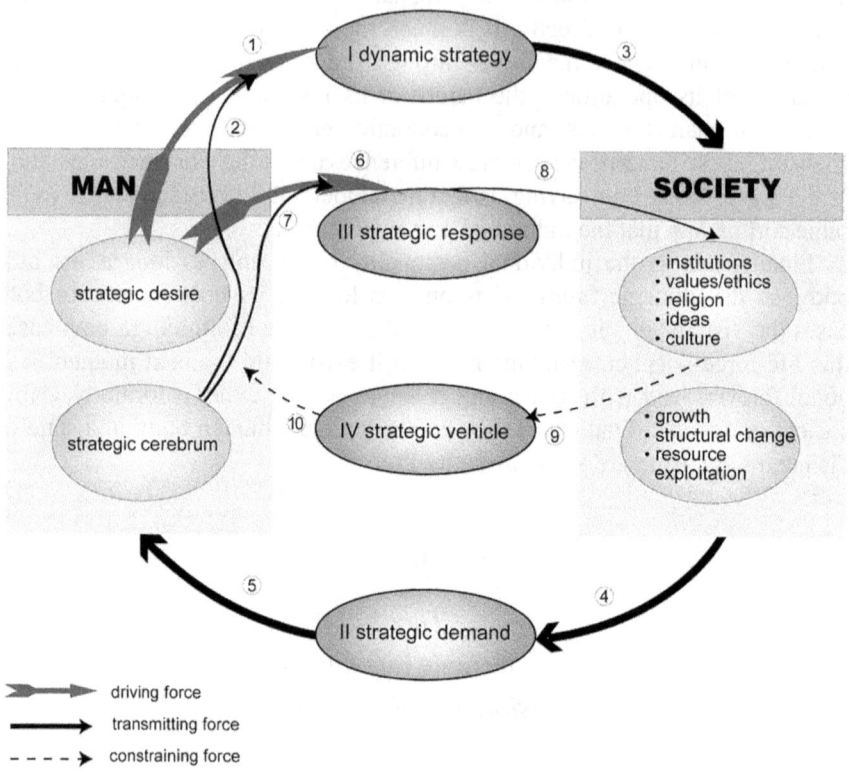

A diagrammatic model of the strategic *logos* is presented in Figure 1. This figure, of course, is merely a two-dimensional representation of a complex, three-dimensional process. Nevertheless, Figure 1 shows the circular nature of interaction between man and society, which lies at the heart of the strategic *logos*. It is an interaction that takes place at four main levels, namely: I the **dynamic strategy** currently pursued by society; II the **strategic demand** that this unfolding process generates for a wide range of strategic inputs; III the individual and collective response to strategic demand; and IV the resulting strategic vehicle that carries society forward in its **strategic pursuit**.

The strategic *logos* is driven by **strategic desire**, which is the motive force that powers the dynamic circle of life. It is at the center of life's pulsating heart, and provides this dynamic mechanism with a self-starting and self-maintaining character. Strategic desire operates primarily by driving both the dynamic strategy being pursued by society and its strategic response. In both cases this is facilitated by the supervisory and planning role played by the **strategic cerebrum**. The great directing force in human society is strategic demand, which changes as the dominant dynamic strategy unfolds. This directing force elicits a response from the people, thereby providing the institutional, organizational, and cultural vehicle necessary to engage in the strategic pursuit. It also provides the medium for natural resource exploitation and for economic growth and structural change required to meet the people's strategic objective of survival and prosperity.

Enough has been said about the main elements of the strategic *logos* to enable us to fire it up and put it through its paces. We begin with man, who is dualistic in nature. He is not only driven by strategic desire to achieve his fundamental objectives of survival and prosperity, but also possesses a highly sophisticated instrument – the strategic cerebrum – that plans and supervises its achievement. This is done through the adoption and exploitation of one of a quartet of dynamic strategies – family multiplication (procreation plus migration), conquest, commerce, technological change – available to that society. As the chosen dynamic strategy unfolds, society increases its access to natural resources, grows, and changes structurally, thereby generating strategic demand for an extensive range of strategic inputs, including land, labor, capital, ideas (technological, strategic, other), institutions (societal rules), societal organizations, values, ethics, religion, and culture. In other words, all human values and institutions are generated outside man by the strategic *logos*, not extruded independently from the mind of man as most scholars claim.

The drive behind the strategic response to this directing demand is, once again, provided by strategic desire, and is guided by the strategic cerebrum. A major outcome of this strategic response is the creation of an institutional, ethical, religious, cultural vehicle capable of carrying the strategic pursuit forward and delivering the material success that meets the needs of strategic desire, which began this whole process. The completion of this circular interaction, however, doesn't lead to equilibrium, because strategic desire is never satisfied. Hence, the circular interaction becomes an upward spiral that continues until the strategic *logos* is exhausted, sending the whole process into reverse.

While this diagrammatic model of the strategic *logos* provides a convenient two-dimensional sketch of a complex dynamic mechanism, its limitations will have become apparent. In the first place, Figure 1 is merely a cross-section of the entire process of circular interaction. A third dimension, time, would show how the strategic *logos* allows a society not only to exploit the initial dynamic strategy, but also how its exhaustion, which threatens the continuing viability of the *logos*, opens the way for the adoption and exploitation of a further dynamic strategy.

A three-dimensional model, by adding a time variable, would demonstrate the **strategic sequence**, which would burrow into the surface of the page at level I. in turn, such a sequence would have a major impact, through a changing strategic demand, on the nature of the strategic vehicle we call civilization.

Reflect, for example, on how different was Greek civilization under the conquest strategy compared with the commerce strategy. Of particular interest in this example is how the strategic sequence of conquest → commerce → conquest resulted in ancient Greece advancing toward, and later retreating from, democratic ecosociopolitical forms. This unfolding strategic sequence was presided over by the Greek *logos*, which was recognized but misinterpreted as the divine *Logos* by Heraclitus of Ephesus, who we met earlier.

Secondly, the strategic *logos* should not be thought of as possessing fixed dimensions as suggested by Figure 1. With time the *logos* grows larger (or smaller if in decline), more complex (representing a spiral rather than an ellipse), and it generates greater (or lesser) levels of population and GDP per capita. Like society, the strategic *logos* is both constantly changing (dynamic) and ephemeral. Some of these matters may be better dealt with by employing conventional **timescapes** showing changes in variables by which the success of societies and civilizations are measured. What we need to remember, however, is that all these outcomes are generated by the strategic *logos*, which is not to be confused with crude representations of it as in Figure 1.

5.

The strategic *logos*, depicted crudely in Figure 1, can be generalized for all "societies" in nature. Similar figures could be drawn for all animal and plant species, which would differ largely in terms of degrees of sophistication of the strategic cerebrum (or, in its absence, the **strategic gene**), in the complexity of the strategic vehicle, or in the type and magnitude of material outcomes. As discussed in *The Collapse of Darwinism* (2003), even simple single-cell life forms adopt and pursue the complete quartet of dynamic strategies. The strategic *logos*, therefore, accounts for the transformation of the "society" of life ranging from the primitive interaction between the simplest forms of life to that between the most complex forms.

Similarly, the strategic *logos* accounts for the emergence of man. It is now clear to me that the *logos* underlies the autogenous process – discussed in detail in *The Collapse of Darwinism* (2003) and *The Selfcreating Mind* (2006) – that accounts for the emergence of the intelligent species we call man. Hence, the box in Figure 1 entitled "Man" can, for other purposes, be renamed "Organism", and the strategic *logos* can be used over vast periods of time to explain **biotransition** itself. In this suggested reconfiguration, the dynamic strategy of genetic change replaces that of technological change, with the other three dynamic strategies – family multiplication, commerce (symbiosis), and conquest – retaining their relevance. Elsewhere I have shown that the great dynasties of the past – such as blue-green algae, reptiles, and dinosaurs – have pursued the strategic sequence of genetic change → family multiplication (or commerce/symbiosis) → conquest, finally going extinct and making way for new unheralded dynasties. By generating man – who has substituted the **technology option** for the **genetic option** – the current mammalian dynasty has been able to avoid extinction. All of this has been due to the role played by the strategic *logos*.

6.

What are we to make of the strategic *logos*? No doubt I will be misunderstood when I call it the ultimate reality or ultimate truth of life. In my philosophical system there are two forms of reality. They are equally real, just different. **Everyday reality** consists of *objects* and physical relationships between objects that can be perceived through the senses. **Ultimate reality**, which I have called the strategic *logos*, is a complex set of invisible relationships between *forces* – such as strategic desire and strategic demand – that can't be perceived through the senses. Through the senses we can only detect the agents (strategists) and outcomes (institutions, organizations, infrastructure, wealth) of those invisible forces. The invisible pattern of forces described in the diagrammatic representation (in Figure 1) of the strategic *logos* can only be apprehended by developing a general dynamic theory that can explain and predict the recurring patterns in everyday reality. This type of relationship between invisible forces and visible objects, which gives rise to observable patterns, is similar to that in the physical world. Ultimate reality, or ultimate truth, therefore, is the dynamic system that is responsible for generating life and all its societal vehicles. Heraclitus, I like to believe, would have been able to embrace the strategic *logos*.

Interestingly, the dynamic-strategy theory was developed not in search of the strategic *logos*, whose existence I had not considered, but rather to explain and predict the recurring patterns that can be found in everyday reality. Only once this theory had been constructed, was it possible to detect the existence of the *logos*, precisely because it is not directly accessible to the senses. Hence, it is everyday reality that leads the way to life's ultimate reality; and it is the dynamic-strategy theory that provides the link between them.

This theoretical link between levels of reality should be Janus-like – working in both directions. Here it might help to play a mind game that has nothing to do with reality. If one could apprehend only ultimate reality – the strategic *logos* – it would still be possible to develop the underlying dynamic-strategy theory by analyzing the relationships between strategic forces. In turn, this dynamic theory could be used to discover everyday reality. Of course, we would need to be very different beings to work in this way, which is clearly out of the question. Remember this is only a game. My point merely is that everyday and ultimate realities are linked through the exercise of **strategic thinking**. The *logos* could not have been discovered in any other way – such as by deductive thinking – for beings like us. The history of philosophy over the past 3,000 years attests to this.

7.

It will be obvious from Figure 1 that the strategic *logos* focuses on the social rather than the physical environment. But it is also clear that physical resources are employed in this system by strategic agents in response to strategic demand. The essential point is that the physical environment is *not* a demand-side determinant of societal dynamics, merely a supply-side constraint. It is for this reason that the natural sciences have made little progress in understanding the dynamics of life.

Darwinism, for example, has provided a distorting legacy, owing to the emphasis it places on the physical environment in driving the dynamics of life. Biological adaptation in a fully populated world is seen by evolutionary biologists as a response to changes in the physical environment. Other natural scientists are also preoccupied with cataclysmic changes in the physical world – plate tectonics, volcanic activity, asteroid impacts, weather changes – which they claim drive the fluctuating fortunes of life. Still others claim that simple physical laws, such as entropy (why not gravity?), can explain life on Earth. Yet, no one has been able to demonstrate how these environmental changes or physical laws can account *systematically* for the great transformations that have taken place in life over billions of years, or for the *systematic* patterns in biological activity.

Only the strategic *logos* can explain the dynamics of life. The *logos* is capable of generating biological and societal change even in the absence of changes in the physical environment. Why? Because it is a self-creating and self-maintaining dynamic system. This is not to deny that changes in the physical environment have some influence on life and human society, just that it takes the form of *random* external shocks that are unable to account for the *systematic* nature of the dynamic process. When a society, species, or dynasty is successfully exploiting a viable dynamic strategy, these random shocks have little affect. Only when a dynamic strategy – or, more particularly, a strategic sequence – has been exhausted, and a society, species, or dynasty is already in decline will a coincidental random shock make its presence felt by hastening the inevitable. And simple physical laws merely provide the passive background conditions of life. It is up to the players to determine whether and how the game of life is to be played.

The strategic *logos* is remarkably resilient. It can be damaged by external shocks if they are sufficiently massive, but usually it quickly repairs itself and resumes its life-generating pulsations. Only small, isolated societies that have all but exhausted their strategic sequence are likely to be terminally damaged by events such as earthquakes, volcanic eruptions, tsunamis, floods, conflagrations, and so on. Interestingly, the only external shock in history that has ever prematurely destroyed a major society's strategic *logos* is conquest – a man-made, rather than a natural, calamity. This, in contrast to natural crises, has happened many times in human history. A few "recent" examples will make the point: Rome destroyed Carthage; Spain crushed the Aztecs and Incas of the New World; and Britain destroyed Australian Aboriginal society. In each of these tragic cases, the strategic *logos* was torn apart, never to be reassembled.

In the absence of conquest, the sole reason for the breakdown of a society's *logos* is **strategic exhaustion**. To employ an analogy, it is like the death of a star. A star dies because the chain reactions that generate its output of heat, light, and energy eventually run out of fuel. In a similar way, the strategic reactions of a pulsating *logos* eventually break down because its strategic opportunities – the wealth-creating capacity of the available dynamic strategies or strategic "fuel" – are eventually exhausted. Rome fell because it was unable to replace its exhausted conquest strategy with a viable alternative, *not* because of changes in the physical environment of the Mediterranean world and *not* because it had run out of natural resources. Volcanic eruptions, like that at Vesuvius on August 24, AD 79, could destroy entire Roman cities, but they had no more than a minor and temporary impact on the strategic *logos* of Rome. The same can be said for any other environmental change in the Mediterranean of that era.

The *logos* can sustain considerable damage without being extinguished. This can be seen in countries that have been devastated during modern total warfare, only to recover rapidly following the cessation of hostilities. Teutonia in the mid-twentieth century is an excellent case study. Having failed in its attempt to conquer Europe, Nazi Teutonia was invaded in 1945 in the west by the Allies and in the east by Moscovia. The resulting impact on the population and infrastructure of Teutonia was devastating. Had the invading forces so desired, they could have extinguished the Teutonic *logos*. Instead it was cut in two: that in the West was revitalized along strategic lines by a massive injection of Allied resources under the Marshall Plan (a plan that was more about reviving the Jeffersonian than the Teutonic economy); and that in the East was taken over by Teutonic antistrategists under orders from Moscow. West Teutonia was able to revive its old *logos* and fashion it into a truly strategic form, enabling it to compete at the highest international level; whereas East Teutonia, under control of Moscovia, was forced to reshape its *logos* in antistrategic form, sowing the seeds of eventual self-destruction.

The concept of an **antistrategic** *logos* is interesting, if oppressive and self-destructive. Refer back to Figure 1. Within an antistrategic *logos*, man is still driven by strategic desire and guided by the strategic cerebrum, but he is not free to explore or exploit strategic opportunities or to follow the lead of successful strategists in other countries. Instead, strategic desire and thought is constrained and redirected – leading to total frustration – by political decree based on a perverted form of idealism. All the major economic, social, and political decisions are made by the small group of antistrategists who have seized power in order to exploit and control the former strategists and to monopolize their sources of income. In terms of Figure 1, the antistrategists, through the imposition of a command economy, determine not only the national "objectives" (it cannot be called a strategy) to be followed, but also the nature of "socialist" (rather than strategic) demand, the "socialist" response, and the "socialist" vehicle to carry it forward, albeit in a limping manner.

By constraining strategic desire and thought, the ruling elite in East Teutonia (following the Moscovian lead) effectively crippled their *logos*. Instead of destroying it outright – as Rome had done in Carthage – the Moscovians consigned it to a slow and inevitable death, just as they had unknowingly done to the Moscovian *logos*. Both had been mortally wounded. As it turned out, the Moscovian *logos* was the first to break down, setting East Teutonia free to be revived, with great difficulty, by its sibling in the West.[4] The lesson here is clear: we manipulate strategic desire and thought at the risk of destroying the *logos* – the dynamic mechanism of life. Antistrategists – including both totalitarian regimes and terrorist groups – are essentially anti life – anti *logos*.

8.

What can the strategic *logos* tell us about truth? Before answering this we need to review the orthodox view of this issue. Academic philosophers write as if truth were a major objective of civilized man. Most philosophers would probably claim that they are driven throughout life by some sort of "will to truth"; and some would even claim that they are in pursuit of an eternal, divine Truth. Lip service is even paid to this notion by various sections of human society – in politics, religion, education, welfare, and, ironically, business and journalism. But, as I've shown elsewhere, truth is always the first casualty of the strategic pursuit, even in religious and philosophical circles.[5]

The key question here is: if truth is not the real objective of man or his society, why do we continue to claim that it is? The answer is tied up with man's **strategic dualism**. Man, as argued here, is driven to survive and prosper by strategic desire, and this objective is facilitated by the strategic cerebrum. The problem for man alone is that the highly developed, self-conscious mind is ruled by reason. And deductively based reason has created an ideal world – to be contrasted with the real world of strategic desire – in which truth rather than materialism is the supposed objective of life. This is what I call the **existential dilemma** of man. As the real world is more powerful than the ideal world – except in cases of seriously disturbed individuals – desire always triumphs over truth. This is true even for those professional groups that claim to be committed to the pursuit of wisdom and truth.

Philosophers profess, as the original Greek word implies, to be "lovers of wisdom". In the tradition of Plato they claim to be primarily concerned with the pursuit of truth. But in reality philosophers are like all other groups of individuals in society. They are primarily concerned with survival and prosperity. The so-called pursuit of truth by academic departments of philosophy is a professional activity designed to generate a comfortable lifestyle. While there is nothing abnormal or unreasonable in this, I have no doubt that the truth of this statement will be vigorously denied.[6] Reality emerges when the pursuit of truth comes into conflict with material issues. In my experience, whenever the survival of a philosophy department is threatened – or is perceived by its members to be threatened – they ruthlessly attempt to eliminate the threat and to justify their actions using untrue statements. Sometimes, even when there is no threat, just the opportunity to "garner" more resources for themselves, philosophers will embark on a conquest strategy and claim that it was all in the best interest of their institution. Of course, not all philosophers operate in this manner, just the majority. As in all walks of life there are exceptions – noble creatures – who refuse to participate in these strategic activities and who, knowingly, suffer the consequences. But, in the main, materialism triumphs over truth. This is why the human race still exists.

Priests claim to be seekers after divine Truth. They also claim a special relationship with a supposed creator of the universe, who is thought to be the source of all goodness and truth. But in reality, apart from the usual exceptions, priests are also primarily concerned with survival and prosperity to which truth is usually sacrificed. In the Western World, the established churches are big business enterprises. They have also been competitively aggressive, following hard on the heels of victorious armies in lesser developed countries to stake their claims on the souls (and a proportion of the possessions) of the vanquished. The Christian Church even planned and led crusades against the forces of Islam in the Holy Lands. A similar role was adopted in the past by Islam against Christian societies.

Priests of all religious faiths have sought power within and for their own churches, often ruling states, such as the Vatican, Media, and Persia. Priests have also pursued comfortable, even opulent, lifestyles at the expense of the world's poorest people. In the contemporary church in the West, priests have, as discussed elsewhere, been guilty of pedophilia – as no doubt they always have – and their institutions have closed ranks against the victims and their families in order to protect the priestly predators. Survival and prosperity rather than truth – with or without an uppercase T – is the real, as opposed to the professed, objective of religious organizations.

9.

If truth is not the real objective of human society what role does it play? It is argued here that the truth, like any other human value including its opposite, is merely a strategic instrument. Both truth and lies will be employed by individuals to achieve their strategic objectives; the choice will depend upon the circumstances. Fiction is also generally preferred to the truth, because of its diverting and entertaining qualities. Reality only becomes the focus of attention when its understanding is essential to the achievement of strategic objectives. If it is necessary to develop new forms of energy or sophisticated weapons, society will fund the necessary research into science and technology. When we have a choice we prefer to spend our time and resources on diversionary entertainment.

Figure 1 suggests that truth (together with all other useful social values) is generated by the strategic *logos*. Truth, as merely one of the **strategic instruments** required in certain circumstances to facilitate the unfolding dynamic strategy, is a response to strategic demand. Values, such as truth, honesty, generosity, justice, are not innate characteristics but rather generalized forms of societal rules required to make civilization work. Rather than elaborating an impossibly long list of detailed rules – one for every conceivable situation in life – human society attempts to economize by inculcating a limited number of general values that, when applied in particular circumstances, lead to predictable response that facilitate the strategic pursuit. These values are taught in the family, school, and church, through public role models, and the media.

Once they reach a more knowing age, however, children are also taught – or learn through experience – that these strategic values should be employed flexibly in order to "get on" in life. While in normal circumstances it is generally expected that the people one comes in contact with will usually tell the truth (or something approximating to it), there will be times when truth will be a liability. At such times the individual, and even society as a whole, will make greater material gains by telling lies. The war on terror is an excellent example. In times of crisis, particularly when the strategic pursuit is under threat, we know that it is best to assume that very few people will tell the truth. Some of course, will tell the truth no matter what. They are the first to perish, as we saw in Nazi Teutonia. Truth, therefore, is not an objective, merely a selective and flexible tool that is highly responsive to strategic demand. Values are external to man and to god. They are generated by the strategic *logos*.

When not required to respond to strategic demand, we all prefer lies to the truth about life. There are a number of good reasons for this. First, lies are necessary if we are to live comfortably with ourselves. This is the basis of my **existential schizophrenia** concept: the need to delude ourselves about our true natures in order to survive and prosper.[7] What we do on a daily basis in response to strategic desire is so repugnant to our rational image of ourselves that we find it necessary to deny our real natures. We deny that we are greedy, selfish, aggressive, and mean spirited, and pretend that we are altruistic, selfless, gentle, and generous. We even fund academic research in universities to "demonstrate" that this is so. We lie about the fact that we lie to ourselves and others.

Second, we need to lie to others to prevent them seeing us as we really are, so as to avoid their condemnation and rejection. And this, despite the fact that everyone else is in the same predicament. It is a case of mutual respect based on deception all round. Only the one who fails to keep up the masquerade is boycotted, not because of his own moral failings, but because he is a mirror to the rest of us – a danger to our mutual self-delusion.

Third, lies, or fiction, distract us from the grinding despair of reality: from having to face, on a daily basis, the grasping materialism of human nature. This preference for fiction is reflected in our demand for spectator sports and other mindless forms of entertainment. Compare the vast amounts of money we, as a society, are willing to pay sportspeople to monotonously and endlessly hit, kick, or throw balls of varying shapes and sizes to each other or into holes, or hoops, or between sticks planted in the ground, or over boundary lines; or to popular singers to belt out eardrum-breaking, mind-numbing sentiments; or to television performers to act out the most banal social relationships (preferably sexual); with the small amounts we pay our serious artists and scholars, who draw our attention to the reality of life.

Fourth, we even lie to ourselves about how wonderful our lives are. This can be seen in the results from surveys around the world that ask people to rate their degree of happiness. Novice researchers are, predictably, surprised to discover that the happiness ratio is usually high and uniform across time and space. All societies, according to these surveys, are approximately equally happy, whether they live in poverty (with high rates of infant morbidity and mortality) or in affluence. The fact is that people need to misrepresent their lives to themselves in order to avoid self-destruction and, thereby, subvert the very objective of the strategic desire that drives us all. The entire point of life is to survive and prosper, not to be happy. We avoid this truth by lying about it.

For those who believe that the results of happiness surveys suggest that people don't want or need material progress, consider the following: Why do poverty-stricken countries bother with economic development if they are really happy with their lot? Why do the disadvantaged migrate in their millions to more wealthy countries? How would people in the First World rate their happiness if they were suddenly reduced to Third-World status? If we can't change our circumstances, we need to lie in order to keep going.

10.

"But," the astute reader objects, "what of the wisemen who have existed throughout the history of civilization? How do we account for them? Men like Kongfuzi (Confucius), Lao Tzu, and Chuang Tzu in the Great-Wall Civilization; Vardhamana, Sidhartha Gautama (Buddah), Patanjali, and Badarayana in Hindustan; Zoroaster, Muhammad, and Ibn Sina in the Middle East; Homer, Heraclitus, Socrates, Plato, Aristotle, Thucydides, Cicero, and Virgil in ancient Greece and Rome; and da Vinci, Kepler, Galileo, Descartes, Newton, Darwin, and Einstein in medieval and modern Europe – to name a few. Are they merely a response to your strategic demand, or is there really a 'will to truth' embodied in mankind after all?"

This is an important issue. Let me say in response that this list of wisemen or **truth-seekers**, which ranges over almost three millennia and four continents, is a very short one. Of course, it is only an illustrative list and could be considerably expanded. Even so, it would still involve a relatively small number of individuals compared to the billions of people who have lived out their lives during the course of human civilization. My point is that if mankind possessed an innate will to truth, the truth-seeker would be commonplace rather than a rarity.

What I will suggest, which is developed more fully elsewhere, is that the truth-seeker is a deviant.[8] All men and women possess varying degrees of the curiosity instinct, but only a very small minority are willing to act on this instinct to pursue truth to, and beyond, the point of social discrimination and psychological disease. Some, like Zarathustra, pursue truth to the point of madness, suicide, or execution. Truth-seeking, therefore, is a perversion that, when indulged in over the long term, leads to the erosion of strategic integration in the individual concerned. While normal curiosity is an aid to prosperity-seeking, its overindulgence leads to a self-destructive form of truth-seeking. The distinction I'm making here is between the average academic, who is a prosperity-seeker responding to strategic demand, and the truth-seeker, who completely ignores strategic demand. At his own peril. Because of its self-destructive nature, truth-seeking could never become an instinct, a "will to truth".

Although the truth-seeker ignores strategic demand, he is not untouched by it. The strategic *logos* defines the society in which he lives. As the truth-seeker is not directly rewarded by the *logos*, he must acquire the necessary surplus to support himself materially in other, less direct, ways. In primitive societies, the material surplus was barely sufficient to allow more than a very few wisemen to practice their craft, usually in their spare time. More advanced societies, in contrast, can generate the material surpluses to allow the emergence of larger numbers of truth-seekers, usually disguised as priests, soothsayers, or academics. Their truth-seeking is funded by wealthy patrons in return for social status and intellectual services; by academic organizations; by the inheritance of wealth; by highly successful strategic adventures in their earlier years; or by indulgent spouses.

The bottom line is that the supply of truth-seekers depends not just on intellectual and instinctual characteristics in the population, but also on the nature of the strategic *logos*. Changes in a society's *logos* can indirectly increase or decrease truth-seeking activity by altering the prosperity or direction of the strategic pursuit. If these changes – such as the exhaustion of a once-dominant dynamic strategy – lead to a reduction in the surpluses available for truth-seeking, the existing wisemen will be discriminated against as the prosperity-seekers compete fiercely for a declining share of the national surplus.

The truth-seeker, therefore, can only operate within the set of material constraints defined by his society's strategic *logos*. But, within these constraints the truth-seeker is driven by his own peculiar desires. Accordingly he generates ideas that are not required by the strategic *logos*, and may even be detrimental to it – ideas that will have no impact on his society until there is a strategic demand for them. Hence, in an authoritarian conquest society, a deviant truth-seeker may wax lyrical about the virtues of democracy, but these ideas will not become popular or be adopted until the conquest strategy has exhausted itself and been replaced either by the commerce or technological strategies, which require less autocratic institutions and organizations in order to be successful. But this can, as in medieval Europe, take 1,500 to 2,000 years to accomplish! Even the witty response of an aging Nobel Prize winner to the question: "To what do you owe your success?" – "Longevity!", is not, therefore, always apt.

Alternatively, Leonardo da Vinci (1452–1519) in the late fifteenth century could design submarines, flying machines, parachutes, and tanks, but none of these ideas would be adopted by his society (or that of Europe) for another 400 years, until the industrial technological strategy had replaced the commerce strategy of his time. And only then, because the commerce strategy had finally exhausted itself, not because of the independent influence of da Vinci's ideas. As it turned out, when the time for these ideas finally came – when there was a strategic demand for them – they had to be reinvented. And, of course, when there was a strategic demand for these ideas, it was the prosperity-seeking intellectuals, and the profit-seeking strategists, who shamelessly exploited the earlier ideas of great men such as da Vinci.

Let me conclude by saying once more that there is no *general* "will to truth". Only a perverse desire by a very small minority of intellectuals to pursue truth whatever the cost. It is precisely this cost, measured in terms of premature death and madness, that prevents the emergence of a universal (instinctual) will to truth. The only reason there are periods in human history when truth about reality unfolds rapidly – periods I have called **technological paradigm shifts** – is because of the systematic emergence of demand for these ideas as the strategic *logos* transforms itself.[9] Without this strategic demand, truth-seeking of all types would disappear from human society entirely. The foundation of, and limitation on, truth-seeking is the strategic *logos* "from which all things follow".

Strategic Desire

1.

The driving force in the strategic *logos*, as we have seen from Figure 1, is strategic desire. It is the strongest and most persistent force in life, responsible for fashioning the nature of all species as well as that of human society. As argued in *The Selfcreating Mind* (2006), strategic desire has shaped the instincts and values that are responsible for human behavior. In the dynamic-strategy theory, this driving force is embodied in what I have called the **materialist organism** in nature and the **materialist man** in human society.

Without strategic desire, no form of life could exist on this or any other planet. It is a force that arises from the biochemical foundations of life: in order to sustain life the first simple cells had to be able to maintain an internal metabolic process to meet their energy requirements. Once an individual metabolic system is established, a simple cell generates a continuous demand for fuel to feed this biochemical process. If this **metabolic demand** for fuel is not met, the cell begins to starve and its structure starts to break down. Impending starvation and collapse, therefore, stimulates the cell to frantic efforts to discover new sources of fuel. Herein lies the source of strategic demand that impels all life-forms, no matter how simple or complex, to struggle to survive and, having survived, to prosper, as insurance against future fuel shortages.

In order to maximize the probability of survival and prosperity, individual organisms adopt (as discussed elsewhere) the most effective of the quartet of dynamic strategies available.[1] Each of these dynamic strategies has a characteristic impact – operating through strategic demand – on the physical (including intellectual) and instinctual traits of organisms in any species, and on the value systems in human society. And those characteristics shape both animal and human behavior.

The dynamic strategies of genetic and technological change generate a demand for physical abilities that provide greater access to new and existing natural resources, for instinctual drives of curiosity and thirst for knowledge, and values (freedom of thought and intellectual property rights) that facilitate innovation. The family-multiplication strategy requires increased fertility and mobility, greater sexual and adventure drives, and values (mutual self-help, and solidarity) that support family formation and migration. The commerce strategy needs greater abilities to monopolize and trade in scarce resources, drives of acquisition and adventure, and values (sharp practices and mercenary attitudes) that favor commercial activities. And the conquest strategy demands the abilities to wage war and administer a larger captive resource base, the drives of aggression and power, and the values (valor, brutality, and teamwork) that support conquest. Changes in physical and instinctual characteristics are effected through strategic selection, and in values through social selection.

Strategic selection, as discussed in detail elsewhere, operates through **strategic imitation** in response to strategic demand.[2] In responding to these different types of strategic demand, the selective organisms will ignore any mutation that doesn't possess the required physical and instinctual characteristics in favor of any mutation that does possess them. The reason is that the characteristics favored by strategic demand increase the probability of survival and prosperity. Individuals possessing the characteristics required by strategic demand in any population will become desirable as comrades and/ or sexual partners (as they can share in their success), whereas the rest will be regarded as undesirable, even as freaks. The desirable will be feted and followed – the process of strategic imitation – whereas the undesirable will be boycotted, attacked, even destroyed by parents, siblings, and neighbors. Through this autogenous process of strategic selection, strategic desire shapes the physical (including intellectual) and instinctual characteristics of individuals in any species, including man.

Strategic demand is also central to the formation of values, which emerge through the process of **social selection**. Some values, which are required to make any strategy work, are of a general nature. These general values include honesty, loyalty, fair dealing, justice, compassion, and so on, and are selected by society to facilitate their strategic pursuit. They are employed in society, as I've explained somewhere else, as a general guide for individuals as they interact in the various spheres of government, law, business, and family. But the way these general values are employed depends on the particular dynamic strategy a given society is pursuing.

In a conquest society, harsher values will prevail, both at home and, particularly, abroad; in a commerce society, values sneered at by a warrior aristocracy, such as those associated with money lending and sharp trading practices, will come to the fore; in a technological society, greater emphasis will be placed on values relating to freedom of thought and respect for intellectual property; and in a society pursuing the family-multiplication strategy – including past primitive societies, the Great Wall Civilization throughout much of the past millennium, Moscovia during the seventeenth century, and the Jeffersonian Republic and Terra Australis during the nineteenth century – family values of mutual self-help and kinship loyalty will prevail.

2.

What has strategic desire – the driving force of the *logos* – got to do with truth? In truth, nothing. While strategic desire is the fundamental force in life, it knows nothing of, and cares nothing for, the truth. The *only* concern of the unconscious organism is to survive and prosper. All methods of doing so are,

Strategic Desire

as far as it is concerned, equally valid. The unconscious organism remains unimpressed by values such as truth, justice, virtue, honesty, and so on.

Accordingly there can be no will to truth associated with the unconscious forces that drive both the individual or his society as some philosophers would like to believe, only an addiction to the most extreme of extreme sports.[3] Even Zarathustra flirted with the idea of a "will to truth", which he thought was associated with an innate "will to power". He taught us that

> The task of true philosophers is '*to create values*' ... Their knowing is *creating*, their creating is law-giving, their will to truth is – will to power.[4]

Zarathustra saw the acquisition of knowledge as power over life. And he saw all "true" philosophers as being driven by this will to truth: "What urges you on and arouses your ardour, you wisest of men, do you call it 'will to truth'."[5] Yet, at the same time, he recognized that truth is not always beneficial to the truth-seeker, and that true truth-seekers had to be special people. Zarathustra tells us the "strength of a mind might be measured by how much 'truth' it can endure".[6]

There is a tragic irony here. Zarathustra was addicted to the truth (as an extreme sport), and suffered greatly because of it. He refused to employ the usual mechanism – existential schizophrenia – for releasing the conscious mind from the tyranny of strategic desire. Instead, he insisted on fearlessly facing the truth about himself and the world. He used truth as a sharp instrument to cut into his own psyche as well as dissecting the great mysteries of life. He became a self-vivisectionist, not out of masochism but in the name of truth. He pushed his body to its limits by refusing to capitulate to bad eyes, blinding headaches, a highly sensitive stomach, frequent vomiting, and chronic sleeplessness. And in the process he became hypersensitive to changes in his physical and social environment. If the weather became too hot, too sultry, too windy, too stormy – or if the social climate became too stimulating, too demanding, or too disagreeable – his health deteriorated rapidly and he would be laid low for days, unable to read, let alone work.

In the last year or so of his sane life, Zarathustra became increasingly manic-depressive, surging suddenly from extremes of elation to those of deep depression. Increasingly he experienced psychotic episodes of delusion. Eventually, at the age of only 45 years, he was unable to shoulder the burden of truth-seeking any further, suffering a massive mental breakdown from which there was to be no sustained recovery. Unable to face reality any longer, Zarathustra retreated into madness.[7] At last his body was liberated from his ruthless intellect, and was able to live on in unaccustomed peace for a further decade.

****

The attitude of most contemporary philosophers toward the truth can be found in the work of Bill Bernard, a fellow of All Heart's College, International

University of Metropolis.[8] Like Zarathustra, Bernard believes in some sort of will to truth, which he prefers to call the "desire for truthfulness". This desire for truthfulness is said to be characteristic of philosophers. Yet while all philosophers have a will to truth, some are skeptical that it can ever be fulfilled. This paradox, Bernard suggests, is the main source of tension in contemporary philosophy. He regards himself as one of the "moderate deniers" – rather than the "radical deniers" – who believe there is pragmatic value, rather than no value at all, in the pursuit of truth. He claims there "is no one reason for preferring the truth ... truthfulness has an intrinsic value ... living in the truth is just a better way to be."

What Bernard does reject is the idea that there is such a thing as "the" truth about either the universe or history. He prefers to think in terms of the existence of "many truths" about these big issues. Bernard claims "there would be such a thing as 'the truth about the past' only if there were one most basic question about the past that was the concern of those enquiring into it, and there is no such question". Also he doubts that such a truth would even be desirable, because

> if 'the truth about the universe' were discovered, future people would have no reason to change it. The theory that expressed it would be ... 'superassertable' ... I do not see how anyone could reasonably think that a large-scale *interpretation* of history might be in this position, or why they should want it to be so. To suppose that future people will need the same things from an *interpretation* of the past as we do surely implies that life as a cultural development will have to come to a stop. [My emphasis.]

Hence, although philosophers have a "desire" for truth, it only extends to *some* truths, not all truths. Certainly not the big truths about the universe and history.

It seems to me that Bernard's negative conclusion about "the" truth arises from an unnecessarily limited conception of what this might be. He sees the truth about history as an "interpretation" of the past rather than an underlying dynamic mechanism embodied in the strategic *logos*. What I have been attempting to show over many years is the possibility of discovering not just "many truths" (or "interpretations"), but one truth that embodies all other truths. This one truth – the strategic *logos* – depends on it being not the "one most basic question about the past that was the concern of those inquiring into it" as Bernard insists, but rather "the" mechanism of life that can explain all questions about the past, and even make sensible predictions about the future. While the strategic *logos* might not be regarded by *all* philosophers as the "most basic question", it certainly was the basic concern of one of the greatest – Heraclitus of Ephesus. We must be able to see beyond "interpretations" and the concerns of the majority of philosophers.

The one truth that encompasses all other truths does not imply, as Bernard claims, that cultural development would come to a "stop" if it were actually discovered. Cultural development continues because the strategic *logos* continues to pulsate, not because we remain ignorant of these pulsations.

Strategic Desire

Knowledge of the one truth is not like the Second Coming of Christ: it will not mean the end of history, just the end of ignorance and superstition. An understanding of the truth is possible and, when there is a strategic demand for it, desirable. Truth, like untruth, has no other "social" justification than that it sometimes facilitates the strategic pursuit. Its "personal" justification is not that "living in the truth" is "a better way to be", but that it enables the successful truth-seeker to understand the true meaning of life. Even at the risk of self-vivisection. Zarathustra is witness to this truth.

Strategic Cerebrum

1.

The strategic dualism in man, which underlies human nature, is the outcome of the relationship between the **unconscious organism** driven by strategic desire and the **strategic cerebrum** ruled by reason. Essentially the human brain is a strategic instrument "employed" by the unconscious organism to supervise its participation in the strategic pursuit, so as to maximize its probability of survival and prosperity. Compared to strategic desire, which stretches back almost 4,000 myrs, it is a relatively recent device. Prior to the emergence of animals with central nervous systems merely 500 myrs ago, its job was undertaken by the **strategic gene**. Even today there are many life forms – including bacteria, viruses, and the entire plant kingdom – that still "employ" the strategic gene to supervise their strategic pursuit and to ensure their survival and prosperity. It was because the strategic gene was unable to cope with the strategic pursuit in the increasingly complex *social* environments faced by some life forms that the strategic cerebrum finally emerged.

It is essential to realize that the brain, even in the most primitive organisms that possess one, is *always* a strategic instrument. At every point in time in its historical development, all the various parts and functions of this new organ were (and are) highly integrated and subordinated to the strategic pursuit. (This has been discussed in detail in *The Selfcreating Mind* (2006).) The healthy integrated brain works not in its own interest, but in the strategic interests of the unconscious organism. Any expansion of cognitive abilities over time – achieved through an increase in the size and complexity of the brain – merely increases the strategic sophistication and capability of the organism. Before any expansion in cognitive abilities, the brain was a strategic instrument; after this expansion it was a more *effective* strategic instrument. It is important, therefore, to abandon any temptation to think of earlier versions of the brain as incomplete or partial in the strategic sense – temptations encouraged by the flawed Darwinian modular theory of the brain. Earlier versions were merely less complex, owing to the less complex nature of the strategic *logos* for a particular life form.

How do we account for the growing complexity of the strategic cerebrum? The answer, as shown in *The Collapse of Darwinism* (2003) and *The Selfcreating Mind* (2006), is **strategic selection**, which completely displaces the Darwinian concept of natural selection. Strategic selection is, as we have seen, the mechanism in nature by which individual organisms play a major role in shaping the physical (including intellectual) and instinctual characteristics they pass on to their offspring. It is important to realize that this mechanism is an integral part of the strategic *logos*. Organisms that are driven to survive and prosper by strategic desire invest metabolic energy and resources in the most cost-effective dynamic strategy available. The resulting combined effect of such investment by all organisms in a particular community or "society" is the generation of **strategic demand** for a range of inputs required in the strategic pursuit. The point that needs to be made here is that these inputs (discussed elsewhere) also include the physical and instinctual characteristics required to participate in an increasingly complex strategic *logos*. It is this response by individual organisms to the biological component of strategic demand that I call strategic selection. Within the compass of the strategic *logos*, strategic selection is activated and shaped by strategic demand. This is an **autogenous**, or selfcreating, process.

2.

For those not familiar with my earlier work, it may be helpful to examine the concept of strategic selection further and to place it within the context of the strategic *logos*. Even those familiar with my earlier work should find interest in seeing how it fits into the strategic *logos*. It is useful to realize that strategic selection is activated by the changing demand generated by the unfolding process of *any* of the four dynamic strategies, not just that of genetic change. We can see the way strategic selection works by briefly examining the process by which the entire quartet of dynamic strategies unfold, which in the natural world progresses through the **strategic sequence** of genetic change → family multiplication (or commerce) → conquest.

Systematic genetic change, which takes place within the strategic *logos*, is a dynamic strategy *deliberately* employed by organisms when circumstances are favorable. Its role is similar to that of technological change in human society. When natural resources are abundant, and competition is minimal, organisms – and hence populations, species, and dynasties – invest much time, energy, and resources in the pursuit of genetic change in order to exploit their good fortune. Organisms respond to these favorable conditions by creating new **genetic styles**, usually called species, so as to reap "monopoly profits" by gaining access to new resources or more intense access to old resources. Speciation, therefore, is the outcome of organisms attempting to gain more favorable access to natural resources. Ironically, this can only occur in a non-Darwinian world which provides guaranteed generous returns and vast periods of time necessary to make the effort worthwhile, and to see it through to fruition. Hence the impotence of Darwin's theory of natural selection.

Genetic change is the outcome not of chance but of *deliberate* and *sustained* decision making – of, in other words, the pursuit of the **genetic strategy**. It involves a change in the way metabolic energy is employed by organisms. Investment in genetic change requires a deliberate transfer of internal energy from an existing to an entirely new biological activity. This can be seen, for example, in early man about 2.4 myrs ago when internal energy was diverted from maintaining a massive jaw, large teeth, and extended gut, to developing and maintaining the large brain needed to construct tools and more complex societies in order to scavenge for meat as well as gather plant materials, and, later on, to hunt large game. This, I've argued elsewhere, was a response to the strategic demand generated by the new meat-and-marrow version of early man's family-multiplication strategy. A strategy that enabled our species to spread throughout the world and greatly increase our numbers. All this took place within a slowly transforming strategic *logos*.

What we need to consider now is how this type of **biotransition** was achieved. Baldly stated it is the outcome of the strategic selection mechanism, which operates through **strategic imitation**. An individual experiencing a beneficial mutation that enables a more favorable access to natural resources will be able to increase its prospects of survival and prosperity. Such success will attract the attention of others, who will seek to emulate it. Those with similar abilities will cooperate with each other to improve their joint prospects. When of the opposite sex, they will also mate together and produce offspring that will, on average, carry the new successful genes. I call this **selective sexual reproduction**. Success attracts and, literally, breeds further success. But it must be emphasized that individuals are attracted to each other not to pass on their genes, as the neo-Darwinists claim, but to increase the probability of their own survival and prosperity.

Mate choice, however, is an essential element in the process of strategic selection. Individuals select mates possessing the phenotypic characteristics they hope will improve their family's access to natural resources in the present and future. Their deliberate selection is based on the observed characteristics that appear to be associated with the success of potential mates. It is their appreciation of conspicuous success rather than an understanding of the nature of these characteristics that is important here. When pursuing the genetic strategy those with sufficient "bargaining power" reject individuals possessing non-resource-accessing characteristics – such as greater fertility or better military characteristics (or connections) – that are not relevant to their joint success in developing a new genetic style. These "aberrant" individuals are regarded as unattractive, even freakish, and, therefore, are avoided.

Similarly, **strategists** following non-genetic strategies find other individuals, who are marginally better able to access new resources, unappealing and unhelpful, because they possess "deviant" physical and instinctual characteristics. Instead they are attracted to those who display characteristics associated with greater fertility, mobility, or military abilities on the one hand, and greater sexual or aggressive drives on the other.

But this is not the whole picture. Strategic selection involves not only selective sexual reproduction but also the culling, both by parents and siblings, of offspring that do not possess the strategically required characteristics.

This process of elimination is widespread in animal and pre-neolithic human societies. By deliberate mate choice, selective breeding, and effective culling, the mechanism of strategic selection by the organism at the phenotypic level shapes the genotype.

It will be clear by now why strategic demand is essential to the strategic selection process. Remove this demand for new genetic (or technological) "ideas" and the dynamic process will break down, even if environmental change generates a steady stream of random mutations. There is just no incentive in these circumstances to develop systematic and directional genetic change. Conversely, if the supply of new ideas were terminated, the materialist organism would merely adopt another dynamic strategy – such as family multiplication, commerce, or conquest – and the dynamic process of the strategic *logos* would continue, even if less efficiently. The fundamental point here is that the strategic *logos* is demand driven.

But why and how does the selective behavior of successful individuals sweep through entire populations? It is, I argue, a further outcome of the strategic imitation mechanism. The material success of strategic pioneers in pursuit of genetic change will soon attract the attention of other individuals, who will attempt to imitate their feeding and sheltering activities. Those with the biological abilities to adopt these new methods will join in, and, through appropriate mate choice, will select for those physical and instinctual characteristics that support the successful genetic strategy. This marks the beginning of a new genetic style. After the passage of many generations, possibly taking tens or hundreds of thousands of years, this imitative process of strategic selection will lead to the emergence of a new species – a new genetic style.

****

Other dynamic strategies of the *logos* operate on the physical and instinctual characteristics of organisms in a similar if less dramatic way. Investment in the **family-multiplication strategy**, for example, involves a redirection of energy by organisms from increasing the intensity of natural-resource access to improving fertility rates and migration skills. This occurs once the genetic strategy has been exhausted – once an optimum number of genetic styles (species) has been created – and when it is more economical to take these styles to the rest of the known world by utilizing underused natural resources.

Investment in the family-multiplication strategy has a less dramatic impact on phenotypic characteristics, but it does involve males in the natural world directing metabolic energy to eye-catching displays, attractive plumage, nest building, and male-to-male combat. They do so to attract or snare mates who they associate with higher fertility rates. Females also view these characteristics to the same ends. Similar processes operate in human society. In these new circumstances, the basis for mate choice switches from intensive resource-accessing abilities to family-forming abilities. And the basis of individual choice is the perception of the relative success of these abilities in the strategic pursuit. This is not about sex for its own sake, which is an important part of "prosperity" once survival has been ensured, but rather about gaining greater family control over natural resources through procreation to enable migration into unused or underused regions. Through strategic selection the embodied physical characteristics that promote greater fertility and mobility together with instinctual sexual and adventurous drives are adopted and passed on to future generations. Other phenotypic characteristics, such as those highly prized under the genetic, commerce, and conquest strategies, are just ignored by ignoring their owners.

The same issues characterize the **commerce (or symbiotic) strategy**, which is employed by some species as an alternative to the family-multiplication strategy. In this case, organisms specialize in abilities that enable them to monopolize certain resources that are in wide demand by other species or societies and to "trade" these resources for others that they require to survive and prosper. There are many examples in both nature and human society. In nature there are symbiotic relationships between algae and coral polyps in coastal waters; algae and fungi (known as lichens) on land; plants that house and feed ant colonies in return for protection; ants that cultivate fungi for food; bacteria that live in the digestive systems of many animals, providing enzymes to break down cellulose. In human society, where this strategy reached its zenith, the great empires of Phoenicia, Greece, and Carthage in the ancient world; the San Marco Republic, the Low Countries, and Engle Land in the premodern world; and the Asian Entrepôt Islands in the contemporary societies. Mate choice, both non-sexual and sexual, in these societies is based on specialized commerce abilities and drives, which are very different to those required by other dynamic strategies within the *logos*.

The **conquest strategy** has always been adopted by animal and human societies once the family-multiplication or commerce strategies have been exhausted. This, finally, is the Darwinian world of intense competition for scarce resources, which leads not to directional genetic change and speciation as required by natural selection, but to war and extinction. While conquest in the short run is a zero-sum game – in that the victor's gains never exceed the vanquished's losses – it does provide fabulous returns to successful individuals, societies, and species. In nature, the victors gain better access to food sources, to favorable habitats and locations, and to sexual partners; and in human society, the successful conquest states acquire additional land, slaves, equipment, infrastructure, treasure, profits, and tax revenue.

To achieve this prosperity, individuals in nature and human society have to invest their energy and accumulated surpluses in the weapons, infrastructure, and organizations required to conduct systematic warfare and to occupy invaded territories. In animal species, individuals, through strategic selection, invest metabolic energy in the development of powerful biological weapons of defense and offense; in plant species, individuals invest internal energy in the production of toxins, thorns, strangling vines, suffocating canopies, or sheer size; and in human society, individuals and the state invest accumulated surpluses in military equipment, war machines, chariots, warships, transport and communication facilities, together with the infrastructure of empire (a mechanism for surplus extraction). Hence, while dinosaurs employed genetic change as a *supporting* strategy to develop biological weapons, mankind uses technological change as a *supporting* strategy to develop non-biological weapons – both within the context of the *dominant* dynamic strategy of conquest. Through a wide-angled lens, the conquest warriors and the great battles of both dynasties look much the same.

The centerpiece of the biology of selfcreation, therefore, is the entirely new concept of strategic selection, whereby individuals embrace the physical, intellectual, and instinctual characteristics required to maximize the probability of survival and prosperity. Selfcreation is a central feature of the pulsating strategic *logos*, which is responsible for the emergence and sustenance of both life and human society.

3.

What type of information is processed by the strategic cerebrum? As the brain's role is to act as a strategic instrument for the unconscious organism, everything else is subordinated to this function. Accordingly, the brain processes information that improves its ability to participate in the strategic pursuit.

Two types of information are processed by the strategic brain: information required for pattern recognition, and information essential for strategic imitation. **Pattern-recognition information**, which is supplied by all the senses, is used in two main ways. First, all functional organisms in a society require simple information about their world in order to find their way around, to carry out essential daily activities, and hopefully, to survive in the short run. Second, a few exceptional individuals will also employ this information to analyze their world and to explore new strategic opportunities. They are the strategic pioneers who blaze new trails in the creation and application of new ideas.

Imitative information is sought and processed by the strategic cerebrum in order to achieve long-term survival and prosperity. As the brain is a strategic instrument rather than a rational machine, it seeks out imitative information about who and what are successful and why, rather than benefit-cost information. It does so in order to imitate conspicuous success in the surrounding world. This leads to the mechanism of strategic imitation by which the successful dynamic strategies of the few are imitated by the opportunism of the many. The modern human brain employs the same type of information, and operates in the same strategic way that less sophisticated animal brains have always operated.

The fundamental issue here is that the human brain emerged to process information required to meet the objectives of strategic desire. As the brain grew in size and complexity it passed a threshold that allowed the billions of neurons to specialize in interactive relationships, which produced both consciousness and then self-consciousness. Both forms of consciousness enabled the strategic *logos* to become even more complex and sophisticated – like the modern metropolis.[1] It became the brain's job to discover what the surrounding physical and social environments are like and what role models should be followed in order to maximize the probability of survival and prosperity. While the brain grapples with the contents of the external world, it is not part of its job description to pursue the truth underlying that world, precisely because that does not contribute to maximizing the probability of survival and prosperity. Pursuit of the truth is the obsession of the deviant few – an obsession characterizing the most extreme of extreme sports.

4.

What then is the relationship between the strategic cerebrum and the truth? Whatever the preoccupations of the brain, the fact that it is not the driving force in life rules out the entrenched idea that man is primarily a truth-seeker. This conclusion has been reinforced by what we have learnt about the role of the brain. The information it collects and processes is required to map and negotiate the contours of reality to meet the objectives of strategic desire. In other words, the strategic cerebrum is interested in reality to the extent that such a knowledge assists the unconscious organism in its pursuit of survival and prosperity. And no further.

This ability to recognize real-world patterns and to generalize about them – what I call **strategic thinking** – emerged with early man some 2 to 3 myrs ago. At the micro level, strategic thinking involved observing and assessing clues about the presence and passage of both animals and other humans, and using those clues to develop simple *inductive* theories (stories really) about the activities of their prey and their competitors. Strategic thinking, at various levels of sophistication, had to be undertaken by all active members of the society of early man. This involved comparing current sense data with memories of patterns in the recent past, and projecting these amended patterns into the present and future. It was an intellectual process that directly assisted their hunting, gathering, and raiding activities.

Some individuals – the wisemen and priests – were also interested in bigger, or macro, issues. They searched for longer term and more complex patterns to be detected in the rise and fall of animal populations as well as of the societies of their human competitors. They also recorded the changing seasons and pondered the rotating patterns in the night skies. The generalizations that the few drew from these macro patterns were used to tell stories about the origins of their tribe, other life forms, gods, and the heavens and earth; and they told stories about the future. They sought out new strategic opportunities and attempted to avert impending disasters. The few were concerned with the bigger issues of life and death that went well beyond the short-term interests of the many.

Strategic thinking, therefore, involves an imaginative response to the changing patterns of nature and society, in order to develop new and better ways to survive and prosper. This is achieved by being able to develop entirely new dynamic strategies and substrategies when the old ones have been exhausted. It involves both individual and group responses. The successful strategic pioneers are followed by all other members of society through the process of strategic imitation discussed elsewhere. This is the process by which individual decision making is transformed into the dynamic strategy of the entire society.

Both micro and macro strategic thinking is, as we have seen, based largely on induction – generalizing from patterns observed in reality. By this I mean that induction is the *main* source of information employed by the strategic cerebrum. This is not to say it is the only source, because deduction – thinking based on a set of logical rules – is also used. While deduction can be a powerful form of thinking in appropriate circumstances, it suffers from what I call the **problem of deduction**: the information embodied in its conclusions is only as good as the information contained in its initial propositions. Rubbish in, rubbish out. Indeed, deductive thinking should be notorious for what it leaves out, rather than famous for what it includes. There is just no substitute for effective pattern recognition and inductive generalization for understanding what is happening in reality, particularly if one's life depends on it. Deductive thinking, on the other hand, is prone to flights of fantasy, which can be very dangerous for one's health in critical situations. Of course it suits the priestly philosophers in their ivory towers, because they are usually isolated from reality.

The strategic cerebrum is a master of strategic thinking, precisely because it was developed by the unconscious organism through the autogenous process of strategic selection for that purpose over the past 600 myrs. Sustained deductive thought, by contrast, was not natural to early man and, even today, is a specialized activity that requires many years of training. Deductive thinking demands a level of sophistication that emerged only with civilization some 6,000 years ago. Indeed, it was strategic thinking that gave rise to civilization, which in turn enabled the development of systematic deductive thought. The rule-based nature of deductive, or logical, thinking arose as part of the institutional response – the development of societal rules – to changes in strategic demand as human society became more complex. This rule-making ability was employed much later to develop logical systems of thought, eventually expressed in mathematical form. Why? Because rule-based thinking made possible the more precise calculations – as opposed to rules of thumb – required in the more exacting task of building cities rather than nomadic shelters.

Even modern humans find logical thought difficult, as our minds are no more sophisticated biologically now than 150,000 years ago when we emerged into a paleolithic culture. Intelligent people not rigorously trained in the rules and procedures of deductive thought consistently fail tests of "rational" ability. Because of this cerebral limitation, human society has for thousands of years trained experts – analytical philosophers and mathematicians – in logical thought and, more recently, has invented rational machines, or computers, to do the hard work of logical thinking for us.

Ordinary humans, meanwhile, continue to do what we are good at – strategic thinking. This is a highly subtle and imaginative art form. An interesting possibility is that as rational machines become more sophisticated they will displace the deductive experts. But even then, machines won't displace the inductive thinking of the strategic cerebrum. To do so it would be necessary to build machines that are independently capable of surviving, prospering, and reproducing themselves as they participate in the strategic pursuit. This will never happen because machines are not and can never be driven by strategic desire, life's fundamental force. We will never have to compete strategically with machines, which will always be our strategic instruments. The unreplicable essence of humanness is our integrated embodiment of strategic desire and strategic thinking, which lies at the heart of the *logos*.

5.

While the human brain developed in order to serve strategic desire, the resulting intellectual capacity could be, and was, employed for nonstrategic – even antistrategic – purposes. This was made possible in the civilized era by the emergence of a specialized class of thinkers, namely priests, who were liberated from the strategic struggle by their overlords in order to pursue their special talents. No longer required to compete in order to survive and prosper, these priestly philosophers had less need to focus on reality. Instead they could indulge their interests in metaphysics and fantasy. They could construct theories of the world as they wanted it to be rather than as it really is. They could focus on idealities rather than on realities.

This metaphysical theorizing could only be achieved, however, once the priestly philosophers had abandoned strategic thinking, which had the nasty habit of challenging fantasy with the cold hard facts of reality. Accordingly, they disparaged strategic thinking as the crude method employed by the herd, and extolled deductive thinking as the sophisticated method of the intellectual elite. By basing their elitist system of thinking on a detailed rule-based method that could only be mastered with years of intensive, specialized study, the priestly philosophers were able to maintain their intellectual "superiority" over the people. In this way they created an aura of mystery that provided the authority needed to protect their privileged status as advisors to the political authority. Their society was prepared to support them materially in this role, because it was believed that the priestly philosophers had a special relationship with the strategic *logos*, which they regarded as divine. Only by retaining the favor of this divinity could their society continue to survive and prosper.

The priestly philosophers – both then and now – perpetuated a fraud over the people and their political leaders, because in reality they never understood the strategic *logos*. They led their societies astray. They lied. Their deductive method created a religious metaphysic from a dynamic reality. They have never had any way of recognizing, understanding, or sustaining the strategic *logos*. Their deductive method was and is totally bankrupt.

Today's priestly philosophers come in two main varieties: the worldly philosophers, and the unworldly philosophers. In their current preoccupations the unworldly philosophers come closest to the priestly philosophers of old. They are concerned with metaphysical issues, ranging from the secular to the religious, that have little to do with the realistic nature of life and human society. These issues include the doctrine of being or existence, rational cosmology (doctrine of the world); the existence of god and the human soul; non-realistic theories of the mind, language, cognitive science, and biology; and flawed theories about the causes and consequences of climate change. Their focus is the ideal not the real. They only attract attention from beyond the narrow confines of their academic discipline when they offend conventional standards: like suggesting that animal life is of equal, if not greater, value than human life; that infants are not yet human; and that buggery is not morally reprehensible. These unorthodox views are defended using arbitrary deductive arguments, which are totally devoid of any understanding of the strategic *logos*. When these unworldly philosophers do focus on the real world – as in the case of climate change – their metaphysical theories lead to dangerous policy conclusions that, if ever accepted, will lead to the eclipse of the forthcoming Solar Revolution (Snooks, *The Coming Eclipse* [2010]). Their gods are completely divorced from material reality.

The worldly philosophers, on the other hand, have nothing to say about God, but they are certain they know everything worth knowing about the material fabric of society. It is a knowledge based not on the careful observation of economic patterns and inductive generalization, but on a set of untested assumptions concerning the tastes, preferences, and motives of an optimizing agent called *homo economicus*. In order to employ mathematics to construct their deductive theories, neoclassical economists assume that *homo economicus* operates in a world in, or tending towards, equilibrium. Hence, their view of the dynamic, pulsating *logos* is a static one! While they claim to understand the economy in the present and to be able to make predictions about its future, in reality they don't even realize that the strategic *logos* exists, let alone have the tools to analyze it. They are, in other words, victims of the "problem of deduction" – the fundamental dynamic system underlying the economy is not even in their field of view.

The worldly philosophers, therefore, are just as idealistic and just as impotent as their brethren in understanding and assisting the operation of the strategic *logos*, as their worldliness extends only to their subject of study – the economy – not their method. Yet, they have the power and authority, which the unworldly philosophers have lost, to mortally damage the *logos*. As I argue in *The Global Crisis Makers* (2000), the neoliberal pursuit of "inflation targeting", which is mistakenly thought to maintain economic stability, actually attacks and weakens the central strategic demand-response mechanism. This causes economic growth to dry up, and, if this policy is maintained over the long run, will actually damage the *logos*. If this occurs, the strategists will become so frustrated in their strategic pursuit that they will throw their political support behind the radical-right parties. The likely outcome, if inflation targeting is not abandoned, is that both the prosperity and liberty of society will be endangered.[2] The dangers of abandoning strategic thinking for metaphysical thinking, therefore, are very real indeed.

The frustration of the strategists is an outcome of the political elite relinquishing strategic leadership. This has enabled the metaphysical (or priestly) philosophers to impose their badly flawed ideas on the strategic *logos*. It happened in the last quarter of the twentieth century. Public attention was only diverted from this long-run problem by the crisis of world terrorism. But, if political leaders fail to abandon their antistrategic policy, this long-term economic and political problem will re-emerge once the short-term international crisis has been resolved.

This is not the first time in world history that the strategic *logos* has been threatened by the metaphysical philosophers. Everyone is familiar with the way the radical Marxists under Lenin were able to hijack the Moscovian revolution, owing to the crisis created by the First World War. Armed with Marxist fantasies, the Bolsheviks mortally wounded the Moscovian *logos*, which eventually expired some seventy years later despite the ministrations of the "experts". Also in ancient Egypt during the 18th Dynasty (fourteenth century BC), Akhenaten ("spirit of the sun-disc") threatened the *logos* of the Nile by changing not only the capital (to Akhetaten – "horizon of the sun-disc") but also the nature of the divinity and the country's dynamic strategy. This new system did not outlive its confused author (see Snooks, *Dead God Rising* [2010]). There are other examples of the strategic *logos* being deliberately and critically damaged through the pursuit of mistaken idealism, but the difference between then and now is that only today has it assumed global proportions. The metaphysical philosophers of the First World are imposing their flawed ideals on both the former Second World recovering from Marxist ideals and the lesser-developed Third World through the IMF, World Bank, and WTO. And there is the very real danger that the climate mitigationists – those economists

Strategic Cerebrum

who employ their short-run, static, marginal theory in a fruitless attempt to solve the dynamic issue of climate change – could derail the forthcoming technological paradigm shift. Probably the greatest lie ever told by orthodox economists is that they have the capability of devising a successful climate-mitigation program, when in truth their theory is totally unable to come to grips with the dynamics of human society. This is the lie that will finally discredit neoclassical economics.

The strategic cerebrum, therefore, has the capacity to lead us far from the truth. Only when it is employing the age-old method of strategic thinking are we able to even approach reality. But, when our intellectual faculties are liberated from a subservience to strategic desire and left to follow their own dictates by employing deductive forms of thought, we are usually unable to find the truth. Left to its own devices, even the strategic cerebrum has no interest in the truth.

6.

It is the priestly philosophers – the metaphysical thinkers – who have convinced most of us that man embodies a "will to truth". One modern dictionary of philosophy begins its entry on truth with the sentence: "Truth is something we all approve of, and aim, or should aim, to achieve." But at the same time these philosophers are skeptical about man's ability to discover the truth. They can't even agree about the nature of truth or of a test for truth. Currently there exist a variety of theories of truth, the most popular being the correspondence theory, the coherence theory, and the pragmatic theory. A brief review shows how the priestly philosophers interested in this issue spend their time.

The correspondence theory, which is usually traced back to Aristotle, is the most widely held theory of truth. Not because it is the most true, but because it is the most accommodating, having been interpreted both strictly and freely. The most strict interpretation claims a strict correspondence between a proposition that is true and a fact that causes it to be true.[3] It is a theory that requires each part of a proposition – nouns, verbs, subjects, and predicates – correspond with parts of reality. This linguistic requirement can only strike the serious social scientist as ridiculous and cause him to be amazed at the ways intelligent people invent to waste their time. There is, however, a looser form of the correspondence theory, which states that something is true if it can be "correlated with a fact", and is false if this can't be done. While this appears to be a sensible basis for empirical work, there are those (the "deflationists") who claim that this raises too many difficulties, and that even the concept of truth is "redundant". There is, they claim, nothing to say about the truth in general. One response to this nihilism has been to develop a freer form of the correspondence theory in which something is said to be true when we agree to repeat or concede it. This, however, is like throwing out the baby with the bathwater: the mundane, trivial, even the false are elevated to the status of truth.

Coherence theory provides a comfortable home for idealists (non-realists) and rationalists (non-empiricists). This theory suggest that something, rather than something else, is true if it "coheres" or is "logically consistent" with a more comprehensive system of propositions than its rivals. No attempt is made as in the correspondence theory, to compare this "something" with reality, only with existing metaphysical systems. This theory of truth was originally developed by the rationalist system-building metaphysicians, such as Leibniz, Spinoza, Hegel, and Bradley, but later it also attracted the interest of logical positivists in the 1920s. Usually coherence theorists argue that only the whole system is really true, while the component propositions are only "partial proximations" to the truth. The problem with this approach to truth is that the priestly philosophers who develop grand systems through deductive thought merely jump to the conclusion that it is automatically true and does not require empirical testing. It probably doesn't worry them that particular parts of their system can be shown to be untrue, because they can retreat behind the argument that as their system is metaphysical it is beyond reality testing. Of course, it is just this argument that makes these metaphysical systems irrelevant to those interested in explaining nature and human society. Zarathustra rejected all grand systems for this reason.

Pragmatism, which arose from the work of nineteenth century philosophers of the Jeffersonian Republic, suggests that an idea is true if it works – if its acceptance brings success.[4] "Acceptance" and "success", however, hardly make something true. As is well known, all manner of fantastic and mutually contradictory ideas are accepted by very large numbers of people around the world. Also, the realist dynamic-strategy theory shows that strategic success depends on the provision – in response to strategic demand – of a large variety of strategic inputs, which include values like untruth as well as truth. In the end, the success and acceptance of ideas are the outcome of the strategic desire of organisms for survival and prosperity. And, as we have seen, strategic desire knows nothing of, and cares nothing for, the truth. Pragmatism is merely the rationalization of materialism.

The priestly philosophers have spent so much of their intellectual energies discussing the *concept* of truth, together with the possibility of its attainment, that they have failed to explore the actual truth of this world. But could it be that the causation flows the other way? Could it be that philosophers spend their superannuated careers discussing empty concepts together with the structure and meaning of language, precisely because they are unable to tell us anything significant about the real world? This interpretation grows ever more appealing. Perhaps the priestly philosophers are ill equipped for the role of truth-seeker, largely owing to their rejection of strategic thinking for deductive or metaphysical thinking.

The history of philosophy shows what happens when metaphysical thinking is employed to build rationalist systems to explain life. The systems of Leibniz, Spinoza, Hegel and Marx are monuments to wasted intellectual effort. This is why Zarathustra rejected these metaphysical systems and opted to focus on moral issues. Metaphysical systems reflect the fantasies of their authors rather than the realities of life. Similarly, those disciplines in the social sciences, such as economics, which have adopted metaphysical thinking, are also monuments to futility. While modern economic theory and the rationalist systems of the seventeenth to nineteenth centuries, share in the victory of fantasy over truth, there is an important difference between them. No strategist today takes the rationalist systems of philosophers seriously; no political leader, fortunately, uses them as the basis for policy formulation. Unfortunately, however, the metaphysical fantasies of neoclassical economists are still taken seriously, and their advice is regularly sought by politicians, and is widely acted upon. This is what makes economists dangerous and philosophers merely irrelevant.

The priestly philosophers, therefore, are both right and wrong. They are wrong when they say that man possesses a "will to truth"; they are wrong when the claim that metaphysical thinking is superior to strategic thinking; and they are wrong in focusing almost exclusively on the concepts, theories, and linguistic vehicles of truth. Yet, on the other hand, they are right to be skeptical about their ability to arrive at the truth about the real world. Only a strategic thinker has any prospect – and with the right preparation it is a good prospect – of discovering the truth. What we need are realist, not rationalist, systems of thought – realist systems like the strategic *logos*.

7.

The strategic *logos* is the fundamental dynamic strategy of life. It is the reality that all serious thinkers have, unknowingly, been searching for ever since the time of Heraclitus of Ephesus. The priestly philosophers who create metaphysical systems have failed, and always will fail, to discover this reality. Their visions are based on fantasy rather than reality. Only more pragmatic thinkers have glimpsed even fragments of this dynamic process, which they usually present in static terms.

The strategic *logos* is the pulsating heart of life. It is the dynamic reality behind the everyday rhythms of existence. It is responsible for the great patterns of life that can be detected in the rise and fall of dynasties in both the natural and human worlds. It is the source of the laws of both life and society that have been discussed elsewhere.[5] It is the elusive presence that all societies have faintly sensed and mistakenly called God. It is the truth "from which all things follow". And finally, the strategic *logos* is indifferent to our existence, not requiring that we know it, or even that we embrace truthfulness.

PART III

TRUTH THE DOUBLE-EDGED SWORD

PART III

THE
DOUBLE-EDGED SWORD

Editor's Preamble III

Truth, according to Herac, is a double-edged sword. Those who attempt to wield it usually suffer lacerations inflicted by themselves as well as others. This can be seen reflected in Herac's own experiences of life. Much of the suffering he endured in the latter part of his life was due to his determination to expose the truth despite the damage he inflicted on himself and the opposition it generated.

Throughout his life, Herac struggled to discover the meaning of existence. It was a quest that began, as quests usually do, with great hope and excitement. While in his teenage years this expressed itself as a search for God, he soon found this metaphysical idea unsatisfactory. God failed the empirical test of reality that Herac always brought to bear on issues of this kind. From this early twenties he turned instead to the writings of the great minds of the past. Modern philosophy, with its preoccupation with empty concepts and the structure of language, however, had nothing to say to him. Herac found it both boring and irrelevant. Even the more interesting metaphysical philosophers of the past failed the same test that had disqualified God. Their "truths" struck him as being merely the fantasies of deductive logic. Herac found more interest and satisfaction in the historians and pioneering psychologists.

As his reading became more eclectic, Herac, for a time, thought that life's meaning might be found in the arts. For a time – from his mid-twenties to this late thirties – he immersed himself in novels, visual art, and music. He even wrote a novel himself, which he made no attempt to publish both because it failed to capture the essence of life for which he was searching and because he realized he lacked talent as a storyteller. By then Herac understood that the arts, as important as they are in lightening the burden of life, could never enable him to discover life's purpose. The arts focused on the creative imagination of man rather than the creative force of life itself. Life's dynamic process was not an extrusion from the creative mind of man, but was an outcome of the interaction between man's whole being – both body and mind, strategic desire and strategic thinking – and his wider social environment. Essentially the arts are, he thought, a diversion from the core reality of life, rather than an explanation of it.

The only creative writer to appeal to Herac was Zarathustra. It was not so much what Zarathustra said about life, but the intellectual example he provided that drew Herac to him. He was attracted by Zarathustra's open and honest quest to understand reality, even though he sensed that Zarathustra's intellectual solutions fell short of what he was looking for. He understood why Zarathustra rejected the grand metaphysical systems of the past, but he felt it ought to be possible to develop a realist system that could explain and predict the entirety of life. Nonetheless, he recognized the dangers of such a quest. Like many others, Zarathustra had been overwhelmed by his pursuit of the truth. Yet, Herac believed he could avoid the worst problems – depression, psychosis, suicide – of this quest. And to a degree he did. Mainly through the benefits that a happy family life can bring, Herac was able to avoid the excessive preoccupation with self and its shortcomings that weighed so heavily on the isolated Zarathustra, despite his imaginary friends Baldy and Adder.

But, of course, what the truth-seeker can never avoid is opposition from the "truth-suppressors" as Herac called them. Certainly this was Herac's unfortunate experience. The closer he approached the idea of the strategic *logos*, the greater became the opposition of the truth-suppressors – the media critics, publishers' readers, and academic "colleagues". Why? Because the reputations and careers of these so-called intellectuals were being challenged by the new ideas about life that Herac was uncovering. If Herac was correct about the strategic *logos* then their standing in the intellectual community, as well as in their own estimation, would be significantly reduced; indeed, their entire careers could even appear meaningless. Herac's more perceptive critics understood this with perfect clarity, and they went all out to destroy his reputation and ridicule his work. They preferred untruth to intellectual irrelevance. The less perceptive critics – particularly those arrogant, youthful products of the decaying culture of the ancient universities of Engle Land (as Herac liked to call it) – always attack and ridicule what they don't understand. As Heraclitus eloquently said so long ago: "Dogs by this same logic, bark at what they cannot understand". If it is beyond their understanding – if it has not been carefully explained to them by their teachers – it must be wrong. As Herac realized, they merely display their foolishness for all time, and become subjects of eternal ridicule themselves.

The combined effect of these truth-suppressors was to choke off Herac's research funding, eliminate his former academic department, mount an untruthful and vicious campaign against him in his own university, subject him to continuous harassment, attack him in the reviewing media, and prevent him finding publishers by misrepresenting his work. This pressure made Herac's life difficult and accelerated the emergence of health problems that ultimately cut his life short.

But the reign of truth-suppressors is limited. Eventually the truth emerges as the old critics pass away and memory of them and their own ideas evaporates. The time for Herac's later and greater ideas has finally arrived. An editor and publisher have been found, and a new audience is waiting. The only problem is that Herac has been dead for many years. While he didn't live to enjoy the triumph of his ideas, his influence and intellectual presence will always remain.

Truth the Vivisector

1.

Truth is a very sharp instrument. It is a double-edged sword with the potential to injure both user and onlooker. It must, therefore, be employed with discretion. One must don appropriate armor to prevent personal damage. Those who fail to take these precautions risk being fatally wounded. Pursuit of truth about oneself is a form of self-vivisection, and about others is a declaration of war. Either use of the sword of truth can lead to tragedy.

It is hardly surprising, therefore, that most people economize on the use of truth. While intelligence is the scarcest resource in the universe, truth is the scarcest value in human society. Truth about ourselves and the rest of the world is usually pursued only when it is essential for our survival and prosperity. This occurs, as I've discussed elsewhere, when there is a strategic demand for truth, mainly affecting the natural and social sciences, rarely the humanities. Fiction is more comforting than reality.

Exceptions do exist, but, as one would expect, they are deviations from the norm. They are the eccentric truth-seekers, who seem to have little regard for their own survival and prosperity. Which is why they are always such a small minority of any viable society: they keep eliminating their self-destructive disposition from the gene pool through early death and an inability to create a stable family life. Hence, while a very small minority of the population is driven to pursue the truth, there is no general "will to truth" in the wider population.

2.

The truth-seeker is a self-vivisectionist. Zarathustra, who believed he could pursue truth in the high mountains of solitude, is a prime example. By exposing his innermost being to the icy winds of self-revelation, Zarathustra eventually destroyed himself. The tension that exists between the material desire that drives us and the rational image we have of ourselves, is too great for most of us to bear for long. We either sensibly protect ourselves against this destructive tension, or we destroy either our minds or our bodies. This **existential dilemma** is the legacy of **strategic dualism**, which is the basis of human nature.

How has man traditionally resolved the tension arising from strategic dualism? How do we protect ourselves against the destructive forces that are endemic to the strategic pursuit? The answer lies in the mechanism I have called **existential schizophrenia** – the *voluntary* "splitting of the mind" achieved by compartmentalizing the outcomes of desire from the intellectual view we hold of ourselves.[1] Somewhat ironically, this separation of our emotional and rational lives enables us to achieve a balance between the body and the conscious mind, between the **strategist** and its **strategic instrument**. Through this balance we achieve **strategic integration**, which resolves the tension created by strategic dualism, and enables us to avoid mental disorders (which my theory treats as **strategic disorders**) and to keep the strategic pursuit on track.

Existential schizophrenia, therefore, is an essential and effective survival mechanism. Despite our self-centeredness and greed, we see ourselves as outreaching and altruistic; despite our cruelty and brutality, we see ourselves as kind and gentle; despite our gross materialism, we see ourselves as spiritual beings. We are masters of the arts of self-deception and self-justification. While we are quick to point out imperfections in others, we have great difficulty seeing in ourselves the very same flaws. We are, nevertheless, fortunate that existential schizophrenia – this mechanism of self-deception – is so effective. Without it we would run the very real risk of opting out of the strategic pursuit in despair and disgust, which would lead to the self-destruction of our species. Of course, a very small minority do just that, and are eliminated from life.

Today, for example, we Metropolitans claim to be unable to understand how other societies are able to survive and prosper by pursuing the dynamic strategy of conquest that requires systematic killing, looting, and enslavement. The answer is that the citizens of conquest societies – such as Macedonia, Rome, medieval Europe, Mesoamerica, Nazi Tutonia, and the Rising-Sun Society – thought of themselves in the same way. Like us they saw themselves as civilized, just, and altruistic. Yet, in view of their bloody occupation – not at all like our virtuous wars in the name of democracy in the Middle East – how could they possibly view themselves in this way? The answer again is: just as we do, through the normal psychological mechanism of existential schizophrenia – through separating out what we do and why we do it, from what we like to think we do and why we do it. When it comes to our own base actions and motives, we look the other way.

****

As shown in *The Selfcreating Mind* (2006), there are varying degrees to which normal individuals have control over the survival mechanism of existential schizophrenia. At one end of the normal range are individuals who possess a relatively good understanding of their own nature and the role desire plays in their lives. While even these individuals are not free from self-deception – reflected, perhaps, in their belief that they fully understand their own motivation – they are more able than most to distinguish between their convenient constructions of "reality" and the real thing. The price of this ability and integrity is a degree of anguish that emerges as they approach the truth about themselves. Many in these circumstances seek refuge from this anguish by prostrating themselves before imaginary divine beings in order to obtain forgiveness and release. The irony here is that these gods owe their very existence to the strategic pursuit that has caused this existential angst (see *Dead God Rising* [2010]).

At the other end of the normal spectrum of self-knowledge are individuals who have at least some difficulty distinguishing between their intellectual constructions of convenience and reality itself. They have a tendency to feel a degree of comfort with untruth. This difficulty sometimes generates faulty decision making, but, by way of compensation, they experience less anxiety in life. The price of bliss, it would seem, can be tabulated in terms of the number of faulty strategic decisions made, owing to self-deception.

It is only a few small steps from this borderline "normal" position to pathological schizophrenia, where one's grasp of reality is completely severed. While the existential schizophrenia mechanism has been overlooked by other social and behavioral scientists, clinical psychiatrists are at least aware of the techniques their patients employ to protect themselves against discomforting and potentially damaging memories and ideas. These techniques are widely known as "defense mechanisms", a term that derives from Sigmund Freud's (1856–1939) early theory of neurosis, in which the "defenses" were viewed as a barrier to eliminating neurotic symptoms. In this tradition, the *Diagnostic and Statistical Manual of Mental Disorders* (*DSM*), which summarizes these defense mechanisms in an appendix, is considering the possibility of including them in their classification of mental disorders, but as yet has "insufficient information to warrant inclusion of these proposals as official categories".[2] It is somewhat ironical that these defense mechanisms, which are essential to the operation of the *normal* existential schizophrenia process, are currently considered by the psychiatry profession as potentially classifiable as mental disorders. No doubt some psychiatrists do treat them as disorders —Freud did – in their patients, often with unhappy outcomes. It would seem that even the sane are regarded as mad by the profession of psychiatry.

What are these "defense mechanisms"? According to the *DSM* they are "automatic psychological processes that protect the individual against anxiety [emotional conflict] and from the awareness of internal or external dangers or stressors".[3] It is the objective of psychoanalysis to expose the traumas that underlie these defense mechanisms in order to release their hidden power. The *DSM* identifies defenses operating at a number of levels, ranging from, at one extreme, the "high adaptive level" – enabling "optimal adaptation in the handling of stressors" by sublimation, suppression, self-assertion, self-observation, humor, altruism, affiliation, anticipation – to the level of "defensive dysregulation", at the other extreme, owing to the failure of the usual defenses and a break with reality leading to delusions and psychotic denial and distortions. Intermediate levels between these two extremes include those called "mental inhibitions" (displacement, dissociation, intellectualization, isolation of emotions, reaction formation, repression, undoing), "image distorting" (devaluation, idealization, omnipotence, fantasy, self-image splitting), "disavowal" (denial, projection, rationalization), and "action" (acting-out and withdrawal).

These clinically observed defense mechanisms are, in fact, the various ways that the conscious mind is able to compartmentalize its participation in, and philosophy of, existence. It enables our kind to avoid acknowledging the unpleasant outcomes generated by the materialist driving force in life – "the horror, the horror" in Conrad's *Heart of Darkness*. It is evidence at the clinical level for the central dynamic mechanism of existential schizophrenia – originally derived from historical observation – and for its breakdown leading to pathological schizophrenia. Individuals – such as Zarathustra – experiencing breakdown or malfunction of this mechanism pass through the spectrum of schizophrenia – the **schizo-spectrum** – and cease to participate in the strategic pursuit. They only continue to survive – although suicide rates are high – because of the protection they receive from family or state. *The truth is that lies are essential for our psychic well-being.*

Zarathustra's life is a tragic example of existential schizophrenia breakdown. Not understanding the importance of existential schizophrenia, Zarathustra abandoned it. As he believed that a person's strength of mind could be measured in terms of how much truth he could bear, Zarathustra refused to resort to voluntary "splitting of the mind". He refused to employ the usual defenses of sublimation, suppression, mental inhibition, image distorting, disavowal, or play-acting. He even finally rejected the psychological buffer of sexual companionship and family. Instead, he looked truth directly in the face; he took up the sword of truth and suffered the lacerating consequences. In the end he employed truth as the self-vivisectionist does the scalpel.

Zarathustra's refusal to employ voluntary existential schizophrenia led, finally, to the emergence of involuntary pathological schizophrenia, as his tortured psyche sought refuge from the self-inflicted agony of truth-seeking. Following a complete nervous breakdown, he experienced periods of surprising lucidity in which he debated with friends and played the piano as skillfully as old, causing some to wonder if this retreat from life was deliberate. But he also displayed characteristics of disorganized schizophrenia with its inappropriate emotions and, later, disorganized speech and behavior. After a number of years of slow but steady deterioration, Zarathustra's disorder developed into catatonic schizophrenia, characterized by motor immobility and mutism. While the first four decades of Zarathustra's life had been a headlong charge into the battle for truth, the final decade was a tragic retreat into madness. Truth had broken him down.

3.

In *The Selfcreating Mind* I provided a more detailed discussion of the malfunction of existential schizophrenia, which may be of interest to some readers. A brief outline will suffice here. The malfunction of existential schizophrenia is a process by which the voluntary "split" between our instinctual and emotional life on the one hand, and our conscious and rational life on the other becomes involuntary. The normal attempt to manipulate our own perceptions of reality gives way in susceptible, or heroic, individuals operating under sustained pressure, to an inability to relate appropriately to reality. Carefully shaped self-delusions are replaced by completely uncontrollable delusions; conscious manipulation of perception is replaced by involuntary hallucination; and individuals suffering these frightening illusions retreat from the everyday world into their own fantasies to live grossly disorganized lives in which language and other forms of communication break down. Unless this degenerative process can be reversed, affected individuals will never be able to reenter the strategic *logos*. Many see this as God having turned his back on them. What begins with the emergence of psychotic symptoms ends in strategic failure.

Figure 2 **The Schizo-spectrum**

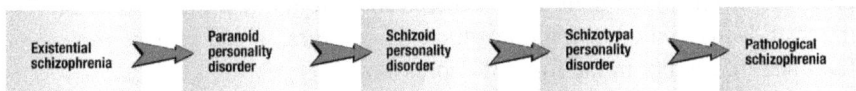

Note: This diagram shows the increasing psychotic state and declining strategic participation of individuals in the population, not necessarily in the lifetime of a single individual.

Source: Snooks (2006).

Breakdown in the normal existential-schizophrenia mechanism generates a spectrum of schizoid states, reflecting increasing psychosis and decreasing strategic involvement. The **schizo-spectrum** presented in Figure 2 begins with the normal condition of existential schizophrenia and passes through a number of personality disorders – paranoid, schizoid, schizotypal – until the involuntary condition of pathological schizophrenia is reached. It should be realized, however, that this schizo-spectrum depicts the progression of schizoid states existing in the population, not necessarily in the individual.

In essence, the schizo-spectrum reflects the progressive breakdown of the survival mechanism employed by the selfconscious organism. It depicts the transformation of **strategic integration** into strategic fragmentation: of the breakdown of the carefully constructed union of strategic desire and reason. Owing to this strategic dualism, psychic integration can only be achieved through self-delusion; and self-delusion involves large doses of untruth.

My concept of strategic dualism, therefore, explains what the evolutionary psychiatrists cannot: why schizophrenia persists in human society despite the fact that their suicide rates are much higher than the population average.[4] While schizoid states are higher among individuals in affected families, they keep emerging in individuals from previously unaffected families, owing to the strategic duality of human nature and the stress of the strategic pursuit. The irony of existence is that we can only survive and prosper as a species by continually placing a minority of individuals at risk – individuals who are unable, or unwilling, to employ the survival mechanism of existential schizophrenia.

Hence, pathological schizophrenia is the eternal price we are forced to pay for the highly beneficial strategic instrument of selfconsciousness, or **strategic awareness** – of being able to reflect upon the desires that drive us in life. Man alone in nature pays this price.

4.

Truth is a doubly dangerous commodity. Its pursuit can result not only in mental disorders, but also in retaliation from others. These others are the **truth-suppressors**, who dominate organizations throughout human society. Usually holding positions of authority, the truth-suppressors can be found in government, law, business, the church, and even – nay, especially – in intellectual groups. They wish to suppress the truth because it either exposes their dishonest/immoral practices or undercuts their achievements and livelihoods. This suppression of the truth leads to the frustration of the truth-seekers, which in turn impacts on their health, usually in the form of depression.

Wherever there is power there is corruption. Most power exists, of course, in government in its various legislative and executive branches. Those who exercise control over a society's public finances and expenditures, or its judicial and enforcement systems, have the means and the opportunity to increase their wealth by diverting some of the national wealth to themselves, either during their time in office or later when calling in earlier favors. Only the "whistleblower" – the person willing to risk retaliation by publicly revealing corrupt practices – stands in their way. Not surprisingly, the response of corrupt individuals in power is to suppress and victimize the whistleblowers.

We are all familiar with the case of the prominent scientist who revealed to the MBC – the Metropolitan Broadcasting Commission – that the President of Metropolis had knowingly exaggerated the military-strike capacity of Babylon in order to convince his people to go to war against them. His real reason, as I have discussed elsewhere, was to serve the interests of big business in Metropolis. The government, with much to hide, applied so much pressure to the whistleblower that eventually he drove out into the countryside and committed suicide. This is merely the latest, and most extreme, of a long list of such cases of retaliation against those exposing the truth. Needless to say, the situation in less democratic countries is much worse, with dissidents being sent to jail on trumped-up charges or just mysteriously disappearing. The truth-suppressors will go as far as their society will allow in order to prevent the truth about their activities being made public. Sometimes even further.

Owing to the vast money-making possibilities in the corporate world, the scope for dishonest dealing is vast. And the temptation for some businessmen in positions of authority is overwhelming. Some individuals and groups regularly divert the resources of their organizations into their own pockets, and then falsify the accounts to cover their tracks. Potential whistleblowers wanting to reveal the truth are subject to financial and physical threats, which, if ignored, are sometimes acted upon. In the case of some well-known urban-development projects in Metropolis, which were delayed by urban environmentalists, the dissident leaders were threatened and, in one famous case, murdered. It is curious that the police failed to arrest anyone for these crimes. Recently there have been a rash of reports that the enterprises controlling team sports have paid bribes to young women to suppress accusations of gang rape. And, of course, the ruthless activities of Mafia-style organizations in Metropolis killing informants, judges, and police officers to disguise their criminal activities is legendary and the subject of popular entertainment.

Even the National Church of Metropolis – the organization that claims to be dedicated to the search for divine truth – has been actively engaged in truth-suppression. Elsewhere I have written about the Church's attempt to suppress the truth concerning sexual crimes committed by its priests.[5] This truth-suppression, which has been undertaken with expensive legal assistance, has had a major adverse impact on the lives of the victims who had the courage to bring the truth to light. Many of the numerous victims experienced psychological problems, and some committed suicide. While these unfortunate people were damaged as children by religious predators – wolves in sheep's clothing – this damage has been compounded by the Church's failure to acknowledge the truth of their claims. Most of the Church's victims were seeking not financial compensation but recognition and justice. The truth-suppressors in the State Church of Metropolis – men, we are told, of the highest moral standards – are even more to blame than the perverted priests who committed the original sins. These perversions could never have become widespread in the Church had upright men refused to look the other way – refused to support the lie.

The truth-suppressors *par excellence*, however, are the academics of Metropolis. One is never surprised when those in the public and private sectors who devote their lives to grabbing wealth and power attempt to suppress truth and to dispose of the truth-seekers. But one is always shocked when those who profess to seek the truth turn out to be doing the opposite. It is the professed purpose of academics to discover and propagate the truth about reality in their area of specialty; and of these it is the philosophers – the "lovers of wisdom" – we look to for guidance on the more general issues of life. Sadly, it is some of these self-styled "truth-seekers" who are the most accomplished truth-suppressors. While I have elsewhere discussed the activities of truth-suppressors within our great universities, here I will focus on their suppression of new ideas more generally.[6]

To continue creating new ideas, a thinker needs to write and publish. Those who believe they can construct complex systems in their heads are merely deceiving themselves, possibly in an attempt to justify their lack of publications.[7] Finding an audience, even a small one, is important to the success of this intellectual process. While it is always possible for even the most isolated thinker to write down his ideas, the incentive to continue to do so depends heavily on whether it is possible to publish them. Nothing is more soul destroying for an innovative thinker than to discover there is no way he can communicate his ideas in published form to a wider audience. The audience need only be large enough to satisfy the thinker that his ideas are being noticed, taken seriously by the more perceptive reader, and that they will survive him. Of course, if he fails to find a publisher, even a small audience is out of the question. No doubt the intellectual lives of many original thinkers have been cut short by the lack of a good publisher.

Let's consider the publishing pattern for a potentially important thinker. His intellectual career will be launched by the publication of precocious work within the boundaries of the academic discipline in which he was trained. At this stage, the young scholar's flair attracts the attention of his teachers, who enthusiastically support his publishing efforts because it reflects well on them to have discovered such a brilliant student.[8] But before long the adventurous young scholar begins to strike out beyond the accepted boundaries of his discipline in a way that challenges and threatens his former teachers and colleagues, who become less enthusiastic and even secretly hostile. At this stage there are still academic publishers willing to support our innovative scholar because some broad-minded experts are still willing to praise the publication of his work.

The **prosperity-seeker** in these circumstances will advance no further. He will revel in his *enfant terrible* image and remain just within the boundaries of what is considered intellectually acceptable. Our **truth-seeker**, however, will not stand still; he will continue to develop his ideas to the point where they threaten to provide the basis for an eventual paradigm shift in ideas, not only in his own specialist area. Once this is widely perceived, all academic support for our truth-seeker evaporates completely. The closer he approaches the truth of his day, the greater is the attempt to suppress it and to dispense with its creator. At this stage, publication through the usual academic publishers, who rely heavily on peer review, is impossible. For our truth-seeker, the process of discovering this is debilitating. Having to suffer scores of rejections is soul destroying – it literally saps one's creative energies.

The only way forward for our truth-seeker is to pay for the publication of his own books or to place them openly on the internet. But this is not a very satisfactory solution: few thinkers can afford the cost of self-publication and, more importantly, the self-published book has only a very limited market. The cost of all this in terms of expended nervous energy is very high and can be extremely destructive. Truth-seekers frustrated in this way, experience extremely severe bouts of anxiety and depression, together with serious physical problems such as cardiac arrhythmia and late-onset diabetes. His problems are compounded if, as is often the case, the prosperity-seekers in his own university see the slowdown in publication as an opportunity to relieve him of research infrastructure. Sometimes this combined pressure leads our truth-seeker into psychosis and a loss of contact with reality – even to suicide. The history of ideas is replete with examples: I will consider one.

Zarathustra's experience is germane to this issue. When in his early twenties, Zarathustra, who was regarded by his former university teachers in classical philology as a future leader of his discipline, found it a simple matter to publish in the very best journals in his field. At that stage he worked precociously within the boundaries of his discipline. Only when he developed his ideas beyond these boundaries – when he began challenging the nature of his discipline – did he begin to experience publishing difficulties. As he refused to heed his colleagues' warnings to return to the fold, Zarathustra eventually found it impossible to find a publisher willing to handle his books. His most famous work – an allegory based on the ancient Persian prophet Zoroaster – is a case in point: as the first three parts, which were published separately by a commercial publisher, found only about forty buyers (owing to hostile academic reviews), the final part had to be published at Zarathustra's own expense. His readers as well as his critics turned their backs on his ideas as they became increasingly unorthodox. Academic publishing houses, which were established to publish important works that do not have a commercial market, had long rejected his work. From that time on, all of Zarathustra's books were published either at his own expense or that of his friends, or remained unpublished at the time of his collapse and even his death. These publication problems added to the pressures that caused Zarathustra to retreat into madness.

With Zarathustra's breakdown, the truth-suppressors considered their work done. But they miscalculated. By the time of his death a decade later, his works were selling in very large numbers. Clearly, the truth can be suppressed for a time, but eventually it will emerge, even if too late to be enjoyed by its liberator.[9] Only those who popularize the work of great thinkers, usually long dead, gain materially from the originator's struggle for the truth. Only the self-confessed plagiarists profit from great ideas, decades or centuries after they have ceased to be at the cutting edge of intellectual ferment; ceased to undermine contemporary intellectual reputations. Contemporary books on Darwinism are just one example among many.[10]

5.

The problem of mood disorders experienced by frustrated truth-seekers invites further discussion. While psychotic disorders are, in my theory of strategic psychiatry, an outcome of malfunctions in the foundations of human nature – namely a loss of strategic integration – neurotic disorders are largely an outcome of **strategic frustration**. Strategic frustration is the psychological response of individuals and groups of individuals to persistent barriers raised against their participation in the strategic pursuit. For the truth-seeker, this frustration is a response to barriers erected against his involvement in the research and publication of his ideas. Strategic frustration, which leads to distressing mood disorders, is the opposite of **strategic satisfaction**, which is the balanced state of mind attained by individuals and groups that are able to participate successfully in the strategic pursuit.

Strategic frustration arises from problems that affect entire societies as well as individuals. At the societal level, it arises from the persistent failure of **strategic leadership**. As a global phenomenon this problem is very modern. It characterizes contemporary governments throughout the First World, owing to their obsession with neoliberal (or economic rationalist) policies, which in turn is an outcome of the triumph of neoclassical (read deductive) economic theory. The problem with this theory is that it has lost contact with reality, and has nothing sensible to say about the dynamics of human society. In particular, it denies that governments should play a proactive leadership role in market economies. The problem for the rest of us in democratic societies is that while our electorates can change governments unwilling to provide strategic leadership, they can't change their neoliberal policies, owing to the tragic fact that *all* major political parties take their advice from neoliberal economists.

The refusal of modern governments to provide proper leadership causes strategic frustration throughout society, which ultimately leads electorates to flirt with far-right political parties. This in turn is likely to lead, on one hand, to societal neurosis of the type experienced in interwar Teutonia, and, on the other hand, to mood disorders in those individuals suffering from the resulting economic difficulties, including the unemployed and the bankrupt. There is some evidence of this in the Rising Sun society, which has languished economically for a generation following the exhaustion of their post-Second World War dynamic strategy of imitative catch-up.

In normal individuals, mood savings involving hypomania and mild depression play an important role in sustaining the strategic pursuit. Feelings of elation arising from successful strategic participation provide the emotional incentive to continue with present strategies, whereas depressed feelings arising from unsuccessful participation provide the emotional incentive to abandon present strategies and circumstances and to seek out new and more profitable ones. These emotional mechanisms are important, because, in their absence, individuals lack the drive and ability to devise and execute successful plans.

These emotions can only be regarded as disorders if they become extremely intense and persistent, to the point that they take on a momentum of their own and bear little relationship to their strategic causes. Mood disorders can be found both in the individual and in society. We have already reviewed the persistent and widespread frustration that arises when a government fails to provide strategic leadership. This lack of leadership disrupts society's dynamic strategy, resulting in slow or negative growth, business failure, and increasing unemployment. The widespread frustration that people experience in these circumstances leads to intense and persistent psychological depression, even suicide, throughout society. It is a form of societal neurosis.

The second source of psychological depression is the lack of flexibility displayed by some individuals in the face of difficult circumstances. It arises from an inability to respond appropriately to a systematic attack – in the form of denial of promotion, actual demotion, or redundancy – on one's participation in the strategic pursuit. There are, of course, always a number of options open to the strategically frustrated individual: they can fight, submit, withdraw to the periphery, or resign and start anew. Many people, however, are unable to make the appropriate choice that would ease their strategic frustration and, hence, they experience prolonged depression. For whatever reason, they are unable to respond to this emotional incentive to improve their participation in the strategic pursuit.

We can now see that the depression experienced by oppressed truth-seekers is a special case of the more general theory about strategic frustration that I developed in *The Selfcreating Mind*. The oppression exercised by the truth-suppressors is triggered by problems that revelation of the truth might pose for these people. The resulting frustration experienced by truth-seekers is even more difficult for them to cope with, because, feeling compelled to follow what they believe to be the true path, they are unable to make the changes that would lead to a less stressful and depressing life.

The Subtle Art of Swordsmanship

Is it possible to seriously pursue truth without inflicting damage on oneself? Is there an art to this pursuit? Could there be a set of rules for successful swordsmanship? If there is, what would they look like? Here are a few possibilities.

- Be firmly grounded.
- Do not climb mountains.
- Do not stray beyond one's borders.
- Do not take on more than one opponent at a time.
- When there are casualties, always look the other way.

These are the types of rules that would prevent our swordsman from coming to too much harm.

On closer inspection, these rules of successful swordsmanship look very similar to those required to be successful in the strategic pursuit, in which we attempt to maximize the probability of survival and prosperity. And, as we have seen, the strategic pursuit can only be successful if we reject the idea of truth-seeking. The implication is that the rules of successful swordsmanship are inimical to those for "successful" truth-seeking. The latter are very different; indeed diametrically opposite, namely:

- Be prepared to fight on broken ground.
- Leave the plains for the mountains.
- Cross all existing borders.
- Take the fight to as many opponents as possible.
- Take responsibility for casualties.

The inevitable conclusion is that truth will always remain a double-edged sword – a vivisector's instrument. Those that live by the truth will surely die by the truth. The swordsmanship of the truth-seeker will always be a difficult and dangerous art. To be a truth-seeker is to become part of a select but perverse fraternity. It is select because it is the most dangerous thing we could opt to do in life – it is the most extreme of all extreme sports; and it is perverse because the entire purpose of life is to survive and prosper, a pursuit jeopardized by truth-seeking. But it is the only way to discover and understand the strategic *logos* – the source of all sustained life. What choice does one have?

PART IV

DOES TRUTH HAVE A FUTURE?

Editor's Preamble IV

It is possible in part IV to bring together a few of Herac's fragmented writings on the role of truth in the future of civilization. These writings have been extracted from his various notebooks. Herac views truth as an "extreme sport" pursued by a few eccentric thinkers prepared to suffer the lacerations that inevitably arise from wielding this double-edged sword. He usually contrasts these **truth-seekers** with the intellectual **prosperity-seekers**, who provide commissioned research for a fee.

Herac ponders the future of truth-seeking in an age of commissioned research even in our leading universities. His own future was at stake here. Being forced from the university system by the truth-suppressors before the usual retirement age, Herac had to cope with an inadequate pension to carry him through the last third of his life. While he continued to be highly productive, the challenging nature of his ideas made it impossible to find a publisher. Nevertheless, Herac carried on, adding one unpublished manuscript to another, all the while fighting off severe attacks of depression. Only his family kept him sane.

From brief comments scribbled in his notebooks, Herac seems to have taken comfort from ancient Greek and Roman writers who, because the printing press would not be invented for another thousand years or more, were likewise unable to find publishers. Yet some works from the best of them have survived. These works survived not just because of luck, but also because other writers found them useful. Take the case of Heraclitus of Ephesus, whose life straddled the turn of the fifth century BC. None of his works survive in complete form, but as many as 130 fragments have been extracted from other works that have survived, because their authors were sufficiently impressed with what Heraclitus had to say. Even these few fragments are sufficient to demonstrate to everyone's satisfaction that Heraclitus was the greatest and most influential Greek philosopher before Socrates and Plato, and to the certainty of some that, owing to an inductive rather than a deductive approach, he was greater even than these.

Notes From the Past About the Future

1.

If truth is always a challenge to the human psyche and often disruptive of the strategic pursuit, does it have a future? Should truth be banned or, at the very least, be issued with a graphic health warning? Like cigarettes? My position is: no, it should not be banned; yes it does have a future; and yes, we should all be aware of its adverse health effects. We should also be aware that most public and private "debates" about the "truth" of any issue are really debates to promote the material interests, however well disguised, of the debaters.

Why does truth have a future despite its inherent dangers? There are two reasons, which if I have time I will expand upon later. First, truth-seeking is the most extreme of extreme sports; and second, it is occasionally required by strategic demand.

2.

Truth-seeking is an extreme sport. For this reason it is both exhilarating and joyful. It is both extremely dangerous and it demands an extremely high level of intelligence and integrity. Indeed, I rate **truth-seeking** as the most extreme of extreme sports. But, you will object, other extreme sports are just as dangerous, and this danger is more direct and emerges more suddenly and dramatically. True, other extreme sports, such as sky-diving, mountain climbing, mountain boarding, and motor racing, can lead to sudden injury and death, but this challenge and danger is of a less sophisticated kind. The unique characteristic of truth-seeking is that the danger arises not from the impact of physical forces on the body, but from the self-imposed disintegration of the human psyche. The balance between body and mind – between strategic desire and reason – is gradually eroded by the truth-seeking process until the self-vivisectionist goes mad or commits suicide. Not in all cases, but in a remarkably high proportion. Injury or death by exposure to physical forces is far more simple and primitive than injury or death by psychic forces. Also, truth-seeking as an extreme sport is something that takes a lifetime of struggle rather than a few seconds of bravado and carelessness. So if its agony and ecstasy you're after, truth-seeking is your ultimate extreme sport.

It is also the extreme sport that makes the greatest demands on the characteristics that most differentiate us from the rest of nature – intelligence. All extreme sports require considerable skills, both physical and intellectual, but it is truth-seeking that requires extreme intellectual input and integrity. All animals are perfectly capable of indulging in dangerous physical activities – indeed the lives of most species consist entirely of this type of extreme "sport"

– but only humans are capable of indulging in the most difficult extreme sport of all. An extreme sport in which the stakes are extremely high, in terms not just of the costs involved but also of potentially beneficial outcomes for our entire species – of technological paradigm shifts. No other extreme sport generates such revolutionary outcomes. And it is a sport that becomes more extreme and bloody as it becomes increasingly out of step with the requirements of society and its strategic *logos*.

As there will always be a demand in human society for the thrills that can be experienced by indulgence in extreme sports, truth will always have its seekers. These ultimate risk-takers should not, however, be confused with the vast majority of academics who, for the most part, labor honestly but conservatively. Most academics are firmly grounded, never leave the plains for the mountains, refuse to approach let alone stray beyond their borders, are careful not to trespass on another's territory, and always look the other way during moral crises. They are intellectual journeymen and journeywomen, not truth-seekers. They have no interest in upsetting the intellectual applecart by exploring genuinely new ideas. They recoil from the possibility of sustaining lacerations from the intimidating sword of truth. Instead they sniff out the truth-seekers and, in concert with their conservative peers, drive them away for fear that their comfortable lives might be disrupted. The academics of Metropolis pursue survival and prosperity, not truth. Needless to say, those academics even more interested in materialism became the managers of intellectual institutions. They even believe they are able to manage "research resources" – or in plain English, research academics – when in fact most would be hard pressed to manage a church fete.

3.

There is another reason truth will always have a future, albeit a precarious one. Sometimes it is required to meet the demands of the strategic *logos*. The strategic *logos*, as I've argued elsewhere, generates a demand for a variety of inputs that include technological and scientific ideas. Individuals and organizations respond to this strategic demand because of the material rewards for doing so. Strategic demand, therefore, is responsible for the routine exploration of reality required in man's strategic pursuit.

This type of strategic response leads to low-risk, systematic research undertaken by teams of conservatively trained scientists commissioned by governments or corporations. The resulting demand-led truths about the real world, therefore, are the outcome of prosperity-seeking rather than truth-seeking. Many of its worthy practitioners differ little from public servants or corporate employees. It is a type of intellectual activity not to be confused with truth-seeking, which is a high-risk lifestyle undertaken by isolated thinkers who are curiosity-driven and self-funded. With a suitable lapse of time, all strategic research is based on the earlier work of the truth-seekers. The big advances are usually generated by solitary truth-seekers, and are only later consolidated and applied by teams of prosperity-seekers in response to strategic demand. Without strategic demand, the work of the truth-seekers would go unnoticed by society; but without the work of the truth-seekers, society would stagnate and collapse.

What of "truth" pursued within the leading universities of Metropolis? It is, in the main, of the prosperity-seeking kind. Universities first emerged, and subsequently developed, to facilitate the dynamic strategies of their societies. Public and private funds are channeled into these intellectual organizations to undertake research that is thought to increase the probability of society's strategic success, as well as to teach the human-capital skills that will facilitate this process. It is an investment in strategic infrastructure designed to generate a positive return in the short run as well as the long run. Possessing varying degrees of intellectual curiosity, interest, and abilities, both the staff and the students of our universities expect to achieve at least a comfortable standard of living by participating in its culture. A measure of this expectation is the loss since the 1980s of our brightest undergraduates – who in earlier, more prosperous, times would have entered academic service – to the corporate sector, owing to the significant relative decline in university salaries. This loss of intellectual quality has added to the bureaucratic nature of the academic sector of Metropolis.

Further, the rapid expansion of the university sector in order to train a larger proportion of the population of Metropolis has led to a crisis in public funding. This in turn has led to university research being heavily financed through external contractual arrangements, with teaching being paid for to a much greater degree by students and their families. All these forces have combined to lower traditional scholarly standards. In particular, most university research has ceased to be curiosity driven, and has become largely "made-to-measure". Corporations and government agencies provide the funds and determine the directions, even the outcomes, of this "relevant" university research. This is a reflection of the fact that universities are not – and have never really been – independent truth-seeking organizations, but rather strategic organizations that respond directly to strategic demand. That demand is more insistent in some periods than others. Universities, therefore, serve not the truth but the strategic *logos*.

With the decline in the amount of "disinterested" public funding – although public funding has never been truly disinterested – per university researcher, universities have become battle rounds for clashes between small minorities of traditional scholars and large majorities of university entrepreneurs and their fellow travelers. The resulting conflicts, predictably, have been one-sided, being resolved in favor of the prosperity-seekers. These prosperity-seekers have ruthlessly obtained a monopoly over public university funds by expelling and marginalizing the truth-seekers.

By the turn of the twenty-first century, university infrastructure in Metropolis was largely in the hands of those who are happy to produce research on demand for whoever is willing to pay for it. Much of this new research was formerly undertaken "in-house" by government agencies, but is now being "out-sourced" to universities, which are forced to hire former bureaucrats for this purpose. To give the appearance of intellectual respectability, even the best universities in Metropolis are widening their definitions of "competitive, grant-based research" to include its opposite – non-competitive, commissioned research. Researchers are being instructed on this new language by university "managers". Hence, research today is responding directly to short-term strategic requirements, and truth is being abandoned in the process.

In the universities of Metropolis, the few remaining traditional scholars – those surviving targeted redundancies – who openly refuse to undertake research on demand have been stripped of all research funding and subjected to continuous harassment. On complaining about this discriminatory treatment, truth-seekers are informed they should – must – apply for outside funding. Of course, to apply for external funding would be to substitute prosperity-seeking for truth-seeking. Even the body established by the government of Metropolis to fund university research – the Metropolitan Research Council (MRC) – is run by prosperity-seekers for the benefit of prosperity-seekers. Truth-seekers may just as well not apply for MRC funds, because they will not receive them. There can be little doubt that, in the university system of Metropolis at the beginning of the new century, the prosperity-seekers have triumphed over the truth-seekers.

4.

What is the future for truth-seekers in human civilization? They have always been a rare and endangered group. Actually, a scattering of isolated individuals rather than a group, because there is no general "will to truth", only an idiosyncratic urge experienced by a handful of deviants, who are driven to understand life and their role in it, whatever the cost. Truth-seeking is an **antistrategic neurosis,** because it undermines the **strategic desire** to survive and prosper..

Recent developments in the university response to the changing strategic *logos* of our society have made it even more difficult for truth-seekers to find a comfortable home in this environment. Many have been forced out of the university system to make way for the prosperity-seeking hacks, while the few who remain are subject to continual harassment. All this adds to other truth-suppressing pressures acting on these isolated individuals. While the journey has never been easy, recently it has become just that much harder. The casualty rates will be high.

Notes From the Past About the Future

   None of this will prevent eccentric individuals pursuing truth, nor will it prevent sudden and unexpected intellectual breakthroughs from occurring in our society. What it does mean is that the cost to individuals will be greater. The truth-seeker of the future will need to become an even more accomplished swordsman.

Editor's Notes

PROLOGUE: **ZARATHUSTRA IS DEAD**
[As truth is not a complete defense against the defamation laws of Metropolis – legislating against truth! – certain details about NUM had to be blacked out.]

1. The Old Realist of the prologue is actually F.S.S. Herac, the author of this allegory. What I have called the Prologue was found among the extant papers of Frederick Herac. See the Editor's Introduction.

2. Talking of a buffoon overtaking the tightrope walker: It was the pompous philosopher who, when Dean of Human Sciences at the National University of Metropolis (NUM), planned and supervised the abolition of Herac's Department of Political Economy. ▇▇ While the pretext was a budgetary crisis, the real reasons were very different. In the first place, the pompous philosopher was ▇▇. And secondly as the pompous philosopher was determined to ▇▇. Abolition of Herac's department would solve all his problems.

   The pompous philosopher went further than this. As the university records show, ▇▇ Herac's department, which had one of the best publication records in the entire university, ▇▇▇▇▇▇▇▇▇▇▇▇. And to round out this ▇▇, the School's philosophers continually told all who would listen that their department was one of the best in the world. Which it wasn't. They were merely effective networkers. Such is the nature of truth in academia.

3. The pompous philosopher was a staunch member of the Metropolitan High Church, playing violin solos on Sundays and preaching whenever he had the opportunity. ▇▇. Herac felt that there was little to distinguish the pompous professor's metaphysical philosophy from this theology. Indeed, the incident that led the philosopher, as Dean, to finally resolve to abolish Herac's department, was the latter's suggestion that it would be more truthful to transfer all the metaphysical philosophers from the Faculty of Human Sciences

Editor's Notes

to the Faculty of Theology. The philosophers' conquest strategy was covertly supported by ▮▮. This ▮▮▮▮▮ subjected the leading truth-seekers to considerable personal pressure to conform to the prevailing mediocrity or leave the institution.

4. To round out this comment by the pompous philosopher on the relative merits of the individual approach of Zarathustra compared with the team approach of his department, I quote from the *Metropolis Times* (2004). The journalist interviewing the pompous philosopher writes: "Dispelling the applicability of examples like Zarathustra – whose philosophical lifestyle consisted of him hiding in the Swiss Alps and 'thinking' himself into middle-age dementia – the Dean advocates a vibrant and interactive job description for philosophers. This job description in the Dean's faculty has led to team research of 'outstanding international quality'." This is probably why everyone today (2044) is familiar with Zarathustra's work but not with that of the pompous philosopher and his colleagues!

PART I TRUTH IN METROPOLIS

The State

1. All quotations from the Athenian-Melian debate were selected by Herac from R. Warner's translation of Thucydides *History* (London: Penguin, 1968) Ch. 7: "Sixteenth Year of War. The Melian Debate", pp. 358–66.

2. All emphasis in this passage from Thucydides is Herac's.

3. Herac's emphasis again, not Thucydides'.

4. The historical and contemporary role of strategic leadership is analyzed in detail in G.D. Snooks, *The Ephemeral Civilization* (1997) and Snooks, *The Global Crisis Makers* (2000). It should be realized that Graeme Donald Snooks is the *nom de plume* used by Herac in his published work. His choice of this name appears to have been because "Snooks" is a corruption of Sevenoaks (sometimes spelt Sennocks) in Kent, Engle Land, where his forebears originated. It is for this reason that I have used Snooks on the title page.

Editor's Notes

The People

1. Here Herac presents us with a puzzle. A mystery. Despite considerable effort on your editor's part, it has not been possible to trace the publications of the authors Herac refers to in these essays. Yet, somewhat curiously, I have been able to trace publications by other authors that are virtually identical! Where this occurs in the text of the essays, I have referenced (in these notes) the authors and works that most nearly echo those referred to, quoted, and critically analyzed by Herac. It is all that an editor dedicated to the truth can do. Is it not?

How do we account for this mystery? The most obvious conclusion is that Herac, a self-proclaimed seeker after truth, was hypocritically weaving a complex web of lies in his notebooks. But what possibly could be his reason for doing so? In all other respects, Herac's work has the ring of truth about it. Could I have been deceived? There is, of course, the fact that Herac employed a *nom de plume* for all his published work. But this doesn't mean that he preferred untruth to truth, fiction to reality. As is well known, anonymity is a most useful way of introducing a liberating degree of freedom – even an objective distance – into one's work that is difficult to achieve when it is closely associated with one's identity. It is a way of letting go in a written work.

But, if Herac was always true to both himself and his world, how are we to explain this puzzle. While I don't necessarily wish to endorse them, there are other explanations (apart from madness, which can quickly be dismissed) that may appeal to some readers. It is, for example, as if Herac inhabited a parallel universe – 11/9, 9/11 is just another example. Yes, I know this suggestion sounds strange, but bear with me while I canvass the possibilities. To put it another way, Zarathustra might have seen it as an example of the eternal recurrence, in which every person (here with different names), every event, every idea, every spoken word will return endlessly. Zarathustra regarded this as the highest truth and the most difficult to bear. The problem is that Herac himself would have rejected such an idea as being entirely metaphysical and, therefore, not worthy of serious contemplation. Accordingly, this is where we should leave this mystery, and allow the reader to make the final judgment. By the way, the closest approximations I can find to the quotations employed in this section are recorded in Bill Bryson, *A Short History of Nearly Everything* (Doubleday, 2003).

It is easier to negotiate Herac's geography than his cast of actors. Although his ancient and medieval worlds appear much the same as ours, considerable differences arise in his modern world. The following table may assist those who still have any doubts after reading the text.

Editor's Notes

Herac's world	Our world
Asian Entrepôt Islands	Hong Kong and Singapore
Babylon	Iraq
Cape Colony	South Africa
Frankish Kingdom	France
Great-Wall Civilization	China
Hindustan	India
Jeffersonian Republic	United States of America
Judaea	Israel
Low Countries	The Netherlands
Media	Afghanistan
Metropolis	Metropolis
Moscovia	Russia
Persia	Iran
Rising-Sun Society	Japan
San Marco Republic	Venice
Setting-Sun Island	not identified
Terra Australis	Australia
Teutonia	Germany

2. Herac was aware of the health problems of intellectual innovators from contacts in his professional life and from details in historical accounts of science. See J. Gribbin, *Science. A History*, 1543–2001 (Allen Lane, 2001).

3. Here Herac is referring to Gitta Sereny, whose biography *Albert Speer: his battle with truth* (Macmillan, 1995) he regarded as a most impressive work. This is clear from his marginal notations in the book.

4. See the autobiography by B. Manz entitled *A Mind in Prison. The memoir of a son and soldier of the Third Reich* (Brassey's, 2000). Note that when Herac deals with important events in the past, he appears to slip from one parallel universe to another that we are more familiar with.

5. Although Herac did not bother about footnotes, I have traced this quotation to ibid: 229.

6. And this to ibid: 232–33.

Editor's Notes

The Intellectuals

1. The dictum "desires drive, ideas facilitate" was coined in Snooks (1996).

2. Concerning the driving force behind ideas, see Snooks (1996; 2003).

3. The strategic *logos*, which is the innovative contribution of this work, is discussed for the first time by Herac in Part II. Although the concept of the strategic *logos* was first developed in this work written in 2003-04, it was first published in *Dead God Rising* (2010).

4. See Gribbin (2002) for details on depression and suicides of major scientists.

5. The distinction between the "secular priesthood" and the "principled" few is made by Noam Chomsky, *Hegemony or Survival: America's quest for global dominance* (Allen & Unwin, 2003).

6. Herac's critical attack on flawed neoliberal policy can be found in Snooks (2000).

7. As I've said before, there are times when Herac appears to inhabit a parallel universe. Certainly in the one I inhabit the relevant authors are Noam Chomsky, Norman Mailer, and Samuel Huntington.

8. As will be clear by now, Herac regarded himself as a strategic thinker.

9. See Chomsky, *Power and Terror* (Seven Stories Press, 2003), and Chomsky *Hegemony or Survival*.

10. All Herac's quotes on linguistics could have come from Chomsky, *On Nature and Language* (Cambridge University Press, 2002).

11. For flaws in the modular mind theory see Snooks, *The Selfcreating Mind* (2005: ch. 10).

12. Such a passage can be found in Chomsky (2002: 139).

13. Everything changed radically between the turn of the twenty-first century and 2044. Metropolis is no longer a democracy, and dissidents are no longer tolerated. Neither Herac nor Linguisky would be safe today.

14. Such a passage can be found in Chomsky (2003b: 216).

15. See *The Global Transition* (Snooks 1999) for a discussion of the transition of the Third World.

16. Time has shown Herac to be correct. Linguisky's (Chomsky's?) heirs in idealism were the first to be eliminated by the antistrategic regime that replaced the strategist government that was in power in the heyday of Herac and Linguisky.

Editor's Notes

17. The reader is referred to Mailer's, *Why are we at War?* (Random House, 2003).

18. As the past half-century has shown, it was the stubborn ecological pursuit of climate mitigation that caused the dynamic process of Metropolis to collapse and our democratic system to disintegrate.

19. Herac's prediction in 2000 about the corrosive effects of neoliberalism on progress and liberty missed the mark, but only because the catastrophic impact of the climate-mitigation program intervened.

20. All Herac's quotations in this section are virtually identical to passages in Samuel P. Huntington, *The Clash of Civilizations* (Simon & Schuster, 1996).

21. Herac is referring here to Alex Kerr, *Lost Japan* (Lonely Planet, 1996).

22. As Herac was writing for himself and a select group of scholars familiar with his ideas, he doesn't always spell out the theories on which his argument is based. Those wishing to follow his discussion about technological paradigms should consult Snooks, *Global Transition* (Macmillan, 1999).

23. Herac probably had in mind works like Felipe Fernández-Armesto's *Civilizations* (Free Press, 2001), which he reviewed critically in *World History* (under the *nom de plume* Snooks) in the early years of the twenty-first century.

24. Herac is referring to the predictions regarding future technological revolutions in Snooks (1996: ch. 13) and Snooks (2010a).

25. This is explained further in Snooks (1997: ch. 13).

The Businesspeople

1. Herac would have been pleased to know that property rights in ideas were finally introduced in Metropolis in the late 2030s, but mortified to learn that they were abandoned, along with all other rights, in 2044 by the New Order.

2. The work to which Herac refers has much in common with Edwin Black's *IBM and the Holocaust* (Time Warner, 2002).

3. The concept of strategic imitation to which Herac refers is developed in Snooks (1996; 1997; 1998b; 1999; 2003).

Editor's Notes

The Clergy

1. The theory of cultural change propounded by Herac is to be found in Snooks (1997), and of religion in particular in Snooks (2010b).

2. Herac discusses the strategic *logos* in detail in the essays I have presented in Part II of this work. The relationship between the *logos* and religion is discussed in detail in *Dead God Rising*. That book discusses these issues more deeply as it was researched and written after the essays published here.

PART II TRUTH AND THE STRATEGIC *LOGOS*

The Strategic *Logos*

1. This is the first essay (written 2003) that Herac wrote on the strategic *logos*. Later (2005-08) he employed this concept to analyze the nature and role of religion in detail. See Snooks (2010b). Herac is quoting here from the translation by B. Haxton entitled *Fragments: the collected wisdom of Heraclitus* (New York: Viking, 2001); with the exception that he has rendered λόγου with the Greek "*Logos*" rather than the English "Word". The quotes are from fragments 1, 2, 92 and 115.

   When Herac died he left behind a manuscript, which he had given up attempting to publish, concerning mankind's confusion of the strategic *logos* with "God". I recently saw this book, entitled *Dead God Rising* (2010) through publication.

3. Herac has in mind the pompous philosopher at the National University of Metropolis (introduced in the Prologue), whose metaphysical thinking was very theological in nature.

4. By using the strategic *logos* to explain the contrasting ecosociopolitical systems of democracy and communism, Herac was breaking new ground. According to the conventional wisdom, without market prices it is not possible to maintain an efficient economic system. What Herac was saying is that, while market signals are important, the fundamental problem in a command system is that its dynamic mechanism – its strategic *logos* – has been irretrievably crippled. Market prices are only a part of this more complex issue.

5. Herac's writings on truth have been collected and printed as part I of this work. The fact that Herac was unable to publish these essays in his lifetime, because of the hostility of publishers' readers', is testimony to their truth. Perhaps this should be seen as the litmus test of truth!

6. This has obviously been written with feeling, because, as detailed elsewhere in my notes, Herac had direct experience of the hypocrisy of academic philosophers. While taking the high moral ground they plundered ("garnered" was their preferred term) his institutional resources.

7. Herac explains more fully the psychological need for existential schizophrenia – selective self-delusion – in his *The Selfcreating Mind* (2006).

8. Herac's more detailed argument about the truth-seeker's motivation can be found in part IV.

9. The technological paradigm shifts to which Herac refers are analyzed in Snooks, *The Dynamic Society* (1996), *The Collapse of Darwinism* (2003), and *The Coming Eclipse* (2010).

Strategic Desire

1. A brief discussion of the theory of dynamic strategies can be found in part II/Strategic *logos*/section 3.

2. Strategic selection and its relationship with strategic imitation are discussed in detail in Snooks (2003; 2004).

3. Herac takes up the idea of truth-seeking as an extreme sport in Part IV/Notes From the Past About the Future.

4. Herac's quote from Zarathustra is similar to that in F. Nietzsche, *Beyond Good and Evil* (J. 211).

5. Similar to Nietzsche, *Zarathustra* (part II).

6. Similar to Nietzsche, *Beyond Good and Evil* (J. 39).

7. It is sometimes argued unconvincingly that Zarathustra's insanity was the result of syphilis. Herac doesn't accept this argument, because Zarathustra's symptoms do not fit the nature of the disease, namely its sudden occurrence, and the long and peaceful period (a decade) between breakdown and death; and because it neglects Zarathustra's long history of steadily worsening neurosis and, finally, psychosis. In short, the conventional hypothesis is untrue.

8. Bill Bernard's work is very similar to Bernard William's *Truth and Truthfulness* (Princeton and Oxford: Princeton University Press, 2002). See particularly pp. 1–7, 257–58, and 263.

Editor's Notes

Strategic Cerebrum

1. The idea of the metropolis was employed by Herac in *The Selfcreating Mind* (2006) as a metaphor for the conscious human mind. This was probably to be expected of a thinker who embraced Metropolis so completely. As he sings to himself at the end of the Prologue: "Metropolis is my university, its bookshops are my library, its cafes and taverns are my refectory, and its thronging crowds are my colleagues."

   Herac thought of the conscious brain as a metropolis in which the billions of neurons, and the million billion connections between them, are represented by millions of citizens and thousands of millions of social interactions. In fact, his analysis of the brain and the metropolis went beyond metaphor: he envisaged both operating as strategic instruments at different levels of the strategic pursuit; and both being part of a more general phenomenon he called "strategic awareness" – consisting of consciousness at the individual level, and of "cultural awareness" at the metropolitan level. Strategic awareness at all levels is the outcome of a high degree of reciprocal interaction between highly specialized strategic agents, which only occurs once the strategic instrument (brain or city) passes a threshold size/complexity. This interaction takes place in the "dynamic strategic core", and involves a process of self-reflection – self-consciousness in the brain and social/political/economic critique in the metropolis – by highly specialized strategic agents (neurons and societal critics).

2. But there is a solution to the problem of modern economics. As shown in Snooks, *Longrun Dynamics* (1998), *Global Transition* (1999), and *The Global Crisis Makers* (2000), there is a way of understanding the strategic *logos* that is useful to imaginative economists and policymakers. There is a new type of economics that is consistent with strategic desire realizing its objectives, and with the need to sustain the strategic *logos*. This is a dynamic economics based on Herac's ("Snooks's") dynamic-strategy theory.

3. The "correspondence" theory was most famously held by G.E. Moore (1873–1958) and Bertrand Russell (1872–1970).

4. Herac probably has in mind the pragmatists C.S. Peirce (1839–1914) and William James (1842–1910).

5. The laws of history and of life are uncovered by Herac in Snooks, *The Laws of History* (1998: pt II) and *The Collapse of Darwinism* (2003: ch. 15).

Editor's Notes

PART III TRUTH THE DOUBLE-EDGED SWORD

Truth The Vivisector

1. Existential schizophrenia as a survival mechanism was first defined and discussed in Snooks *The Ephemeral Civilization* (1997). It was also subsequently employed in *The Laws of History* (1998a) and *Longrun Dynamics* (1998b). The psychological basis for this normal mechanism, together with its relationship to pathological forms of schizophrenia were first discussed in detail in *The Selfcreating Mind* (2006). Its relationship with religion is analyzed in *Dead God Rising* (2010).

2. Herac is quoting here from *DSM* (2000: 759) on defense mechanisms.

3. The *DSM* (2000: 807) and defense mechanisms again.

4. Evolutionary psychiatry was fashionable in psychiatric and philosophical circles in the few decades that straddled the turn of the twenty-first century. It encountered considerable critical attention, particularly from Herac ("Snooks") in *The Selfcreating Mind* (2006). This bizarre intellectual fashion came too late to enjoy a long life, owing to the more general collapse of Darwinism predicted by Herac ("Snooks") in his book of the same name, published over forty years ago in 2003.

5. These writings by Herac have been collected and presented in part II of this book.

6. See part II below for further discussion of academic truth-suppression.

7. At the time he wrote this, Herac had, under the *nom de plume* Snooks, already published a dozen books in this series on what has become known as the "Quest for the Strategic *Logos*". There is no way he could have developed such a complex system in his head without commitment to paper. The old oral tradition that once flourished at the ancient universities of Engle Land was a hollow one, amounting to local reputations based on posturing in college common rooms. Of course, the swing to the other extreme in the new universities has been just as pointless, producing a great flood of badly conceived and written books on trivial subjects. Not worth destroying good forests for.

8. This, as Herac well understood, was not always the case. His collected papers show that when he was appointed by the National University of Metropolis to replace his old PhD supervisor as Head of the Department of Political Economy, he discovered in the old departmental files a copy of a report written by his professor at the request of a journal seeking guidance on an article the young Herac was attempting to publish from his thesis. This article, as it turned out, was an early contribution to the impact of chaos in the social

sciences. His professor, perhaps feeling threatened by his former student, actually recommended that the article not be published. Happily the journal editor ignored this advice.

9. As in the case of his hero Zarathustra, Herac's work was also suppressed. Only now, some twenty-five years since Herac's death, do I detect a growing interest in it. Hence this volume. It is difficult, of course, to compete with someone like Zarathustra, who paid the price of madness for his philosophy. The public usually judges thinkers not by the brilliance of their ideas, but by the entertainment value of their lives. You have to have a gimmick: it helps sales to be either a mad or a crippled "genius".

Like Zarathustra, Herac encountered increasing opposition to his path-breaking ideas. This opposition was expressed in sarcastic reviews of his books and in indignantly negative reports commissioned by potential publishers. Because of these truth-suppressors, Herac's final series of manuscripts were not published in his lifetime. His friends, according to the correspondence I have read, believed that this pressure contributed to his premature death in relative obscurity.

10. Herac was correct about the collapse of Darwinism. The very peak of popular books on Charles Darwin – about 150 years after the publication of *The Origin of Species* (1859) – coincided with the publication of Snooks' *The Collapse of Darwinism* (2003), which brought the whole house of evolutionary cards crashing down once the importance of his ideas had seeped into intellectual consciousness.

Glossary of New Terms and Concepts

The editor has compiled this glossary, which includes the new terms and concepts employed by the author in his analysis of truth and its relationship with the strategic *logos*. All new theories require new terms and concepts, and, hopefully, this glossary will assist readers in understanding them. When a new term or concept is first mentioned in one of the book's four parts, it appears in bold type. Italics in the glossary indicate that additional concepts are also defined here.

Antistrategic countries (ASCs) are societies that have been hijacked by radical organizations interested only in rent-seeking and in suppressing the potential *strategists*. It is important to draw a distinction between ASCs or command economies and antistrategic policies adopted by Third-World countries that may be rent-seeking but do not attempt to suppress emerging strategists. See also *SCs*.

Antistrategic disorders are mental illnesses that adversely affect not only the individual's strategic role but also the viability of his society's dynamic strategy. This is most evident in criminals, but also in other *antistrategists*. The main disorder of this type is antisocial personality disorder (or physchopathy).

Antistrategic intellectuals base their views on deductive thinking, and see their role as attacking and destroying key strategic organizations in the public and corporate sectors. They regard *strategists* and *strategic intellectuals* as enemies of their idealism. See also *nonstrategic intellectuals*.

Antistrategic *logos* is condemned to certain self-destruction, because local *strategists* are not free to explore or exploit strategic opportunities domestically or to follow the lead of successful strategists in other societies. Both strategic demand and thought are constrained and redirected by political decree. All major economic, social, and political decisions are made by a small group of *antistrategists* who have seized power. See also *strategic logos*.

Antistrategic neurosis. *Truth-seekers* suffer from an abnormal urge to understand life and their role in it, whatever the cost in terms of their psychic and/or physical health. It leads to a less than successful participation in the *strategic pursuit*. This can be thought of as a neurosis.

Antistrategists comprise those individuals and groups in society who engage in rent-seeking rather than profit-seeking. Essentially they attempt to siphon off the productive surpluses generated by the *strategists*, and in doing so undermine the viability of their society. The antistrategists range from criminals who break societal laws, through opportunists who exploit legal

Glossary of New Terms and Concepts

loopholes, to revolutionaries who in times of crisis attempt to hijack their society and institute repressive economic and political systems (command systems). Also see *antistrategic disorders* for an explanation of antistrategists.

Autogenous mind. See *selfcreating mind*.

Biotransition is the term used in this work in place of the misleading term "evolution", which has been irreparably contaminated by Darwinian natural selection. It involves the transmutation of species arising from genetic change and is part of the wider process of the dynamics of life.

Cultural-awareness is the self-reflective condition that emerged in human society, owing to the high degree of reciprocal interaction between highly specialized *strategists* and the cultural critics they support, in response to *strategic demand*. It is an expression of *strategic-awareness* that occurs at the societal level, just as is consciousness that occurs at the individual level.

Commerce strategy. The dynamic strategy of commerce, or symbiosis, is a more specialized means of achieving prosperity, practiced by a variety of plants, bacteria, viruses, insects, and other animals, and, most spectacularly, by some human societies. It can be thought of in nature as an alternative *dynamic strategy* to *family multiplication* and in human society as an alternative to *conquest*. Under this strategy an organism/society that manages to gain a monopoly over an important resource or location may exchange it for a resource or locational access held by a different organism/society. This exchange is to their mutual advantage.

Conquest strategy. This has played a major role in the dynamics of both life and human society. In life, conquest has been responsible for the elimination – the extinction – of those species and dynasties that had exhausted their *genetic styles* and/or *genetic paradigms*. By doing so they provided other species and potential dynasties with the opportunity to show what they could do. If the dinosaurs, for example, had not eliminated themselves through their world wars, the mammals would never have had the chance to show what their passion for the intellect could do on life's stage. And in human society, conquest was responsible for taking the agricultural revolution around the world – at first the Old World and then the New World – thereby ultimately exhausting the neolithic technological paradigm (by the mid-eighteenth century in the Old World) and making way for the Industrial Revolution (1780 to 1830). This transforming role could only be identified in retrospect. In prospect, conquest has always been adopted because, once a species' *family-multiplication strategy* had been exhausted, it was the only way that organisms could hope to survive and prosper.

Deduction. See *problem of deduction*.

Glossary of New Terms and Concepts

Dynamic strategies. To achieve its objective of survival and prosperity, the *materialist organism* must find a way to gain consistent, long-term access to the resources required for generating metabolic energy and for providing shelter. It must pursue a dynamic strategy that will deliver a reliable return on the energy it expends in its participation in life. The most appropriate dynamic strategy will depend on the physical environment – on the availability of natural resources – and on the degree of competition with other organisms in their own and neighboring species. The dynamic strategies of life are four-fold: *genetic/technological change, family multiplication, commerce* (symbiosis), and *conquest*. These strategies are "dynamic" because they are employed by organisms (including man) to maximize the probability of survival and prosperity over the lifetime of the individual, and because, when successful, they lead to the transmutation of species, to population increase, to geographic expansion of the species or dynasty, and to biological or economic growth (an increase in "output" per unit of input).

Dynamic-strategy theory is a general dynamic theory that transcends the specialist preoccupations of both the biologist and the social scientist. It can explain the dynamics of both life and human society. This theory was first presented in Snooks (1996; 1997; 1998a; 1998b; 1999; 2003).

Eternal recurrence in reality is the ultimate outcome of the exhaustion of the resource-accessing capacity of life's *genetic option*. Subsequent biological activity involves the rise and fall of life's dynasties without any improvement in their access to Earth's resources. This is the *great wheel of life* (see Figure 13.4 in Snooks 2003). The only way to break out of this eternal recurrence is through the replacement of the genetic option with the *technology option*. In Nietzsche's philosophy the eternal recurrence is given a metaphysical interpretation.

Everyday reality consists of objects and physical relationships between objects that can be perceived through the senses. Patterns can be recognized in these relationships and inductive theories can be developed to explain them. See also *ultimate reality*.

Existential dilemma of man is the outcome of *strategic dualism*, which involves a biological distinction between the *unconscious organism*, driven by *strategic desire*, and the *strategic cerebrum*, dominated by reason. Hence, it involves an eternal tension between desire and reason in man, which can lead to mental disorders.

Existential schizophrenia is a non-pathological condition required to resolve the problem of *strategic dualism* in man. It involves the need to divide our lives into mutually exclusive compartments – what we do and what we pretend we do – to enable our minds to coexist with our bodies. When this mechanism

Glossary of New Terms and Concepts

breaks down, psychotic mental disorders – see *schizo-spectrum* – emerge in susceptible individuals. This concept was first introduced in Snooks (1996).

Family-multiplication strategy involves the exploitation of unused resources through procreation and migration to new regions. By increasing the size of the extended family and gaining greater control over natural resources, the family head is able to achieve the universal objectives of survival and the maximization of material advantage. This is the force that drove the primitive dynamic, which has been called here the *great dispersion*. Family multiplication is a strategy pursued by plants as well as animals and humans.

Fatal forgetfulness occurs when governments appear to forget the role that political leaders have always played in facilitating the strategic pursuit. It involves a loss of *strategic leadership*.

Genetic option. In the history of life, organisms have been able to improve their access to the Earth's resources through the genetic option – the use of the *dynamic strategy of genetic change* – and, when it was totally exhausted, the *technology option*. With each *genetic paradigm shift* the capacity of the genetic option was progressively exploited until it was finally exhausted by the time the dinosaurs were in their prime (80 myrs ago). The technology option, however, only displaced the defunct genetic option when the intellectual capability of the hominids enabled them to employ the *technological strategy* (2.4 myrs ago). During the almost 80 myrs between these events, nature was dominated by the *great wheel of life*. If life had relied only on the genetic option it would never have escaped the *eternal recurrence*.

Genetic paradigm. This is the genetic basis on which an entire *dynasty of life* gains access to the Earth's resources. Each paradigm consists of a series of *genetic styles* – more commonly known as species – which employ specialized genetic techniques to survive and prosper.

Genetic strategy. The most controversial feature of the *dynamic-strategy theory* is its treatment of genetic change. Rather than viewing the emergence of species as the outcome of either "divine selection" or "natural selection", it is seen as the result of *strategic selection*, or self-selection writ large. Genetic change in other words is a *dynamic strategy* that is deliberately pursued by organisms – similar to the role of technological change in human society – when the circumstances are favorable. Organisms select those mutations that assist their dominant dynamic strategy and they ignore the rest. They do this by cooperating and mating with those individuals who have an edge in accessing natural resources as demonstrated by their material success. This occurs not just when pursuing genetic change as a dominant dynamic strategy, but also sometimes under the non-genetic strategies in response to the strategic demand that they generate for military weapons (*conquest*) and fertility/mobility aids (*family multiplication*). Accordingly, the concept of strategic selection is far more general in its application than Charles Darwin's concept of natural selection, to which he was forced to add "sexual selection" as a separate and puzzling process. This is why the dynamic-strategy theory, in contrast to Darwinian evolution, is a *general* dynamic theory.

Genetic styles. Within any *genetic paradigm* there is a series of genetic styles that are the outcome of species pursuing the *dynamic strategy of genetic change* in order to gain access to the Earth's resources and hence to survive and prosper. See also *technological styles*.

Global strategic transition is a complex dynamic process by which an increasing number of *nonstrategic countries* (NSCs) are drawn into the vortex of dynamic interaction between the world's most economically advanced nations. This dynamic process, by which the strategic core engulfs the strategic fringe, is an outcome of the global unfolding of the industrial technological paradigm. See Snooks (1999).

Great wheel of life. This is the mechanism of the *eternal recurrence* (Figure 13.4 in Snooks 2003). It is the process of biological baton-passing whereby a dynasty emerges to exploit a *genetic paradigm*, exhausts their version of it, collapses and is followed in the same way by a new dynasty operating within the same paradigm. The great wheel of life rotates without gaining traction, without being able to generate a new paradigm shift to replace the old exhausted paradigm. Without gaining more intensive access to the Earth's natural resources. The great wheel of life comes into operation in a mature life system when the *genetic option* has been exhausted. At this point in time it is no longer possible through genetic change to increase the global level of the biomass of life. The only way to break out of this eternal recurrence is through the replacement of the genetic option with the *technology option*.

Herac, F.S.S. In the parallel world of this book, Herac, F.S.S. is closely associated with Heraclitus of Ephesus.

Imitative information is sought and processed by the strategic cerebrum to achieve long-term survival and prosperity. Essentially, this constitutes information about who and what is successful and why. The objective is to imitate conspicuous success. It is the basis of Snooks' concept of *strategic imitation* by which the successful strategies of the few are copied by the many. See also *pattern-recognition information*.

Logosian demand. See *strategic demand*.

Materialist man, a subset of the *materialist organism*, is a central concept in longrun dynamics. Materialist man should be contrasted to the neoclassical concept of *homo economicus*. Rational economic man is not a dynamic force in society, but rather an abstract collection of preferences and rational choices concerning consumption and production – a set of optimizing conditions.

Economic theorists have divorced these behavioral outcomes from more fundamental human motivational impulses. Economic man is a mathematical convenience. Materialist man on the other hand is a real-world decision-maker who attempts to survive and, with survival, to maximize material advantage over his lifetime. This does not require perfect knowledge or sophisticated abilities to rapidly calculate the costs and benefits of a variety of possible decision-making alternatives, just an ability to recognize and imitate success.

Materialist organism. A systematic examination of the history of life undertaken in the dynamic-strategy project (Snooks, 1996; 1997; 1998a; 2003) suggests that organisms attempt at all cost to survive *and*, having survived, to prosper – to maximize their consumption subject to the prevailing physical, social, and genetic/technological constraints. This is the dynamic concept of the materialist organism. It is the all-important driving force in the dynamic system, striving at all times, irrespective of the degree of competition, to increase its access to natural resources. It is this most basic force in life – which Snooks has called *strategic desire* – that accounts for the dynamic-strategy theory's self-starting and self-maintaining nature. More intense competition merely raises the stakes of the strategic pursuit. Also see *materialist man* and *metabolic demand*.

Metabolic demand is the demand generated by an organism's metabolic system for organic resources (fuel) in order to sustain life. It is the source of *strategic desire*, which is the driving force in life.

Metaphysical thinking is the outcome of the exclusive use of deductive logic. It ignores empirical evidence and forms the basis of theorizing about issues that can be neither verified nor falsified scientifically. It is the type of thinking responsible for theological and other fantastical systems. See also *strategic thinking* and *problem of deduction*.

Nonstrategic intellectuals are interested neither in facilitating nor undermining the strategic pursuit, only to live outwardly successful and comfortable lives. They support the powers that be, whether democratic or fascist, to maximize research funding and salaries. They are driven neither by reality nor ideality, but by self-interest. They embrace both lies and truth according to their purpose. See also *strategic intellectuals* and *antistrategic intellectuals*.

Outsiders. See *risk-takers* and *truth-seekers*.

Pattern-recognition information. There are broadly two types of information processed by the *strategic cerebrum*: information required for pattern recognition, and information required for *strategic imitation*. Pattern-recognition data, which are supplied by the senses, are employed both to undertake daily activities (short-term survival) by all organisms, and to explore new strategic opportunities by a few exceptional individuals (long-term survival). Also see *imitative information*.

Problem of deduction. We are told repeatedly of the "problem of induction" – the lack of mechanical rules for drawing inferences from empirical data – but the more serious "problem of deduction" is ignored. Only by the systematic examination of empirical data is it possible to derive realistic premises. It is not sufficient to argue that those logical models based on unrealistic assumptions will be weeded out through a process of empirical falsification – a process Karl Popper calls "error elimination" – because in reality very few theories are rejected in this way. Old theories just fade into the background when new unverified theories come along, often to be revived at a later date. Also, it is highly likely that, without the assistance of systematic observation, the deductivist will completely overlook some of the main explanatory variables.

Prosperity-seeker is the opposite of *truth-seeker*. They have much in common with *nonstrategic intellectuals*.

Reality. See *everyday reality* and *ultimate reality*.

Risk-takers in this work are the *truth-seekers* in life. They indulge in the "extreme sport" of exploring the nature of *strategic dualism*, and suffer the psychological, physical, and social consequences. They are self-vivisectionists. Theirs is the life of the *outsider*.

Schizo-spectrum is the range of schizoid states (see Figure 2 above) that reflects increasing psychotic characteristics and decreasing strategic involvement. It is the progressive outcome of a breakdown in the normal condition of *existential schizophrenia*, which is necessary for the survival of selfconscious life forms.

Selective sexual reproduction is based on those perceived characteristics in other individuals that will improve the prospect of survival and prosperity of the selecting individual. If this perception turns out to be correct, those physical and instinctual characteristics will also be passed on to the individual's offspring. Mate choice is an important technique for implementing all four *dynamic strategies*, not just of *genetic change*. Selective sexual reproduction provides individuals with greater control over their dynamic strategies, which is the reason for the emergence of sex some 1,000–600 myrs ago.

Selfcreating mind. It arises from an autogenous process of *biotransition*. The theory of the selfcreating mind is part of a more general theory – the *dynamic-strategy theory* – that Snooks has been developing since the late 1980s to explore the fluctuating fortunes of life and human society. As the selfcreating mind is shaped by *strategic selection* in response to *strategic demand*, it is the outcome of individual choice. The human mind is definitely not the outcome of an artificial filtering device, such as natural selection.

Glossary of New Terms and Concepts

Social selection is the process by which human values are formed. Essentially they are a response to *strategic demand*, which is generated by an unfolding *dynamic strategy* within the *strategic logos*.

Societal neurosis is the outcome of widespread *strategic frustration*, whereby the material aspirations of the majority of citizens are blocked. This occurs when governments are unwilling or unable to provide *strategic leadership*.

Strategic agents. In Snooks' general theory of *strategic-awareness*, highly specialized strategic agents generate self-awareness by interacting with each other in the *strategic core*. At the level of human society they consist of human individuals that generate *cultural-awareness*, and at the level of the human brain they consist of neurons that generate selfconsciousness.

Strategic-awareness. A general theory of strategic-awareness has been developed in *The Selfcreating Mind* (Snooks, 2006). It encompasses individual selfconsciousness, together with *cultural-awareness* at the metropolitan, national, and global levels. Strategic-awareness at the societal level means that the citizens are aware of their society's economic/social/political role in the *strategic pursuit*. This occurs when a society passes a size/complexity threshold that enables the generation of a high degree of specialization and, hence, of a self-reflective ecosociopolitical culture. In the same way, individual selfconsciousness is the outcome of the brain, in its historical development, exceeding a size/complexity threshold and generating a similar degree of highly specialized neural interaction. Underlying this self-reflection at both the societal and individual levels is the emergence of the dynamic *strategic core*.

Strategic blindness is displayed by antistrategic countries (ASCs) that suppress their *strategists* and appropriate their surpluses. Accordingly, they fatally wound their *strategic logos* and are unable to detect the signs – market signals – needed to maximize the strategic pursuit. Eventually, all antistrategic societies (like the former USSR) grind to a halt and collapse.

Strategic cerebrum. Organisms in pursuit of survival and prosperity control their dynamic strategies through what Snooks calls *strategic instruments*. These strategic instruments include brains in organisms that possess them and special genes in those that do not. These instruments are the strategic cerebrum and the *strategic gene*. A watershed occurred in life, some 500 myrs ago, when some organisms were able to replace the strategic gene with the strategic cerebrum.

Strategic core. In the *dynamic-strategy theory*, the concept of the strategic core – which is generated by the interaction of *strategic agents*, whether individuals or neurons – operates at the societal (global, national, metropolitan) and cerebral levels. It was first suggested at the societal level in Snooks (1996;

1999), and is similar to the "dynamic core" concept at the cerebral level suggested by Edelman and Tononi (2000). While Edelman and Tononi employ it as a descriptive concept, in this work it is part of a general dynamic theory. The strategic core is a response to *strategic demand*, which changes as the prevailing dynamic strategy unfolds. This concept is essential to an understanding of *strategic-awareness* at both the societal and individual levels.

Strategic countries (SCs) are those countries that have been fully incorporated into the *global strategic transition* (GST) through their successful pursuit of the prevailing technological strategy. These societies constitute the steadily growing *strategic core* at the global level.

Strategic demand is the central concept in the dynamic-strategy theory of both life and human society. It is the core force in the *strategic logos*. It is an outcome of the unfolding dynamic strategy that is driven by *strategic agents* exploring their strategic opportunities, and exerts a longrun influence over the employment of resources, the institutional and organizational structure of animal and human society, the genetic and technological structure of organisms and human societies, and the nature of the human mind. Shifts in strategic demand occur as the dominant dynamic strategy unfolds and as one dynamic strategy replaces another. These shifts elicit changes in the way organisms employ resources and interact with each other.

Strategic desire. The attribute that first separated living from non-living cells some 4,000 myrs ago was not the ability to reproduce systematically but the intense need to obtain organic material to fuel their internal metabolic systems. This need to meet *metabolic demand* is called strategic desire. It is the driving force in life. Replication (or *family multiplication*), which is merely one of the *dynamic strategies* employed by organisms to survive and prosper, is secondary to strategic desire. Without strategic desire, life would not exist.

Strategic disorders. In the dynamic-strategy theory, mental disorders are treated as strategic disorders – disorders arising from the breakdown in psychological mechanisms that have emerged in the distant past to enable man to participate successfully in the *strategic pursuit*. These disorders are either strategy-challenging (largely neurotic) or strategy-terminating (largely psychotic). *Strategic psychiatry* aims at reversing the breakdown in these mechanisms to enable patients to rejoin the *strategic pursuit*.

Strategic dualism. While human nature is a reflection of our capacity to engage in the strategic pursuit (*strategic power*), that capacity possesses a destabilizing potential for some individuals. This problem is an outcome of the tense relationship between the *unconscious organism* and the *strategic cerebrum* in mankind. The unconscious organism is driven by *strategic desire*, while the strategic cerebrum, which supervises our participation in the *strategic pursuit*, is ruled by reason. Strategic dualism, which has nothing to do with Cartesian dualism, is a materialist concept. It has biological foundations.

Strategic exhaustion is the outcome of the depletion of the wealth-creating capacity – or strategic opportunities – of the *strategic logos*. The collapse of a *strategic logos* is like the death of a star, which occurs when the fuel that supports the chain reactions generating heat, light, and energy is totally exhausted. But there is a fundamental difference: the *logos* is based on dynamic strategies, not chemical compounds.

Strategic followers travel in the wake of the *strategic pioneers*. They seek information not about the benefits and costs of materialist alternatives, but about who and what is successful, and why. The successful pioneers are emulated by large numbers of followers. This is the mechanism of *strategic imitation*, which is central to the development of all species.

Strategic frustration, which is the outcome of barriers raised to the *strategic pursuit*, operates at both the societal and individual levels. At the societal level, governments unable or unwilling to provide adequate *strategic leadership* provoke strategic frustration amongst the population, who then turn to radical groups to find relief. Snooks calls the resulting disruption of society, *societal neurosis*. At the individual level, strategic frustration emerges when persistent barriers are raised against their participation in the strategic pursuit. This frustration leads to distressing mood disorders, such as manic depression. *Strategic satisfaction* is the opposite of strategic frustration.

Strategic gene. Organisms in pursuit of survival and prosperity control their *dynamic strategies* through what Snooks calls *strategic instruments*. These strategic instruments include brains in organisms that possess them and special genes in those that do not. These instruments are the *strategic cerebrum* and the strategic gene. Strategic genes are used by organisms to respond to the changing physical and social environments, which determine the availability of nutrients and presence of competitors, and to activate the most appropriate dynamic strategy. When nutrients are abundant this will be the *family-multiplication strategy*; when competition is intense it will be the *conquest strategy*. In lower life forms, therefore, these strategic genes play the same role as central nervous systems in higher life forms – they select and supervise the most appropriate dynamic strategy to fulfill the *strategic desires* of the *materialist organism*. As such they do not drive life, they merely facilitate it. It is essential to realize that these strategic genes emerge in response to the driving ambition of their organisms. They do not have an independent existence or any driving ambitions of their own as claimed by the neo-Darwinists. It is significant that, in some forms of life, organisms replaced the strategic gene with the strategic cerebrum about 1,000 to 600 myrs ago.

Glossary of New Terms and Concepts

Strategic imitation. It is in the process of strategic imitation, by which the vast majority of organisms emulate the action and values of successful *strategic pioneers*, that societal "rules" are created and employed. Institutions are needed to economize not on benefit–cost information, as the economic institutionalists or rationalists argue, but on intelligence. This is true not only in animal society where intelligence is particularly scarce, but also in human society where most individuals find intellectual activity difficult and unhelpful. Intelligence is the scarcest resource on Earth, and probably non-existent in the rest of the Universe. The rule-makers, therefore, are the *strategic followers*, who demand guidance in their strategic pursuit; while the rule-breakers are the strategic pioneers, who attempt to break out of the restrictions of institutional conventions as they follow their new visions. As the "followers" constitute the vast majority of organisms in life, "rules" are essential to the dynamics of both animal and human society even though they are purely a response to it.

Strategic instruments are agents or values employed by organisms (including man) to supervise or facilitate their *strategic pursuit*. The agents include the *strategic gene* in primitive life forms and the *strategic cerebrum* in more advanced life forms. The values, such as truth, honesty, generosity and justice, are not innate characteristics of man, but rather generalized forms of societal rules required to make civilization work. Values economize on impossibly long and complex lists of rules. Values are a response to *strategic demand* and, hence, are external to man.

Strategic integration. The *dynamic-strategy theory* shows that psychotic disorders arise from a breakdown in the individual's strategic integration. This problem arises from the dual basis of human nature (*strategic dualism*). The task of *strategic psychiatry* is to reverse the process of breakdown in order to restore the strategic integration of the individual.

Strategic intellectuals are concerned to understand reality. They are empiricists who gather and examine data about the real world, and who employ the inductive method to construct theories to explain these real-world patterns. They employ *strategic thinking* rather than *metaphysical thinking*. They expose false ideas, which are based on metaphysical thinking. Ideas that could retard the successful unfolding of the prevailing dynamic strategy. They recognize that desire drives and ideas merely facilitate. See also *antistrategic intellectuals* and *nonstrategic intellectuals*.

Strategic leadership. In animal societies, males battle with each other to gain control over the sources of their *dynamic strategy*, which are territories that provide access to food and shelter. They battle, in other words, to become the leading *strategist* in their group. The conflict between them is part of the struggle for "political" control of their "society". Having maintained or achieved this strategic control, which ensures his survival, the strategic leader is in a good position to maximize his prosperity, which involves the consumption of food, sex and, for the time being, leisure. Procreation assumes greater significance when it is part of the dynamic strategy of *family multiplication*, but even then it is a means to a more important end.

Strategic *logos* is the great creative system of life – the great pulsating heart of each and every living system. It is an invisible circular process of interaction between man and his society (see Figure 1). It is a complex strategic demand–response mechanism. It is also a self-starting and self-sustaining process that continues to pulsate until the entire sequence of dynamic strategies available to a given society is completely exhausted. In the case of the world's most successful societies, such as ancient Rome and ancient Egypt, this can last for between one and three millennia. Eventually, however, the strategic society collapses because its *logos* finally exhausts itself. It is the strategic *logos* that generates all culture, religion, values, institutions, progress, liberty, and even man himself. It is from the strategic *logos* that "all things follow". See also *strategic exhaustion*.

Strategic pioneers are those innovators who employ and invest in aspects of a new and emerging dynamic strategy. They operate on the basis not of detailed benefit–cost information but of *pattern-recognition information*. When successful they are imitated by the rest of society – by the *strategic followers*.

Strategic power. While each species possesses a defining set of innate characteristics, they cannot capture the essence of its nature. This is because the expression of these characteristics changes with strategic circumstances. The real nature of a species, including human nature, resides in its strategic power, which is its capacity to engage successfully in the *strategic pursuit*. This is demonstrated by the *dynamic-strategy theory*. Human nature, therefore, is the expression of the way our species employs its strategic power through our instinctual, emotional, and intellectual faculties in response to *strategic demand*. Hence, while the particular set of characteristics that *describe* human beings in a given society will change over time (according to the dynamic strategy employed and the stage of its unfolding process), the essence of human nature – its strategic power – remains the same.

Strategic psychiatry is based on Snooks' dynamic-strategy theory applied to the human mind. This theory identifies the source of mental disorders (here called *strategic disorders*) as the breakdown of those psychological mechanisms required by individuals to participate successfully in the *strategic pursuit*. The objective of strategic psychiatry is to reverse these strategic malfunctions to enable patients to rejoin the strategic pursuit. This requires strategic retraining.

Glossary of New Terms and Concepts

Strategic pursuit. All life is dedicated to the strategic pursuit, in which the pioneering *strategists* explore the material potential of the most effective *dynamic strategy* and its substrategies. It is important to focus on the strategic pursuit rather than the means (family multiplication, conquest, commerce, technological change) by which this driving force is translated into a material surplus. In the life sciences both the neo-Darwinists and the neoliberal economists have focused on static physical structures rather than the dynamics of the strategic pursuit. In doing so they have failed to develop general dynamic theories.

Strategic satisfaction is that balanced state of mind attained by individuals and groups of individuals when they are able to participate successfully in the *strategic pursuit*. This state of mind results in viable individuals and societies. It is the opposite of *strategic frustration*.

Strategic selection is a central concept in this work. It is a dynamic process in which organisms are themselves responsible for selecting or rejecting benign (non-lethal) mutations. It operates through the *strategic imitation* process. If an individual experiences a beneficial mutation that enables better access to natural resources – within the context of the *dynamic strategy* it is pursuing – that individual will increase its prospects of survival and prosperity. This success will attract the attention of others. Those with similar abilities will cooperate with each other to improve their joint prospects. The point of strategic selection is that individual organisms – rather than gods, genes, or blind chance – are responsible for selecting comrades, mates, and siblings that have the necessary physical and instinctual characteristics to successfully pursue the prevailing dynamic strategy. It is important to realize that strategic selection operates under varying degrees of competition, not just under intense Darwinian competition, and that it responds to each of the four dynamic strategies, not just the *genetic strategy*. Also it is associated with the welfare of the self and not that of future generations. Strategic selection is a form of self-selection at the "societal" level which replaces the "divine selection" of the creationists and the "natural selection" of the Darwinists.

Strategic sequence. Typically, organisms in a species will pursue a sequence of strategies from the time they begin to diverge from the parent species until they finally go extinct. The sequence prior to the emergence of human society 2 myrs ago was typically *genetic change, family multiplication* or *commerce*, and *conquest*. Each *dynamic strategy* is exploited until it is exhausted, which leads to a temporary crisis until a new strategy can be employed in their *strategic pursuit*. If, in a normally competitive environment, a new strategy is not adopted by a species following the exhaustion of an old strategy, that species will collapse and go extinct prematurely. Human societies also pursue strategic sequences, with similar outcomes. Accordingly this strategic sequence leads not to a linear development path but to a series of waves consisting of phases of expansion, stagnation, crisis, decline, and renewed expansion.

Strategic struggle is the main "political" instrument by which established individuals/species (old *strategists*) attempt to maintain their control over the sources of their prosperity, and by which emerging individuals/species (new strategists) attempt to usurp such control. Although it employs "political" instruments it is fundamentally an "economic" struggle – a struggle for survival and prosperity in the face of scarce resources. In the process these individuals/species employ the dynamic tactics of order and chaos. See *strategic leadership*.

Strategic thinking is the type of thinking that comes naturally to the *strategic cerebrum* that emerged about 500 myrs ago in order to supervise the *strategic pursuit* of the *unconscious organism* in an increasingly sophisticated social environment. It is an inductive form of thinking that employs *pattern-recognition information*. It is to be contrasted with rationalist thinking based on benefit–cost information, which emerged with human civilization a mere 6,000 years ago.

Strategists comprise the dynamic group in animal and human society that invests time and resources in pursuing and profiting from one of the four *dynamic strategies*. The strategists are a diverse group. We must distinguish between the *strategic pioneers* (the more ambitious and less risk-averse) and the *strategic followers*; between the old strategists (supporters of the traditional strategy) and the new strategists (supporters of the emerging strategy); and between the surplus-creating strategists and the surplus-consuming strategists. While there is synergy between the pioneers and the followers and the surplus-creators and surplus-consumers, the old and new strategists are generally involved in a struggle against each other for control of society's dominant dynamic strategy. See *strategic struggle*.

Technological paradigms (TPs) are economic eras, ranging from a few hundred to a couple of million years, defined by the fundamental technology they employ. The palaeological TP (1.9 myrs BP to 10,600 years BP) was based on hunting technology; the neolithic TP (10,600 years BP to AD 1780–1830) was based on agricultural technology; and the modern TP (since 1780–1830) is based on industrial technology. See also *technological paradigm shifts*.

Technological paradigm shifts. The progress of human society takes place within a dynamic structure defined by the great technological paradigm shifts in which growing resource scarcity is transcended by mankind breaking through into an entirely new technological era, thereby opening up extended possibilities for further economic growth. This involves the introduction of an entirely new set of techniques, skills, institutions, and outcomes. There have been three great technological paradigm shifts in human history: the

Glossary of New Terms and Concepts

palaeolithic paradigm shift when hunting displaced scavenging; the neolithic paradigm shift when agriculture displaced hunting; and the industrial paradigm shift when urban centers displaced rural areas as the major source of growth (Snooks 2003: Figure 13.2 and 13.3).

Technological strategy. This strategy is the dominant dynamic of modern society and, in the past, has been employed by economic decision-makers to transcend exhausted technological paradigms. It was the outcome of the Intelligence Revolution and enabled life to escape the *eternal recurrence*. The technological strategy was at the very center of the Palaeolithic (hunting), Neolithic (agricultural), and Industrial (modern) Revolutions or *technological paradigm shifts*. And it will be the dominant dynamic strategy of the future. Unlike the *conquest* and *commerce strategies* it leads to an increase in material living standards not only for its host civilization but for human society as a whole.

Technological styles. Within the modern technological paradigm, the dynamic *strategists* of competing nation-states attempt to secure a comparative advantage in their pursuit of extraordinary profits by developing new technological substrategies or technological styles. These technological styles – which historically have included: steam-powered iron machinery using coke (1780s–1830s); steel, synthetic chemicals, and complex machinery (1840s–1890s); electricity and the internal combustion engine (1900s–1950s); automated processes, microelectronics, lasers, new construction materials, and biotechnology (since 1950s) – emerge within the existing industrial paradigm as it unfolds at the global level. In dynamic-strategy theory technological styles are analogous to *genetic styles*.

Technology option. The emergence of intelligence enabled the most intellectually advanced line of the dynasty of mammals to replace the *genetic option* with the technology option, which was to spawn a series of *technological paradigm shifts* and, within each of these, a series of *technological styles*. This released life from the *eternal recurrence*.

Timescapes are those portraits of reality provided by a visual representation of longrun quantitative and qualitative data. These portraits emerge from the statistical record of the course taken by life and human society over vast expanses of time. They show us the nature of real-world relationships, such as the great waves of life and of economic change. They provide a glimpse of dynamic processes operating in life and in society, and constitute the building blocks of existential models. As fact is stranger than fiction they provide a breadth of vision required to build realist dynamic models that is missing in the deductive approach.

Glossary of New Terms and Concepts

Truth-seekers are deviants in human society. They are outsiders, who respond not to a general will to truth – a figment of the philosopher's imagination – but to the thrill of participating in the most extreme of extreme sports. They pursue the truth about themselves and their world far beyond the point at which it ceases to be advantageous to them. Instead they suffer discrimination, mental disorders, and even premature death for their quest. They are self-vivisectionists. Theirs is an underground activity.

Ultimate reality is a complex set of invisible relationships between forces (rather than objects) – such as *strategic desire* and *strategic demand* – that cannot be perceived through the senses. Snooks calls this ultimate reality the *strategic logos*. This invisible pattern of forces (see Figure 1) can only be apprehended by developing a general dynamic theory that can explain and predict the recurring patterns in *everyday reality* that are detected by the senses.

Unconscious organism. The dynamic-strategy theory embodies the concept of *strategic dualism*, based on the biological fact that human beings are a fusion of the unconscious organism that can trace its origins back to the beginning of life some 3,000 myrs ago, and the *strategic cerebrum* that first emerged merely 500 myrs ago. The unconscious organism, which is driven by *strategic desire*, attempts to survive and prosper through the adoption of one of a quartet of *dynamic strategies*. This was achieved at first by the *strategic gene*, but, in some species, more recently by the strategic cerebrum. The strategic cerebrum is just an instrument developed through *strategic selection* to facilitate the strategic pursuit.

Zarathustra is dead: an allegory about the strategic *logos*.

References

This list of references was compiled by the editor, not the author. It is an attempt to reconstruct the list of books that the author might have used in writing the notes and essays compiled in this work. The list is based on internal textual evidence together with the annotated books in what remains of the author's library. No doubt it would have been more comprehensive had the author published this book himself. It should be remembered that thousands of additional sources are to be found referenced in the Snooks editions listed here. There remains, of course, a mystery about many of the authors mentioned in the text, who, along with Herac himself, appear to inhabit a parallel universe. In these cases one can merely list the authors and works that they appear to parallel in our universe.

Editor's List

Beck, S. and M. Downing (eds) (2003). *The Battle for Iraq. BBC news correspondents on the war against Saddam and a new world agenda*. London: BBC.

Black, E. (2002). *IBM and the Holocaust. How America's most powerful corporation helped Nazi Germany count the Jews*. London: Time Warner.

Blackburn, S. and K. Simmons (eds) (2003). *Truth*. Oxford: OUP.

Broinowski, A. (2003). *Howard's War*. Melbourne: Scribe.

Bryson, B. (2003). *A Short History of Nearly Everything*. London: Doubleday.

Campbell, J. (2002). *The Liar's Tale. A history of falsehood*. New York and London: WW Norton.

Camus, A. (1966). *The Outsider*. London: Penguin.

Casson, L. (2001). *Libraries in the Ancient World*. New Haven and London: Yale University Press.

Cate, C. (2003). *Friedrich Nietzsche. A biography*. London: Pimlico.

Chomsky, N. (2002). *On Nature and Language*. Cambridge: CUP.

Chomsky, N. (2003a). *Power and Terror. Post-9/11 talks and interviews*. New York: Seven Stories Press.

Chomsky, N. (2003b). *Hegemony or Survival. America's quest for global dominance*. Sydney: Allen & Unwin.

Collinson, D., K. Plant, and R. Wilkinson (2000). *Fifty Eastern Thinkers*. London and New York: Routledge.

Conrad, J. (1999). *Heart of Darkness*. London: Penguin.

Dostoyevsky, F.M. (1972). *Notes from Underground*. London: Penguin.

Diagnostic and Statistical Manual of Mental Disorders (DSM), 4th edition (TR). Washington DC: American Psychiatric Association.

Edelman, G.M. and G. Tononi (2000). *Consciousness. How matter becomes imagination*. London: Penguin.

Ellenberger, H.F. (1970). *The Discovery of the Unconscious*. London: Allen Lane.

Fernández-Armesto, F. (1998). *Truth. A history and a guide for the perplexed*. London: Black Swan.

Fernández-Armesto, F. (2001). *Civilizations. Culture, ambition, and the transformation of nature*. New York: Free Press.

Gribbin, J. (2002). *Science. A history, 1543–2001*. London: Allen Lane.

Grimal, P. (ed.) (1965). *World Mythology*. London: Hamlyn.

Hayman, R. (1981). *Nietzsche. A critical life*. London: Quartet Books.

Heraclitus (c. 460 BC), *Fragments, the collected wisdom of Heraclitus* (trs. B. Haxton). New York: Viking.

Huntington, S.P. (2003). *The Clash of Civilizations and the Remaking of World Order*. New York: Simon & Schuster.

Hollingdale, R.J. (2001). *Nietzsche. The man and his philosophy*. Cambridge: CUP.

Kaufmann, W. (1973). *The Portable Nietzsche*. New York: Viking Press.

Kaufmann, W. (1974). *Nietzsche. Philosopher, psychologist, anti-Christ*. Princeton: PUP.

Kerr, A. (1996). *Lost Japan*. Melbourne: Lonely Planet.

Kriwaczek, P. (2003). *In Search of Zarathustra. The first prophet and the ideas that changed the world*. London: Phoenix.

Leick, G. (2001). *Mesopotamia. The invention of the city*. London: Penguin.

Leiter, B. (2002). *Nietzsche on Morality*. London and New York: Routledge.

References

McCalman, I. (2003). *The Seven Ordeals of Count Cagliostro*. Sydney: Flamingo.

Mailer, N. (2003). *Why Are We at War?* New York: Random House.

Manley, B. (1996). *Historical Atlas of Ancient Egypt*. London: Penguin.

Manz, B. (2000). *A Mind in Prison. The memoir of a son and solider of the Third Reich*. Washington DC: Brassey's.

Marshall, P. (2002). *The Philosopher's Stone. A quest for the secrets of alchemy*. London: Pan Books.

Nietzsche, F. (1872, 1874, 1886). *The Birth of Tragedy* (trs. R. Speirs). Cambridge: CUP, 2000.

Nietzsche, F. (1873, 1874, 1876). *Untimely Meditations* (trs. R.J. Hollingdale). Cambridge: CUP, 2003.

Nietzsche, F. (1878, 1879, 1880, 1886). *Human, All Too Human* (trs. M. Faber and S. Lehmann). London: Penguin, 1994.

Nietzsche, F. (1881, 1887). *Daybreak. Thoughts on the prejudices of morality* (trs. R.J. Hollingdale). Cambridge: CUP, 2001.

Nietzsche, F. (1882, 1887). *The Gay Science* (trs. W. Kaufmann). New York: Vintage, 1974.

Nietzsche, F. (1883, 1884, 1885). *Thus Spoke Zarathustra* (trs. R.J. Hollingdale). London: Penguin, 1971.

Nietzsche, F. (1886). *Beyond Good and Evil. Prelude to a philosophy of the future* (trs. R.J. Hollingdale). London: Penguin, 1973, 2003.

Nietzsche, F. (1887). *On the Genealogy of Morals* (trs. D. Smith). London: Penguin, 1972.

Nietzsche, F. (1889). *Twilight of the Idols* (trs. R.J. Hollingdale). London: Penguin, 1972.

Nietzsche, F. (1888, 1895). *The Anti-Christ* (trs. R.J. Hollingdale). London: Penguin, 1972.

Nietzsche, F. (1888, 1908, 1911) *Ecce Homo* (trs. R.J. Hollingdale). London: Penguin, 1992.

Nietzsche, F. (1968). *The Will to Power* [a selection from the notebooks] (trs. W. Kaufmann and R.J. Hollingdale). New York: Vintage.

Nietzsche, F. (2003). *Writings from the Late Notebooks* (trs. K. Sturge). Cambridge: CUP.

Porter, R. (2000). *Quacks, Fakers and Charlatans in English Medicine*. Brunscombe, UK: Tempus.

Price, S. and E. Kearns (eds) (2003), *The Oxford Dictionary of Classical Myth and Religion*. Oxford: OUP.

Sereny, G. (1995). *Albert Speer: His battle with the truth*. London: Macmillan.

Snooks, G.D. (1993). *Economics Without Time. A science blind to the forces of historical change*. London/Ann Arbor: Macmillan/University of Michigan Press.

Snooks, G.D. (1996). *The Dynamic Society. Exploring the sources of global change*. London and New York: Routledge.

Snooks, G.D. (1997). *The Ephemeral Civilization. Exploding the myth of social evolution*. London and New York: Routledge.

Snooks, G.D. (1998a). *The Laws of History*. London and New York: Routledge.

Snooks, G.D. (1998b). *Longrun Dynamics. A general economic and political theory*. London/New York: Macmillan/St Martin's Press.

Snooks, G.D. (1999). *Global Transition. A general theory of economic development*. London/New York: Macmillan/St Martin's Press.

Snooks, G.D. (2000). *The Global Crisis Makers. An end to progress and liberty?* London/New York: Macmillan/St Martin's Press.

Snooks, G.D. (2002). "Uncovering the laws of global history". *Social Evolution & History* 1: 25–53.

Snooks, G.D. (2003). *The Collapse of Darwinism, or the rise of a realist theory of life*. Lanham, MD and Oxford: Lexington Books, Rowman & Littlefield Group.

Snooks, G.D. (2005). "The origin of life on Earth: A new general dynamic theory". *Advances in Space Research* 36: 26–34.

Snooks, G.D. (2006). *The Selfcreating Mind*. Lanham, MD and Oxford: University Press of America, Rowman & Littlefield Group.

Snooks, G.D. (2007). "Self-organization or selfcreation? From social physics to realist dynamics". *Social Evolution & History* 6: 118–44.

Snooks, G.D. (2008). "A general theory of complex living systems: exploring the demand side of dynamics". *Complexity* 13 (July/August): 12-20.

References

Snooks, G.D. (2010a). *The Coming Eclipse, or the triumph of climate mitigation over Solar Revolution.* Canberra: IGDS Books.

Snooks, G.D. (2010b). *Dead God Rising. Religion & science in the universal life-system.* Canberra: IGDS Books.

Sobel, D. (2000). Galileo's Daughter. *A drama of science, faith and love.* London: Fourth Estate.

Tanner, M. (2000). Nietzsche. *A very short introduction.* Oxford: OUP.

Wachsberger, K. (gen. Ed.) (1998). *Banned Books: Literature suppressed on political, religious, social, and sexual grounds.* 4 vols. New York: Facts on File Inc.

Waterfield, R. (2000). The First Philosophers. The presocratics and the sophists. Oxford: OUP.

Acknowledgements

I have been fortunate to obtain technical support from two excellent colleagues. Debbie Phillips of **DP+** skillfully transformed my handwritten manuscript into a legible typescript, and Julie Hamilton of **Mirrabooka Marketing & Design** expertly converted this typescript into a publishable book, as well as stylishly designing the book's cover.
I am indebted to both.

And finally, in addition to being the father of my two wonderful grandchildren, Adrian Snooks has been a source of unfailing encouragement and advice.

About the Author

Graeme Donald Snooks is the Executive Director of the Institute of Global Dynamic Systems (IGDS) in Canberra. For twenty-one years between 1989 and 2010 he was the foundation Coghlan Research Professor in the Institute of Advanced Studies at the Australian National University. More than two decades ago he embarked on an ambitious research program to develop a realist dynamic theory of the changing fortunes of human society and life from their beginnings. This has given rise to the widely acclaimed dynamic-strategy theory (recently published in *Advances in Space Research* and in *Complexity* the journal of the Santa Fe Institute), which Professor Snooks is employing to rethink all aspects of the life sciences. This is the first general dynamic theory in the history of human thought to employ an effective demand-side approach. The significance of this is that all supply-side theories are fundamentally flawed.

The results of this research have been published in a number of well-received trilogies, including the global history trilogy (*The Dynamic Society, The Ephemeral Civilization,* and *The Laws of History*), the social dynamics trilogy (*Longrun Dynamics, Global Transition,* and *The Global Crisis Makers*), and the dynamics of life trilogy (*The Collapse of Darwinism, The Selfcreating Mind,* and *Dead God Rising*). Future volumes will explore the dynamic nature of human values and will provide an overview of the entire research program. The core discovery of this work is the universal life system, analyzed for the first time in *Dead God Rising* and *The Death of Zarathustra*.

About IGDS Books

IGDS Books is the imprint of the publishing activities of the Institute of Global Dynamic Systems in Canberra. It is the mission of IGDS Books to publish innovative work that pushes beyond the existing frontiers of knowledge – a challenge that major scholarly publishers have abandoned in this electronic era. As Executive Director of the Institute, Professor Graeme Snooks oversees the activities of IGDS Books.

For information about the Institute or **IGDS Books**, see the Institute's website, or contact Professor Snooks at seouenaca@gmail.com.

Other **IGDS Books** include:

G.D. Snooks, *THE COMING ECLIPSE – or The Triumph of Climate Mitigation Over Solar Revolution* (August 2010)

G.D. Snooks, *DEAD GOD RISING. Religion & Science in the Universal Life-System* (November 2010)

G.D. Snooks, *THE DEATH OF ZARATHUSTRA. Notes on Truth for the Risk-Taker* (March 2011).

G.D. Snooks, *ARK OF THE SUN. The Improbable Voyage of Life* (forthcoming 2011).

For information about and orders for the Institute's publications – books and working papers – please contact the Institute Administrator at institutegds@gmail.com.

www.ingramcontent.com/pod-product-compliance
Lightning Source LLC
Chambersburg PA
CBHW050632160426
43194CB00010B/1643